THE MATTHEW MYSTERIES

A Revelation of the Higher Wisdom Concerning the Church, Israel and the Gentiles in Prophecy

By
Gary T. Whipple, Th.M.

Schoettle Publishing Co., Inc.
P.O. Box 1246
Hayesville, N.C. 28904
U.S.A.
1995

THE MATTHEW MYSTERIES

Copyright ©1994 by Gary T. Whipple

All rights reserved. No part of this publication may be reproduced, stored in a retrieval system, or transmitted in any form or by any means - electronic, mechanical, photocopy, recording, or any other - except for brief quotations in the printed reviews, without the prior permission of the publisher.

ISBN: 1-56453-087-6

Printed in the United States of America

ACKNOWLEDGMENTS

We gratefully acknowledge the work of Mrs. Christine Bacchus and Nellie Whipple (my wife) for their labors of love in proof-reading the manuscript of this book. Also, we give thanks to God for the prayers and support of our church, Lamp and Light Baptist Church, during its writing.

TABLE OF CONTENTS

Introduction 1
Chapter 1   The Royal Line of the Kingdom 5
Chapter 2   The Announcement of the Kingdom 19
Chapter 3   The Message of the Kingdom 33
Chapter 4   The Credentials of the Kingdom 55
Chapter 5   The Invitational Boundary Line of the Kingdom ... 79
Chapter 6   The Qualificatons of the Kingdom 91
Chapter 7   The Rejection of the Kingdom 119
Chapter 8   The Mysteries of the Kingdom, Part One 139
Chapter 9   The Mysteries of the Kingdom, Part Two 165
Chapter 10   The Mysteries of the Kingdom, Part Three 181
Chapter 11   The Church of the Kingdom 213
Chapter 12   The Trees of the Kingdom 253

Subject Index 283
Scripture Index 287

FOREWORD

This is the completion of a two volume set that I have wriitten on the "kingdom truths" Where the first volume, *Shock and Surprise Beyond the Rapture*, dealt mainly with scriptures out of the epistles, this deals mainly with scriptures out of the book of Matthew.

Matthew is one of the most misunderstood books in the Bible. Yet, in it we learn directly from the teachings of Jesus concerning His coming kingdom. When the reader understands the scriptures that are expounded upon in both volumes concerning the kingdom, he will surely see that most of the Bible cannot be completely understood without the truths that they teach.

As in the first volume, I have struggled in this volume to put a sea of knowlege into every drop of language. Hence, the reader should not lightly read its pages, but should go back and make a full study of each truth revealed.

Finally, I felt led of the Lord to expound upon specific scriptures in Matthew that reveal the gross errors of the church today.

Gary T. Whipple

October 1, 1994

INTRODUCTION

This book was written to present an overview of the teachings of the book of Matthew and to give an intensive study of its thirteenth chapter.

The reader will soon come to see that Matthew is probably one of the most misunderstood of all the books of the New Testament. This is due to misunderstanding its scope of teaching and the terminology used to present its message.

Each of the four gospels presents a different emphasis on Jesus Christ's ministry while He was on the earth. John emphasizes His Deity and calls Him the "Son of God." Luke emphasizes His humanity and calls Him the "Son of man." Mark emphasizes His miraculous "works." Matthew emphasizes Him as the "King" – King of the Jews (He was born with this title) and the coming King of kings to rule over the earth during His millennial reign.

When attempting to show an unregenerated person how to be saved, one should use the book of John rather than the book of Matthew; because initial salvation is not emphasized in Matthew's gospel as it is in John's (John 20:31). Matthew is written to those who are already saved, showing them how to inherit the coming kingdom. Therefore, the scope of Matthew's gospel is not the salvation of the spirit of man (eternal life), but the salvation of the soul of man (millennial life). It does not emphasize the *gift* of salvation, which allows one to enter "heaven"; but the *prize* of salvation, which allows one to enter the "kingdom of heaven." Hence, the book of Matthew does not major on first tense salvation, i.e., salvation from the penalty of sin, but second tense salvation, which is salvation from the power of sin.

1

Second tense salvation begins at the moment one is saved (trusts Jesus as Saviour) and continues throughout his life on the earth. Its purpose is to save one who already belongs to God from the power of sin in his life by producing righteous works through him. Third tense salvation is the future redemption of the body of the believer at the rapture of the church. The church will be raised from the dead and caught out with the remaining living ones. They will all stand at the judgment seat of Christ and be judged according to their works (2 Cor. 5:10). These works will be either works of the flesh (unrighteous) or works of the Spirit (righteous). The believer must have righteous works to enter (inherit) the kingdom of heaven (Heb.1:14b). This kingdom is a literal, visible kingdom that will be established on the earth for a thousand years at His return.

The power of second tense salvation, or continuing salvation (salvation of the soul) while in this life, is produced by the Holy Spirit (already residing in the believer) as the believer continues to study the Word of God (Rom. 10:17). This, in turn, causes the believer to have continuous faith, repentance, and commitment of his life to Christ, so his life becomes automatically controlled by Christ. Christ's control of his life allows the Holy Spirit to produce His works of righteousness through the believer. These righteous works are necessary for a believer to gain rewards (rule and reign with Christ in His kingdom). (Note: see author's book *Shock and Surprise Beyond the Rapture* for details concerning these different salvations.)

TWO KINDS OF WORKS

In Matthew, the reader will recognize two kinds of works that can be produced by the believer; works of the flesh and works of the Spirit. It is within this framework of thought that the book of Matthew was written. Jesus came to Israel (His people) in order to find good fruit (works of the Spirit). Instead, He found only evil works (works of the flesh). They had turned from God's righteousness and were trying to establish their own righteousness by keeping the law.

Matthew teaches that Jesus came to the Jews first to offer the kingdom to Israel. Since entrance into the kingdom was an offer based on having righteous works, Israel was not in a position to inherit the kingdom and to rule over the nations of the earth. Therefore, the call for repentance went out from the preaching of John the Baptist and from Jesus – but to no avail. Israel, as a nation, rejected Jesus and finally crucified Him.

Before this occurred, the message of Jesus began to change, as recorded in the eleventh chapter of Matthew. He turned from Israel and began to offer the kingdom to individual Jews and Gentiles, which He will later reveal in the sixteenth chapter of Matthew as the "church." A formal rejection of Israel is taught in the twenty-first chapter, where Jesus formally withdrew His offer to Israel and gave the kingdom to the church.

The kingdom, then, has been formally given to the church based on works of righteousness (salvation of the soul). Believers who allow the Holy Spirit to produce these works through them in this lifetime will inherit the kingdom (receive a reward). Believers who produce works of self-effort in this lifetime will suffer loss of the kingdom at the judgment seat of Christ (1 Cor. 3:1-15). It is this qualification for entrance into the kingdom that the parables of Matthew chapters twenty-four and twenty-five address. They are written to the church and not to Israel.

CLOSING THOUGHTS

The major outline of Matthew is as follows:

I. The kingdom is proffered to Israel on the basis of national repentance (Matt. 1-10).

II. Israel refuses to repent (Matt. 11-12).

III. Jesus begins His rejection of Israel and to form His church (Matt. 13-21).

IV. Jesus formally rejects Israel, taking the kingdom from them and giving it to the church (Matt. 21:43).

V. Jesus prophesies Israel's punishment during the church age and the tribulation period (Matt. 24:1-31).

VI. Jesus instructs the church through parables on "how to enter the kingdom" (Matt.24:32-25:30).

VII. Jesus prophesies His judgment of the nations upon His return to establish His kingdom (Matt. 25:31-46).

VIII. Israel formally rejects Jesus and crucifies Him (Matt. 26:1-27:66).

XI. Jesus is bodily raised from the dead, instructs His disciples and ascends into heaven (Matt.28).

CHAPTER ONE

THE ROYAL LINE OF THE KINGDOM

Since Adam's fall, God's revealed goal has been to establish a literal, corporeal, physical kingdom of God on the earth, with Jesus Christ as its King. By understanding this introductory truth, the reader will soon discover that Matthew teaches a scope of truth different from that of John. In John, the main scope of teaching is the new birth (salvation); in Matthew, it is the kingdom (rewards of the saved).

REVELATION OF THE KING

"The book of the generation of Jesus Christ, the son of David, the son of Abraham" (Matt.1:1).

In the opening verse of Matthew, God reveals His Son, the Lord Jesus Christ, as the one who will be the future King who will rule over the earth. He also presents Christ's genealogical credentials and His Messianic titles, the "son of Abraham" and the "son of David." This was necessary to prove to Israel that He was of the royal line of David and the Promised Seed of Abraham. Thus, His Messianic titles were established in the very first verse of Matthew. In the remaining portion of the first chapter, His full genealogical credentials were recorded from Abraham down through Joseph (Mary's husband). This is called the *royal line* although Joseph was not His natural father.

Mary, His natural mother, gave to Jesus the *legal line* to the throne of David; she was a lineal descendent of Abraham and of David through Nathan. Nathan, David's other son by Bathsheba, was older than Solomon; so he became the legal heir to the throne and passed the title down to Jesus through Mary. The genealogy of the royal line is listed in Luke 3:23-38 and traces Jesus' lineage back to Adam and God. It proves that Jesus was the Divine man (the Son of man).

> "And Jesus himself began to be about thirty years of age, being (as was supposed) the son of Joseph, which was {the son} of Heli" (Luke 3:23).

Additionally, in Luke 3:23, Joseph is identified as the **"son of Heli,"** who was actually Mary's father and Joseph's father-in-law, because fathers-in-law were called "fathers" and sons-in-law, "sons." Also, **"as was supposed"** would have been more accurately translated "according to law," thus revealing Jesus as the legal heir of Joseph.

The Royal and Legal Lines Compared

> "{Is} this man Coniah a despised broken idol? {is he} a vessel wherein {is} no pleasure? wherefore are they cast out, he and his seed, and are cast into a land which they know not? (29) O earth, earth, earth, hear the word of the Lord. (30) Thus saith the Lord, Write ye this man childless, a man {that} shall not prosper in his days: for no man of his seed shall prosper, sitting upon the throne of David, and ruling any more in Judah" (Jer. 22:28-30).

Joseph's position as the unnatural father of Christ may present a problem to the casual reader of the Word. However, as we look closely at the royal line of Christ, we see that God used Joseph to safeguard the virgin birth of Jesus Christ and to thwart the efforts of Satan in his attempt to keep Jesus Christ off the throne of David.

God accomplished this by revealing in his genealogy that Joseph could not possibly have been Jesus' natural father. There had been a corruption of the royal line, of which Joseph was a member (see above scripture verse 30), because of Coniah (same as Jechonias in Matt. 1:11-12). The royal line stopped when God declared that no man of the seed of Coniah (son of King Jehoiakim) could prosper, **"sitting upon the throne of David and ruling any more."** Therefore, Jesus could not have been physically out of the royal line and also sit on David's throne. God solved this problem by

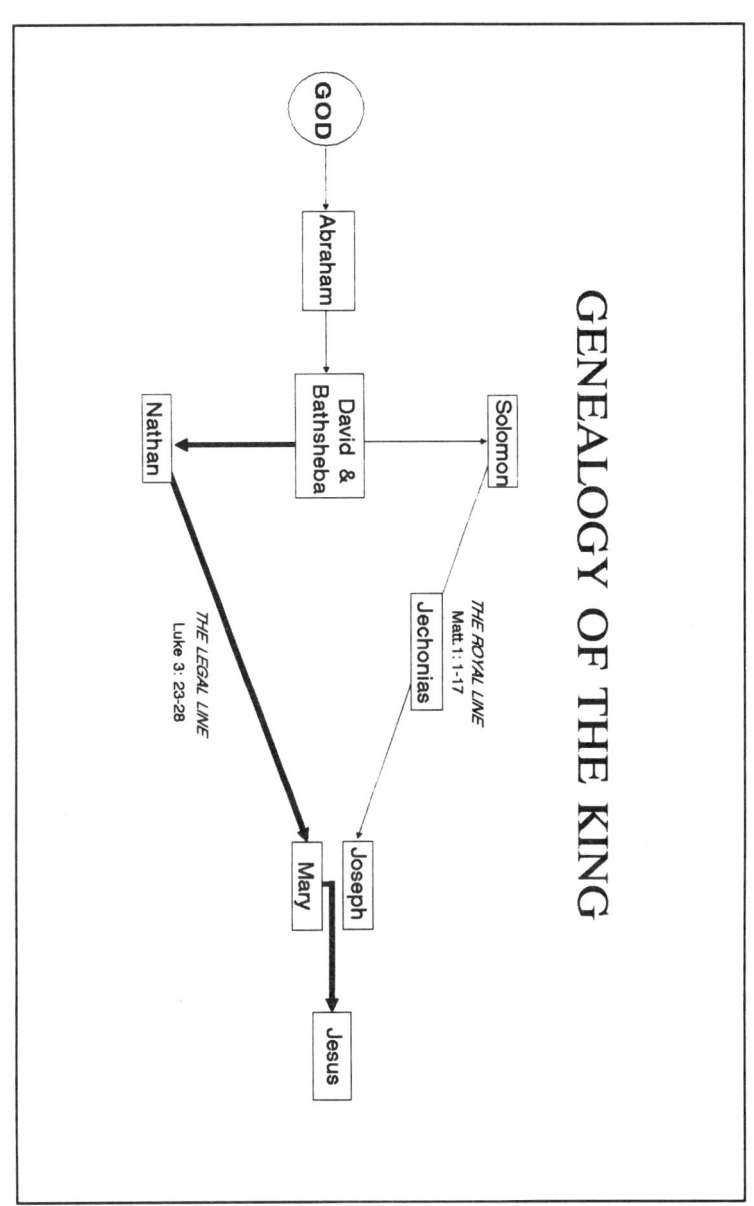

having Joseph marry Mary after she conceived by the Holy Spirit. This made Jesus the legal heir of Joseph and the legal heir to the throne of David.

The reader may be tempted to question this solution, thinking that the genealogy of Jesus must be from father to father. However, there is no spiritual law of God that excludes women from the genealogy of Jesus. As examples, Matt. 1:3 tells us that the royal and legal seed came through Thamar, who was a prostitute. In Matt. 1:5, the line continued through Rachab, the Canaanite, and Ruth, the Moabitess.

The Orthodox Jews totally reject this genealogical record that authenticates Jesus as their Messiah. They look forward to another that will be their Messiah, not knowing that if Jesus is not their Messiah, there can be no other. They do not realize that all genealogical records of the Messiah were destroyed in the first century. Hence, anyone who claims to be the Messiah today will be unable to authenticate his claim, since there are no records.

THE BEGINNING OF THE SEED

The book of Genesis is the germ seed of the kingdom; the book of Matthew is the announcement of the kingdom. The germ seed begins in Gen. 3:15, when it presents the coming King as a man — the Godman who is the Seed of the woman (the virgin birth). Still further in Genesis, we will recognize Abraham as the first foundational stone of the kingdom truths. It was to Abraham and his seed that God first gave the promises of the kingdom. As the centuries passed, his seed (collectively) multiplied until finally his Seed (singularly), the Lord Jesus Christ, invaded human history as the Seed of the woman, and made the announcement recorded in Matthew that the kingdom was at hand.

While this is historical, it is also doctrinal. The historical order of Genesis is the doctrinal order of the New Testament. With this in mind, we will present in the remaining portion of this chapter both the historical and the doctrinal orders that teach of the coming kingdom.

God's Original Plan

After God regenerated the earth from its condition of ruin and chaos (Gen. 1-2), He created man in His own image and placed him as the ruler over His restored creation (Gen. 1:26). However, Adam sinned. By sinning, he forfeited the rights of rulership to Satan, and Satan became the god of this age under the *rule of rulership*. This rule allowed him to rule the earth until another man could be qualified to take his place. Since no man of Adam's seed could be qualified, because of sin (Rom. 5:12), another Man, who was not of Adam's seed, would have to be found to restore the integrity of God's Word. Satan, believing that all men had to be the seed of Adam, thought he had legally thwarted God's plans. He reckoned that he would remain as ruler over the earth forever. But God's solution to this seemingly impossible situation was in His plan from the beginning; it had already been decreed in His secret council that His King would not be the seed of Adam, but the Seed of the woman.

The expression *seed of the woman* declares that the virgin Mary would be the natural mother of the new King and God would be His father. Since He would be the Seed of the woman, He would be born without the stain of sin (note: the stain of sin is passed down from father to son, making every person, male and female, the son of Adam). It follows that as a man, Jesus Christ, who is the Seed of the woman (without Adam's stain of sin), would qualify to rule over the earth; while, at the same time, as God, He would be impeccable and incapable of sin. This, in turn, would make His rule eternal.

The revelation of this plan from God was first uttered after Adam's fall and is recorded in Gen. 3:15. God used only one verse of prophecy to announce His glorious victory in the coming King, the Lord Jesus Christ, and to declare the utter defeat of Satan.

"And I will put enmity between thee and the woman, and between thy seed and her seed; it shall bruise thy head, and thou shalt bruise his heel" (Gen 3:15).

In this verse, God clearly stated that the Seed of the woman (Jesus Christ) would come, and He would be opposed by the serpent (Satan) and the seed of the serpent (antichrist). Satan would bruise His heel (on the cross), and He would bruise (Gr. *suntribo*, meaning to crush completely) the head of the serpent (Satan) (at His second coming) (Rom. 16:20). In view of this prophecy, the careful student of the Word will identify many time-honored and fundamental doctrines of the Bible; for example, the virgin birth, the first coming of Jesus Christ, the hatred of Satan for Israel, the death of Jesus Christ on the cross, the coming antichrist, the second coming of Jesus Christ and the ultimate destruction of Satan. Historically speaking, one can trace this promise of a coming Redeemer and King throughout the Old Testament and into the first book of the New; from Eve to Shem, to Abraham, to Isaac, to Jacob, to Judah, to David, to Mary, to Jesus.

In light of the fact that the Seed (the Promised Redeemer and King) must come through a line of redeemed men, God must have begun His redemptive work of grace with Adam and Eve; a work of redemption that would continue for six thousand years, with its full payment culminating on the cross of Calvary. For it was there that God would personally pay for the sins of the world with the death of His Son, Jesus Christ. God would then qualify a portion of those believing in His Son to be co-heirs with Him in His coming rule over the earth.

When God delivered His first message of redemption to Adam and his wife in Gen. 3:15, they believed. Thus, by grace through faith, they were redeemed. In two places of God's Word, we see the action of their faith after they believed in the coming "seed of the woman." First, in verse 20, when Adam gave his wife the name Eve, which means "mother of the living," or "mother of every father's family." It apparently was then that Adam believed that Eve was the woman that God spoke of; the woman who would bear the Seed. Therefore, he appropriately gave her a name that expressed his faith in God's word (note: before this time, God had called Adam's wife "Adam," Gen. 5:2). Second, this faith is seen in Eve when she named her first born son "Cain" (Gen. 4:1), which means "I got me a man from God." Again, we see faith in action. Eve believed that she was the woman in God's prophecy and that Cain was the Promised Seed.

A Look at the Redemption of Adam and Eve through Typology

Before we leave this section, which reveals God's original plan, we need to examine, through typology, the doctrinal teaching of redemption. Types are exact foreshadows of truth, used by God in the Old Testament to teach of His redemptive work and of His coming kingdom in the New Testament. It is the doctrinal truths of the New Testament that cast their shadows into the Old. The longest of these shadows of truth reaches back into the first chapter of Genesis.

As an example, the shadow, or typical picture, of salvation in Adam and Eve is confirmed to us by God when He made coats of skins and clothed their nakedness (Gen. 3:21). God must have slain an innocent animal (possibly a lamb) before He made these coats. In typology, the slain animal is an emblem, or foreshadow, of Jesus Christ (the Lamb of God), who willingly died on the cross. The coats of skins, therefore, typify the coats of righteousness procured by the shed blood of Jesus Christ on the cross, which are imputed to all believers at the moment of faith in Jesus Christ. Notice carefully when the skins were provided. They were not put on Adam and his wife until after they had believed (verse 20).

To add to this typical picture, God reveals that before He had clothed them with skins, Adam and Eve were wearing aprons of fig leaves made by their own hands. Fig leaves are a type of man's own works, and making them into aprons is a type of the lost man's attempt to cover his sins (nakedness). Therefore, these fig leaf aprons typically speak of man's own self-righteous coverings of works, and is particularly an emblem of all religious

11

institutions that teach salvation by works.

THE SEED OF ABRAHAM

> "Now the Lord had said unto Abram, Get thee out of thy country, and from thy kindred, and from thy father's house, unto a land that I will shew thee: (2) And I will make of thee a great nation, and I will bless thee, and make thy name great; and thou shalt be a blessing: (3) And I will bless them that bless thee, and curse him that curseth thee: and in thee shall all families of the earth be blessed" (Gen 12:1-3).

In Abraham, God begins to reveal the "Promised Seed"; the One who would be the "Royal Seed" (Jesus Christ); the One who would depose Satan as ruler over this earth and become the ruler Himself; the One who would fulfill the goal of prophecy for a Man to rule over the earth. Also, God begins to reveal, through Abraham's life, that which is necessary to qualify one to have a part with the "Promised Seed" in ruling over the earth.

The Natural Seed of Abraham

The "natural seed" of Abram began with Ishmael, who became the father of the Arabian people. However, Ishmael was rejected as the "son of promise" (heir to the land), since he represented the fruit of the flesh of Abram. He was born of Hagar, the Egyptian handmaid of Sarai, the wife of Abram. Consequently, Ishmael came to portray Abram's and Sarai's lack of faith in God's Word. For God had proclaimed that He would give the couple a child through their faith (works of the Spirit) and without their own efforts. Hence, all of Abram's seed through Ishmael and, later, through the sons of his second wife, Keturah, represent works of the flesh and are, thus, the natural seed of Abraham (Gal. 4:22-27).

The National Seed of Abraham

When Abram and Sarai finally came to trust God for a child without adding any works of the flesh, God gave them Isaac, the "son of promise." Out of Isaac came his son, Jacob, who, in turn, became the father of the twelve tribes of Israel through his own twelve sons (each being a father of one of the twelve tribes). As a result, these twelve tribes became the "national seed" with rights under the Abrahamic covenant to inherit the land. However, the land given to Abram and his "national seed" has never been completely occupied (Gen. 15:18) and cannot be until Jesus Christ, the "Royal Seed," returns to the earth to reign over it for a thousand years.

The Royal Seed of Abraham

Out of the "national seed" came Jesus Christ, the "Royal Seed." His lineage was through the tribe of Judah, the family of David and the virgin Mary. He was the fulfillment of the prophecy given to Adam and Eve that spoke of the coming "seed of the woman." He is the greater son of Abraham and, as such, is the heir to the promises made to Abraham by God.

> "Now to Abraham and his seed were the promises made. He saith not, And to seeds, as of many; but as of one, And to thy seed, which is Christ" (Gal 3:16).

The word *seed* in the Hebrew is both a singular and collective noun, depending on its contextual setting. In the above verse, we are told that its singular use points to Christ and to the ultimate fulfillment of the promises made to Abraham and his seed. As a result, Christ is the legal heir and owner of the land of Palestine, plus all other lands that fall within the scope of the inheritance (Gen. 15:18).

The Spiritual Seed of Abraham

The "spiritual seed" of Abraham represent all people, both Jew and Gentile, who have come out of the "Royal Seed" (Jesus Christ) through faith. God informs us that all nations (Gentiles) who have the same faith as Abraham (believing God's Word concerning the Promised Seed — Jesus Christ) will become the seed of Abraham — not the seed of his flesh, but of his faith. **"Therefore {it is} of faith, that {it might be} by grace; to the end the promise might be sure to all the seed; not to** that only which is of the law [Israel], but to that also which is of the faith of Abraham [the church]; who is the father of us all, (As it is written, I have made thee a father of many nations,)..." (Rom. 4:16-17a)

The Ruling Seed of Abraham

The "ruling seed" represent believers who will receive a reward at the judgment seat of Christ because they produced righteous works in this life (1 Cor. 3:13-14). They will be selected out of the spiritual seed (those from all nations who trusted Christ) at the judgment seat of Christ and will inherit the kingdom. **"For we must all appear before the judgment seat of Christ; that every one may receive the things {done} in {his} body, according to that he hath done, whether {it be} good or bad"** (2 Cor. 5:10). Those who fail to produce righteous works (works of Christ through them) will not receive a reward; i.e., not be members of the ruling seed. **"If any man's work shall be burned, he shall suffer loss: but he himself shall be saved; yet so as by fire"** (1 Cor. 3:15).

It is worthy to note that the "national seed" (Israel), as the "children of the kingdom" and "those who were bidden" (Matt. 8:12; 22:3), had the privilege of becoming part of the "ruling seed" of the kingdom, but rejected it. If they had only believed as Abraham believed and, as a result, repented nationally and brought forth spiritual fruit, they would have had the privilege of becoming the "wedding guests" in the literal coming kingdom of Christ. This would have given them power as kings to rule over cities in the coming kingdom (Matt 22:1-14). However, they rejected the offer and, consequently, the privilege was withdrawn and given to the church (Matt. 21:43). Only an individual Jew, by renouncing his position as an Israelite under law and becoming a member of the church through faith in Jesus Christ, the "Promised Seed," would still have this privilege. This privilege would then not only be an invitation for them as believers to become the "wedding guests," but also a higher opportunity to become the "bride of Christ" (Rev. 19:7b-8).

The Bride of the Royal Seed of Abraham

Contrary to that taught by most teachers, all believers during the church age are not counted by God as being automatic members of the "bride of Christ," but only those believers who attain to the highest level of rule. Those of the bride will be joint-heirs with Christ in His coming kingdom because of the suffering they endured with Christ in this present world. Scripture teaches that all the saved during the church age are heirs of God, but only those who suffer with Christ are joint-heirs with Him (Rom. 8:16-17). Therefore, the bride of Christ will be a higher selection out of the saved, and will rule "over much" or "over all that He has" (Matt. 24:45-47; 25:21-23). (For a detailed study of this subject, see chapters eight and nine of the author's book *Shock and Surprise Beyond the Rapture*.)

In conclusion, the highest position in the coming kingdom of heaven will be given to those of the church who will be called "joint-heirs with Christ" (the bride). They will come out of the wedding guests (the ruling seed); who, in turn, will come out of the spiritual seed (all the saved); who will, by faith, spiritually come from Christ (the Royal Seed); who physically came out of the national seed (Israel); who, in turn, physically came out of the natural seed of Abraham; who physically came out of Eve, to whom the promise was first made. See diagram, p. 17.

THE SEED OF DAVID

In Matt. 1:1, Jesus was not only called the "seed of Abraham", but also the "seed of David". Thus, through the tribe of Judah and the house of David came the Royal Seed, Jesus Christ.

> "Behold, the days come, saith the Lord, that I will raise unto David a righteous Branch, and a King shall reign and prosper, and shall execute judgment and justice in the earth. (6) In his days Judah shall be saved, and Israel shall dwell safely: and this {is} his name whereby he shall be called, THE LORD OUR RIGHTEOUSNESS" (Jer. 23: 5-6).

"And, behold, thou shalt conceive in thy womb, and bring forth a son, and shalt call his name Jesus. (32) He shall be great, and shall be called the Son of the Highest: and the Lord God shall give unto him the throne of his father David: (33) And he shall reign over the house of Jacob for ever; and of his kingdom there shall be no end" (Luke 1: 31-33).

The Jewish leaders of Jesus' day failed to recognize Christ as the "son of Abraham" and the "son of David." Yet, Jeremiah, one of their own prophets, was very clear when he said that He would be born the Seed of David, would sit upon David's throne (a literal, earthly throne) and that He would be Jehovah in the flesh (THE LORD OUR RIGHTEOUSNESS). On the other hand, the liberal theologians of today are trying to destroy the writings of Luke by spiritualizing them. They teach that the throne of David is in the heart of man and that Jacob and Israel have become the church; thus making the rule of Jesus occur in the heart of the church only.

However, when Jesus announced to Israel that the kingdom was at hand (book of Matthew), it was to be a literal kingdom, with its King (Jesus Christ) sitting upon a literal throne. Nevertheless, Israel rejected Him and His kingdom and, as a result, the kingdom was postponed for two thousand years. At the close of these two thousand years (the church age and the seven year tribulation period), the nation of Israel will finally inherit all the land that was promised to them as the saved national seed of Abraham. Nevertheless, their loss of the privilege of ruling and reigning with Christ in His coming kingdom (the kingdom they rejected) will be forever. Only those Jews who are individually saved during the church age, who turn their backs on Judaism, will have this opportunity as members of the church.

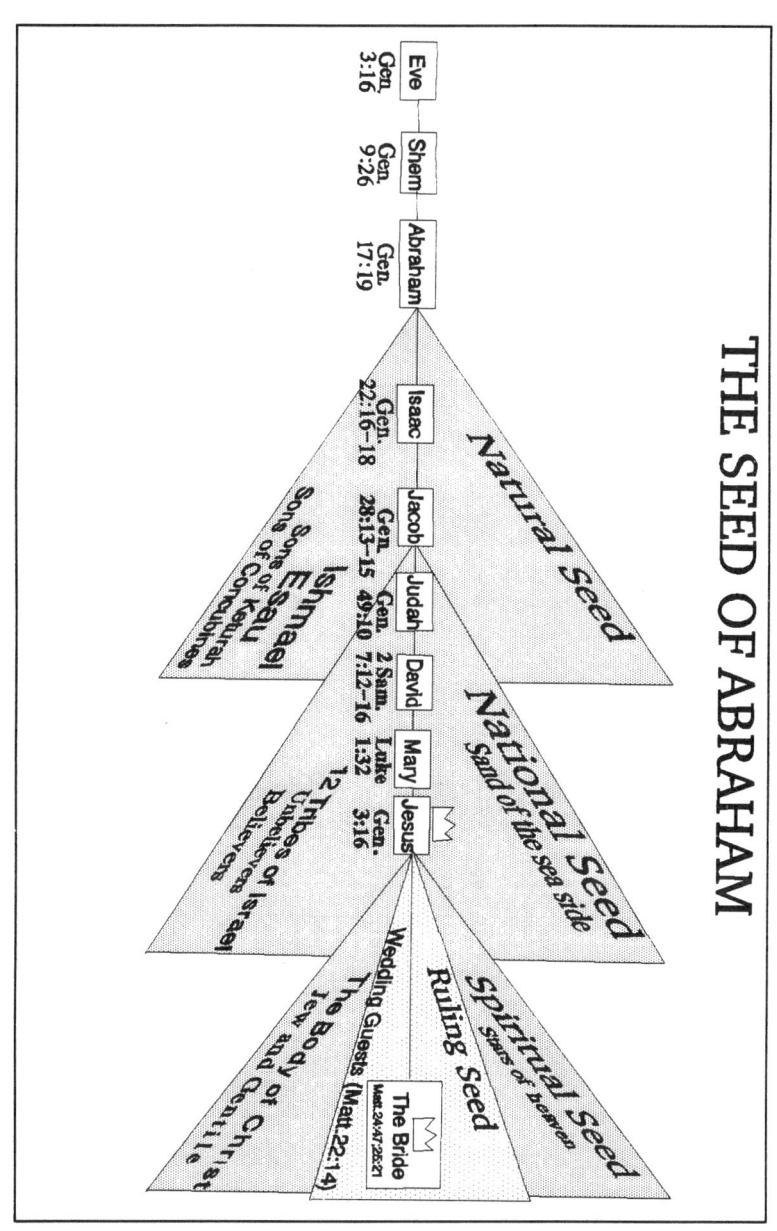

NOTES

CHAPTER TWO

THE ANNOUNCEMENT OF THE KINGDOM

Jesus Christ invaded human history about four thousand years after Eve first learned of the coming "seed of the woman." Thirty years after His birth, the book of Matthew records, He entered into His public ministry. It was then that He began to announce the coming kingdom of heaven. This announcement was for Israel to "repent," because the kingdom of heaven was about to appear (Matt. 4:17). We would think that Israel (the national seed of Abraham) would have believed Jesus and, as a result, responded to this message; particularly since He authenticated His message by performing signs and wonders. But they were not interested. They didn't even search out the signs of His coming recorded in the Old Testament. If they had checked the scriptures, they would have discovered the following signs.

THE GEOGRAPHICAL SIGN

> "But thou, Bethlehem Ephratah, {though} thou be little among the thousands of Judah, {yet} out of thee shall he come forth unto me {that is} to be ruler in Israel; whose goings forth {have been} from of old, from everlasting" (Micah 5:2).

In this verse, it is clearly prophesied that the Messiah would be born in Bethlehem. When the wise men of the east came into the court of Herod inquiring where the young child Jesus was, they alarmed Herod so much that he sent soldiers to Bethlehem to kill all the male children up to two years of age (Matt: 2:7,16).

THE CELESTIAL SIGN

> "I shall see him, but not now: I shall behold him, but not nigh: there shall

come a Star out of Jacob, and a Sceptre shall rise out of Israel, and shall smite the corners of Moab, and destroy all the children of Sheth" (Num. 24:17).

In this prophecy, Balaam spoke of a Star arising out of Jacob and a Sceptre out of Israel. The old rabbis, from time immemorial, associated the star that appeared in the east with the star of Jacob prophesied by Balaam. There were many that recognized the significance of the star, but the large majority of Israel ignored it.

THE GOVERNMENTAL SIGN

"The sceptre shall not depart from Judah, nor a lawgiver from between his feet, until Shiloh come; and unto him {shall} the gathering of the people {be}" (Gen. 49:10).

This prophecy came from Jacob when, on his deathbed, he revealed to his sons the things that would happen to them in the last days. Simply expressed, this prophecy tells us that when the sceptre (the sign of Israel's governmental power) had departed from Judah, the Messiah would be on the earth. The sceptre is the visible symbol of the power of government, which allows it to execute capital punishment. So what Jacob said, in effect, through this prophecy was that when Judah could no longer execute a sentence of death on a criminal, Shiloh (the Lord Jesus Christ) would have come.

In John 18:28-31, we read of Jesus being taken to Pilate by the Sanhedrin to be sentenced and executed. When Pilot said, **"You take Him and judge Him according to your laws,"** they answered, **"It is not lawful for us to put any man to death."** The sceptre had departed from Judah and every Jew should have been aware of this prophecy and realized that Shiloh had come.

THE CHRONOLOGICAL SIGN

"Seventy weeks are determined upon thy people and upon thy holy city, to finish the transgression, and to make an end of sins, and to make reconciliation for iniquity, and to bring in everlasting righteousness, and to seal up the vision and prophecy, and to anoint the most Holy. (25) Know therefore and understand, {that} from the going forth of the commandment to restore and to build Jerusalem unto the Messiah the Prince {shall be} seven weeks, and threescore and two weeks: the street shall be built again, and the wall, even in troublous times. (26) And after threescore and two weeks shall Messiah be cut off, but not for himself: and the people of the prince that shall come shall destroy the city and the sanctuary; and the end thereof {shall be} with a flood, and unto the end of the war desolations are determined. (27) And he shall confirm the covenant with many for one week: and in the midst of the week he shall cause the sacrifice and the oblation to cease, and for the over spreading of abominations he shall make {it} desolate, even until the consummation, and that determined shall be poured upon the desolate" (Dan. 9:24-27).

Probably the most amazing of all signs is the chronological sign, which reveals the very year in which Christ would be crucified on the cross. Daniel was studying the book of Jeremiah and realized that the seventy years of captivity of the children of Israel was almost completed (Dan. 9:2 Jer. 25:11-12; 29:10). He was thinking that at the expiration of the seventy years, the Lord would come. But while Daniel was in prayer over the matter, the Lord sent the angel Gabriel to further instruct him that the Messiah would not appear to Israel at this time, and they must wait (after the conclusion of their captivity of seventy years) until seventy weeks had expired before the Messiah would appear and the kingdom would be restored to them. The Hebrew term *seventy weeks* means "seventy sevens," or four hundred ninety years (one "week" is equal to seven years). According to the angel's message from God, the seventy weeks cover the time from the going forth of the commandment to restore and build Jerusalem, which was in the month of Nisan (March) in the twentieth year of Artaxerxes Longimanus, the Persian king (about 453 B.C.), to the second coming of Christ (Neh. 2:1-5).

The first period of seven weeks in this prophecy refers to the time it would take to restore and to build Jerusalem. History tells us that it took forty-nine years. This forty-nine years gives us the key to the meaning of "week"; for if seven weeks are equal to forty-nine years, then each week is equal to seven years.

The second period of threescore and two weeks, or four hundred and thirty-four years (one week equals seven years), refers to the time from when Jerusalem would be restored and built to the coming of the "Messiah the Prince" (Jesus Christ). Hence, the total of seven weeks and threescore and two weeks tells us that four hundred eighty-three years was to pass from the commandment to restore and build Jerusalem to the first coming of Christ and His death on the cross; i.e., being "cut off" (see verse 26).

The Seventieth Week

At this point in our prophecy, many have become confused over the seventieth week, or last seven years. The question may be asked, "Shouldn't the last week of this prophecy have begun at the cross and continued for seven years, and shouldn't Christ have come back at that time?

No, after Christ was crucified, God stopped the time clock of this prophecy, because Christ had been rejected and God would no longer be dealing with Israel. As a result, they would be scattered throughout the world for two thousand years until God had finished dealing with His other people, the church. After the rapture, God would once again gather all of Israel into the land and begin dealing with them in judgment and tribulation until a remnant would be saved. Like pulling the plug on an electric clock, God had stopped this prophetic clock at the end of the sixty-ninth week. When He starts it again, Israel must go through the last seven years (the seventieth week) of Daniel's prophecy, which is the "great tribulation" and the "time of Jacob's trouble." But only a remnant, one third of them, will come out alive. This last week of Daniel's prophecy is recorded in verses 26 and 27.

In verse 26, after the cutting off of the Messiah, we are introduced to the people of the prince that shall come and destroy the city and the sanctuary (Jerusalem and the rebuilt temple). Many think that this prince refers to Titus and the Roman legions that destroyed Jerusalem in AD 70; but the Hebrew definite article tells us that he is the antichrist, whose coming has been announced and expected. He is, evidently, the same as the "little horn" of the seventh and eighth chapters of Daniel. Titus and the destruction that he accomplished can only be viewed as a type of antichrist. Therefore, after Messiah was cut off in the beginning of this verse, a time gap of over two thousand years was placed by God between Christ's death and the appearance of this prince (in the middle of verse 26) who would prevail unto the end, which is the end of all things determined by God for Israel. These are a flood, a war and desolations. The flood is a figure that refers to the desolating judgment of God, and here, specifically, the last outpouring of his wrath, in which the prince shall be destroyed (compare Isa. 10:20-24; 30:27-33). The war and desolations speak of the nations invading Israel; they are also a part of the flood of God's wrath.

In verse 27, we see the details of these events of the tribulation period. Lest the reader become confused, this method of giving the major points of prophecy first and then its details later is employed by God throughout the books of Daniel and Revelation. In verse 26, we see the major points of the coming antichrist and his people during the tribulation period — his coming, their attack on Israel, and their destruction by God. But in verse 27, the focus is on the antichrist himself when he comes to Israel claiming to be their Messiah and **"confirming the covenant with many for one week,"** or seven years. The use of the word *confirm*, not "make," shows that antichrist will be counterfeiting Christ's authority to confirm the Abrahamic covenant. He will be saying, in effect, "Follow and worship me, for it is the time for you to enter the kingdom and share in the promises of Abraham." He will allow them to build their temple and reinstitute the temple worship sacrifices to convince them that he is Christ. This will be the greatest confidence game in human history, for he will thoroughly convince many Jews (not all) with signs and miracles that he is Christ (1 Cor. 1:22). But in the middle of the week, or three and one half years later, he will become the "beast" of Revelation. He will cause the sacrifice and the oblation to cease in the temple and, in its place, he will have idols of himself erected. The worship of Jehovah will be transferred to himself; and he will exalt himself above all that is called God or that is worshiped. He will seek to slay all the Jews by ultimately convincing the nations of the world to bring their armies against them. God says that He will then destroy those nations and pour out His determined wrath upon antichrist (the desolate; Heb. *desolator*) and destroy him at His coming.

This will occur when Messiah appears in the heavens and then goes forth to make war on the nations to utterly destroy them (Rev. 19:11-21). He will also rescue the remnant of Israel, judge the nations and set up His kingdom.

His sixfold purpose for Israel that is mentioned in our text will then be fulfilled. When He returns, He will:

Finish the Transgression:

This refers to the transgression of Israel, which can be finished only when the nation is converted at Christ's coming. The finishing of the transgression speaks of the turning away of "ungodliness from Jacob" (Rom. 11:26-27).

Make an End of Sins:

The Hebrew says to *seal up sins*. Sins are the symptoms of Israel's revolt and the figure of sealing them is connected to prison. Hence, sealing them up signifies their arrest and custody. This verse could also refer to Satan, the author of Israel's sins, being sealed in the bottomless pit at Christ's coming (Rev. 20:1-3).

Cover Iniquity:

This means, according to the scriptural figure, to make reconciliation, or atonement, for iniquity; to expiate by sacrifice. While in the previous purposes, the refining process of judgment upon members of the Jewish nation was referred to, this purpose speaks of another way to remove sin and to identify the holy seed, who will be saved. Though the atonement on the cross was made for Israel's sins, it will not be applied to Israel, as a nation, until Christ returns and they look upon Him whom they have pierced (Zech. 12:10; 13:1). For Jews, as a people, there is no expiation in this present dispensation; if an individual Jew is to have the benefit of the death of Jesus Christ, he must willingly resign his nationality and become a member of Christ, in whom there is neither Jew nor Greek.

Bring in an Everlasting Righteousness:

When Israel's transgression has come to an end and her sins are shut up, then everlasting righteousness will be brought in. This will be done by the introduction of the new covenant, when God will no longer write on tables of stone, but will put His law in their inward parts and write it upon their hearts (Jer. 31:33-34).

Seal Up Vision and Prophecy:

When Israel's sins are sealed up, there will no longer be a need for vision and prophecy.

Anoint the Holy of Holies:

This probably refers to the anointing of the "most holy place," or the "holy of holies," of the "millennial temple," described by Ezekiel in the 41st chapter. There will be no ark of the covenant with its mercy seat in the "most holy place" of the millennial temple (Jer. 3:16), only the royal throne where the Messiah will sit as the "King Priest" (Zech. 6:12-13) whose anointing is referred to here.

Closing Thoughts Concerning This Sign

The Jews living during the days of Christ could have figured out the first sixty-nine weeks of this self-explaining prophecy and, as a result, have recognized Jesus as the Messiah when He began to preach, "Repent, for the kingdom is at hand." They had the key to understanding the meaning of the seventy weeks. They knew that the temple was completed in forty-nine years (or seven weeks in Daniel's prophecy). Hence, the next sixty-two weeks, from the completion of the temple to the coming of Messiah, would have to be four hundred and thirty-four years. The accuracy of this time scale is amazing. Jesus was crucified (cut off) on the third day after Israel officially rejected Him on Palm Sunday (the last day of the sixty-ninth week) of that year. Yet, the Jews were blinded to these things, especially to His death.

THE SIGN OF JOHN THE BAPTIST

John the Baptist was the first to announce the kingdom. He was chosen by God to be the forerunner of Jesus Christ and the **"voice of one crying in the wilderness, Prepare ye the way of the Lord, make His paths straight"**(Matt. 3:3). Isaiah prophesied John's coming and mission. He was to be like one who goes before a king in his journeys, making the crooked paths of his travel straight and the rough places smooth (Isa. 40:3). John's purpose was to point to and announce to Israel the arrival of the King, Israel's Messiah, who was already in their midst. Hence, his message was to **"repent, for the kingdom of heaven is at hand"**(Matt. 3:2).

When the leaders of Israel learned that John was baptizing scores of repenting Jews in the river Jordan, their curiosity got the best of them and they sent priests and Levites to him inquiring who he was (John 1:19-23). They wanted to know if he was the Christ, and he said, "I am not." They asked him if he was Elias (Elijah), and he said, "I am not." They asked him if he was that prophet (spoken of by Moses in Deut. 18:18), and he answered, "No!" Little did they know when they asked John this last question that the prophet spoken of by Moses was none other then the Lord Jesus Christ, who was in their midst. Finally, they asked him to tell them who he was, and he answered, **"I am the voice of one crying in the wilderness, Make straight the way of the Lord, as said the prophet Esaias [Isaiah]."** This statement alone, without knowledge of any of the other signs mentioned above, should have been enough to reveal to the leaders of Israel that the Messiah had come and the kingdom was about to appear. All they needed to do was to read the book of Isaiah in its fortieth chapter, verse 3. But they were so entrenched in Judaism that they turned a deaf ear.

John the Baptist was not only a preacher of the "gospel of the kingdom," but also a prophet. Jesus called him the greatest of all the prophets (Luke 7:28). He prophesied of Messiah's coming judgment, and His power to save. In Matt. 3:10, he informed Israel that judgment was near, with the figure of an ax which is laid to the root of the trees, poised to cut them down. The figure of trees in scripture is an emblem of either nations or apostate men, depending on the context (compare Luke 21:29 with Jude 1:12). In John's prophecy, it emphasizes men who will be cut down in judgment and cast into the fires of judgment. Notice that this judgment is not a judgment of unbelievers, but of men who belong to God and who fail to bring forth good fruit. The immediate context speaks of these as being the apostates of Israel — the Pharisees and Sadducees, who said, in verse 9, that since they had Abraham as father, they needed nothing else. But John, in verse 7, called them vipers and revealed God's wrath that was to come upon them.

In verse 11, John begins to prophesy of the two baptisms of the coming Christ; baptisms that were to be totally different from John's, which was the baptism of repentance. John's was with (Gr. in) water, Christ's would be with (Gr. in) the Holy Ghost and in fire. Add to this Christ's command for Christian baptism, and we have a total of three baptisms in which every Christian must be baptized to enter the coming kingdom.

The Baptism in the Spirit

The first baptism of Christ mentioned in verse 11 is "baptism with (Gr. in) the Spirit." This occurs at the very moment a lost person first trusts Jesus as his Saviour. He is immersed by Christ into the Holy Spirit, and immediately becomes a member of the body of Christ (the church). Contrary to what others teach concerning this baptism, the Holy Spirit (or Holy Ghost) is not the baptizer, but the element in which the person is baptized. It is Jesus who is the baptizer. We see this in 1 Cor. 12:13, where we read, **"For by one Spirit are we all baptized into one body, whether {we be} Jews or Gentiles, whether {we be} bond or free; and have been all made to drink into one Spirit."** The second word of this verse (by), which is the Greek preposition *en,* should have been translated "in" and not "by." It is the same word that was used by John the Baptist in our text, but translated there as "with." One certainly cannot be baptized (Gr. immersed) with water. For immersion means "in." Hence, as John the Baptist immersed "in" water, so Christ immerses "in" the Spirit. It is amazing how one little mistranslated Greek preposition could have brought so much confusion to the church; confusion that is responsible for forming the false doctrine of the "baptism of the Holy Spirit"; .i.e., the Holy Spirit coming upon the believer sometime after he is saved and baptizing him. No, no, a thousand times! There is but one work of grace for the believing sinner. When he is saved, he is simultaneously immersed by Christ "in" the Spirit, which makes him a member of the body of Christ. This is positional grace, which gives him peace "with" God. Only after the believer grows in this grace does he begin to experience standing grace, which continually gives him the peace "of" God. Perceptively, a Christian should not be striving to possess more of Christ, but striving to allow Christ to possess more of him.

The Christian Baptism

The second baptism is called Christian baptism. Though this baptism is not in view in our Matthew text, it is, nonetheless, commanded of each new believer by our Lord (Matt 28:19). This baptism is an immersion into water, symbolizing the believer's testimony that he has judicially died in Christ, was buried with Christ and has arisen to a new life.

The Baptism of Fire

Being contrary once more to what others have taught, the baptism of fire in our text is not the baptism of the Holy Ghost or the baptism of power from the Holy Ghost. It is the future fire at the judgment seat of Christ, in which every Christian must be baptized to have his works tested, whether good or bad (2 Cor. 5:10). This baptism is particularly descriptive in 1 Cor. 3:15, where it says: **"If any man's work shall be burned, he shall suffer loss: but he himself shall be saved; yet so as by [Gr. through] fire."** The term *through fire* in this verse suggests a literal immersion into fire, which will destroy only the chaff, or bad works, of the Christian at the judgment seat of Christ.

This is further seen in the 12th verse of Matthew 3, which reads: **"Whose fan {is} in his hand, and he will thoroughly purge his floor, and gather his wheat into the garner; but he will burn up the chaff with unquenchable fire."** The symbol, *fan,* in Christ's hand is a shovel-like device that was used by the reapers of John's day to scoop up their harvested wheat and throw it into the air so that the wind could separate it from its chaff (bad works). By using this method of separation, the wheat would fall directly to the barn floor while the chaff would blow away. Then the reaper would gather the wheat into the garner, but the chaff would be burned up. Hence, in this verse, John is prophesying the coming judgment seat of Christ in heaven for the church, since the church is always symbolized by wheat. However, it also speaks of the coming judgment of Israel on earth during the "great tribulation period," when God will refine His earthly people by burning off the chaff in His furnace of affliction (Isa. 48:10). For only the remnant will be saved.

IN CONCLUSION

With all these signs in evidence, the Jews still would not accept that Jesus of Nazareth was their Messiah. The Jews did not see — they did not understand — they were blinded; because they had turned from the Old Testament that recorded these signs and read only the traditions of men. They cared not for the Word of God, and they missed the greatest opportunity of their lives. For two thousand years, the nation of Israel has paid and paid in agony, tragedy and suffering untold; all because they did not believe in the signs of the times. No wonder Jesus called them hypocrites.

The first twelve chapters of Matthew show clearly that the message of the kingdom, i.e., the gospel of the kingdom, was given by Jesus to Israel only and was accompanied by the baptism of John the Baptist (a baptism of repentance, not salvation). After John the Baptist was slain and the leadership of Israel refused to repent, the offer of the kingdom was withdrawn. This withdrawal occurs at the close of the twelfth chapter, but is not historically completed until about forty years after the cross.

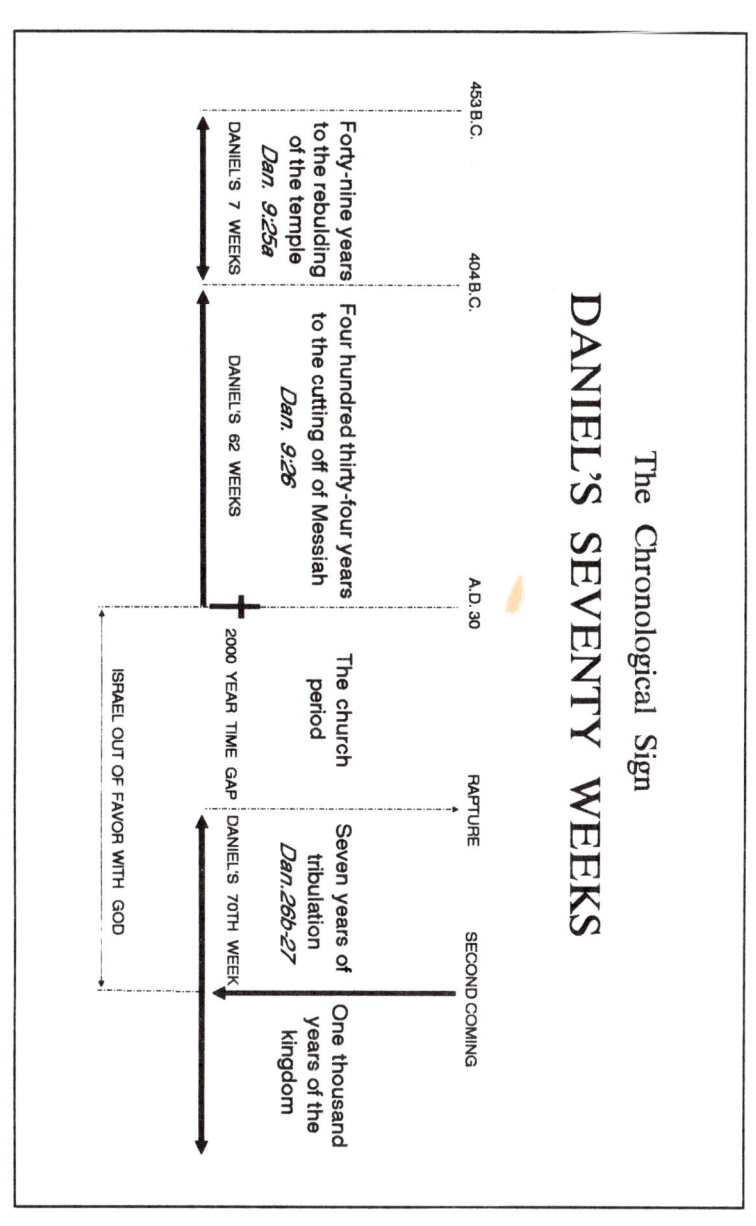

NOTES

CHAPTER THREE

THE MESSAGE OF THE KINGDOM

When Jesus Christ entered His public ministry, His message was the same as John the Baptist's: "Repent for the kingdom of heaven is at hand" (Matt. 3:2; 4:17). One may ask why Jesus did not preach the message of John 3:16 in Matthew. The answer is twofold. First, the message of John is not written generally to Israel, but to all nations that they might believe that Jesus is the Christ (John 20:31). Second, John 3:16 could not be preached until after the crucifixion, since it is a different gospel, the gospel of grace. In view of this, it is important for the reader to understand that the mission and message of Jesus, while in the flesh, was only to the lost sheep of the house of Israel. It was the "gospel of the kingdom" that He preached and not the "gospel of grace."

This truth is seen in Matt. 15:24 and 26, when a Gentile woman came in faith asking Him to heal her daughter. Jesus said, **"I am not sent but to the lost sheep of the house of Israel..."** and, **"It is not meet to take the children's [Jew's] bread and cast it to the dogs [Gentiles]."** However, the woman, by faith, took the position of a little house dog who rightfully has the privilege to eat the crumbs that fall from the table of the children (the Jews). She recognized that she, as a Gentile, had no part yet in the blessings of God, which were only for the Jews. This act of faith resulted in Jesus healing her daughter; for God honors all faith.

This message is again revealed in Matthew when Jesus sent His disciples out to preach. They were told not to go to the Gentiles, but to the lost sheep of the house of Israel, and as they went, they were to preach, "The kingdom of heaven is at hand" (Matt. 10:6-7).

THE FIVE GOSPELS

For centuries, the church has been confused over the interpretation of the book of Matthew. The major reason is that they have not discerned the difference between the five distinct gospels that are in the Bible (also called five aspects of the gospel of God). These are: the "gospel of the kingdom," the "gospel of grace," the "gospel of glory," the "everlasting gospel" and "my gospel" (Paul's gospel). In Matthew, it is the "gospel of the kingdom" that Jesus preached to the Jews.

Each gospel is but an aspect of the one gospel of God, emphasizing a different facet of truth that determines its title. Hence, the good news of God is a muti-faceted truth.

The Gospel of the Kingdom

"From that time Jesus began to preach, and to say, Repent: for the kingdom of heaven is at hand" (Matt. 4:17).

The first gospel of this multi-faceted truth is called the "gospel of the kingdom." It was first preached by John the Baptist and then by Jesus to the Jews. It was the good news that the kingdom was about to be established on the earth. This would have fulfilled the covenant that God had made with David pertaining to his house and his throne; the same covenant that would raise up David's Seed (Jesus Christ) to sit on his throne and rule over the house of Israel forever (Luke 1:30-33).

Therefore, when Jesus Christ first appeared in Israel preaching, "Repent: for the kingdom is at hand," He was offically offering the kingdom to Israel based on their national repentance for disobeying God's commandments. Israel rejected the offer by refusing to repent and, as a result, crucified Christ. In spite of this rejection, God, in His great love and patience, elected to give Israel a probationary period of time after the crucifixion (about forty years) during which they could repent. This probationary period necessitated that the "gospel of the kingdom" would be preached to national Israel during the same time that the "gospel of grace" was being preached to the Gentiles (up to about A.D. 63).

During the early church period, the "gospel of the kingdom" included a different message from that preached before the crucifixion. Before the crucifixion, the gospel of the kingdom called upon national Israel to repent for their disobedience to God's commandments; after the crucifixion, it called upon them to repent for rejecting and crucifying the Lord Jesus Christ.

The gospel of the kingdom was preached during the early church period to individual Jews, calling upon them to *repent* and be baptized in the name of Jesus Christ (Acts 2:38). At the same time, the gospel of grace was being preached to individual Gentiles, calling upon them to *believe* on the Lord Jesus Christ (Acts 10:43; 16:30-31; Rom. 1:16).

Forty More Years:

The probationary time period that God gave to national Israel in which to repent ended around A.D. 63. This extended time beyond the cross was given as an answer to Jesus' dying prayer on the cross. For it was there that He prayed, **"Father, forgive them; for they know not what they do."** To let the Jews know that Jesus' prayer was answered, God informed them through Peter's second sermon that He would allow Israel more time in which to repent because of their ignorance in crucifying their Messiah (Acts 3:17). Scripture tells us that this time ran out in about A.D. 63. History informs us that God waited about seven more years before He destroyed the city of Jerusalem in A.D. 70.

During Peter's sermon, he told his Jewish hearers, **"Repent ye therefore, and be converted, that your sins may be blotted out, when the times of refreshing [the establishing of the kingdom] shall come from the presence of the Lord"** (Acts 3:19). Peter's message was not the "gospel of grace," but the "gospel of the kingdom." It was preached here as it was in his first sermon (Acts 2:38) and would continue to be preached to Israel until the last of the Jewish leaders (in Rome) would reject God's offer for the final time. The "gospel of the kingdom" ceased to be preached around the year A.D. 63 when God set Israel aside. About seven years later, He scattered them throughout the world.

The Future Preaching of This Gospel:

The "gospel of the kingdom" will not be preached again until after the church is raptured and the dispensation of grace is over. During the tribulation period that follows the rapture, 144,000 Jewish evangelists will be sealed by God to preach to the Gentiles. They will go throughout the world (excluding Israel) preaching the "gospel of the kingdom." Scripture tells us that the end (of this present age) will not come until this gospel is preached in all the world (Matt 24:14).

Many Christian writers, not knowing the difference between the "gospel of the kingdom" and the "gospel of grace," have erroneously taught that the gospel of Matt. 24:14 must be preached throughout the world before the rapture can occur. However, this verse does not speak of the "gospel of grace," but the "gospel of the kingdom." The reference to the end in this verse is not the rapture of the church, but the revelation of Jesus Christ at His coming to set up His kingdom. Hence, this scripture correctly says that the "gospel of the kingdom" must be preached throughout the world (during the tribulation period) before Christ will appear to set up His kingdom. This preaching of the kingdom will be done by the 144,000 sealed Jews throughout the world. No scripture teaches that the "gospel of grace" must be preached to every creature in the world before the rapture can occur.

Repent versus Believe:

The command to "repent" in the gospel of the kingdom is a national command. That is, the leadership (scribes, Pharisees and other leaders) of Israel were commanded to repent and turn back to God, thus causing the nation to turn back to God.

The gospel of grace tells us that the way of salvation for all men during the church age is to believe on the Lord Jesus Christ. Repentance is not a part of this gospel. The word *repent* cannot be found one time in all the pages of John's gospel, which tells all people how to be saved (John 20:31) The apostle Paul tells us in Eph. 2:8-9 that salvation is by grace through faith, and not of ourselves. It is NOT OF WORKS lest any man should boast. This scripture leaves out repentance, because repentance before faith is a condition, or a work; and if a work, then also a boast.

The only time the word *repent* is used during the church age is when our Lord gives a warning in six of the seven letters that He sent to the seven churches of Revelation (Rev. 2:5; 2:16; 2:21; 2:22; 3:3; 3:19). In each letter, our Lord was/is telling a church to repent and turn back to God. Since all the individuals of these churches were/are already saved (except for most of Thyatira) and had apostatized (fallen away) from God, He was/is warning them of the consequences if they do not turn back (repent).

"Repent" is used in the scriptures mainly as a demand from God to those who already belong to Him and have spiritually fallen away. Hence, it not only is a word used by our Lord for Israel (nationally speaking) as a condition to inherit the kingdom (Acts 5:31); it is also a condition for Christians who desire to please God in order to inherit the kingdom. The results of repentance are manifested in the Christian's life by a continuous confession of his sins (1 John 1:9).

Many evangelists have tried to use Acts 20:21 to prove that a Gentile must repent before he can be saved. **"Testifying both to the Jews, and also to the Greeks, repentance toward God, and faith toward our Lord Jesus Christ."** They have called upon the lost in revival meetings to repent and then believe to be saved. However, Paul is speaking about two different peoples in this verse — Jews and Gentiles — and about two different gospels. Thus, to understand this scripture more fully, it could rightly be interpreted, "Testifying both to the Jews, repentance toward God, and to the Greeks, faith toward our Lord Jesus Christ."

One of the few times that repentance is used differently in the scripture is in Paul's sermon at Mars' hill (Acts 17:30). His use of the term here is a general call for all men to repent, i.e., for the entire human race, who turned away from God while in Adam, to turn back to him.

The Gospel of Grace

> "For I delivered unto you first of all that which I also received, how that Christ died for our sins according to the scriptures; (4) And that he was buried, and that he rose again the third day according to the scriptures" (1 Cor. 15:3-4).

The second gospel of this multi-faceted truth of God is called the "gospel of grace." It was first stated in Paul's letter to the Corinthians. However, contrary to what some teach, grace did not begin with Paul, but at the cross; for it was at the cross that the law was fulfilled in Christ. The cross fulfilled the dispensation of the law and ushered in grace. Fifty days later at Pentecost, the church began. It was made up of Jews who were saved under the preaching of the "gospel of the kingdom" and, later, of Gentiles who were saved under the preaching of the "gospel of grace." After national Israel was set aside in A.D. 63, the "gospel of the kingdom" was no longer preached. Instead, the "gospel of grace" was preached exclusively to both the Jews and the Gentiles.

It is important for the reader to note the difference between these two gospels in the early church (before A.D. 63). The comparison is demonstrated by the apostle Paul when he was asked by the Philippian jailer (a full blooded Gentile), **"Sirs, what must I do to be saved?"** Paul's answer was, **"Believe on the Lord Jesus Christ and thou shalt be saved..."** (this is the gospel of grace). He did not say, **"Repent, for the kingdom of heaven is at hand"** (Matt. 4:17); or, **"Repent, and be baptised in the name of Jesus Christ for the** remission of sins" (Acts 2:38); or, "**Repent therefore, and be converted, that your sins may be blotted out**"(Acts 3:19). These verses speak of the "gospel of the kingdom," which was for the lost Jew. The earliest accounts of the gospel of grace being preached, before the time of the Philippian jailer, were to the Ethiopian eunuch (Acts 8:37) by Philip and to Cornelius by Peter (Acts 10:44-45). Both were full-blooded Gentiles and neither was told to repent. They were saved by believing on the Lord Jesus Christ.

It is also worthy to note that the "gospel of grace" was preached at the same time that the "gospel of the kingdom" was preached — up until the time of Acts 28:28 (about A.D. 63). It was here that Paul preached the "gospel of the kingdom" to the Jewish leaders in Rome, until they rejected it. Then the Holy Spirit said, through Paul, "**For the heart of this people is waxed gross, and their ears are dull of hearing, and their eyes have they closed; lest they should see with {their} eyes, and hear with {their} ears, and understand with {their} heart, and should be converted, and I should heal them. Be it known therefore to you that the salvation of God is sent unto the Gentiles, and that they will hear it**" (Acts 28:27-28). Thus, in A.D. 63, the probationary time period established by God for the nation of Israel ran out.

Israel had refused to repent when Jesus came preaching, and they hanged Him on the cross. Then they refused to repent for crucifying the Lord of Glory. At this time (A.D. 63), they rejected the "gospel of the kingdom" for the last time, and this salvation was taken from them and given to the Gentiles. From this time on, the "gospel of grace" would be preached to the Gentiles and the individual Jew. A dispensational boundary line had been crossed. From then until the rapture, God would be dealing only with the church, which would be composed of the individual Jew and Gentile with each being saved under the preaching of the "gospel of grace."

The Nature of the Two Gospels:

(1) Under the preaching of the "gospel of the kingdom," the poor were cared for out of the common treasury (Acts 2:44-45; 4:34-35); under the preaching of the "gospel of grace," every man is to provide for his own (1 Tim. 5:8).

(2) Under the preaching of the "gospel of the kingdom," they were not to provide gold, nor silver, nor an extra cloak (Matt. 10:9-10); under the preaching of the "gospel of grace," they are to provide things honest in the sight of all men (Rom. 12:17).

(3) Under the preaching of the "gospel of the kingdom," a rich man had to sell all that he had and give it to the poor to enter the kingdom (Mark 10:21); under the preaching of the "gospel of grace," rich men are told to do good with their riches and be ready to distribute to the needy (1 Tim. 6:17-19).

(4) Under the preaching of the "gospel of the kingdom," there appeared signs and wonders, which served to authenticate those who were preaching it; under the preaching of the "gospel of grace," only the Word being illuminated by the power of the Holy Spirit serves to authenticate those who are preaching it.

(5) Under the preaching of the "gospel of the kingdom," those who preached it were to go only to the lost sheep of the house of Israel (Matt. 10:5-6); under the preaching of the "gospel of grace," those preaching it are to go to the Jew first and then also to the Greek (Gentile) (Rom. 1:16).

The Gospel of Glory

"In whom the god of this world hath blinded the minds of them which believe not, lest the light of the glorious gospel of Christ, who is the image of God, should shine unto them" (2 Cor. 4:4).

The third gospel of this muti-faceted truth of God is the "gospel of glory." It was obscured in the translation of the King James version of the Bible. To understand this, the above verse should have been translated the "gospel of the glory of Christ," instead of the "glorious gospel of Christ."

The established principle of this gospel is the coming glory of Christ, which will be revealed to the entire universe when He returns to establish His kingdom. Most Christians teach only of His first coming and His humiliation on the cross, and never mention His coming again in glory. Others not only teach of His first coming, but also His secret coming to catch-out (rapture) the church. However, the good news that Christ is coming in His glory and that every eye shall see Him should also be preached and taught by Christians during this church age. They would be emphasizing both His cross and the crowns He has won — the Saviourship and the Kingship of our Lord Jesus Christ.

The Everlasting Gospel

> "And I saw another angel fly in the midst of heaven, having the everlasting gospel to preach unto them that dwell on the earth, and to every nation, and kindred, and tongue, and people" (Rev. 14:6).

The fourth gospel of the multifaceted truth of God is called the "everlasting gospel." This is the only gospel that is to be preached by an angel. The establishing principle of this gospel is that His creation is to sanctify and to glorify God as the creator of all things. It will be preached at the closing of this present age during the great tribulation, when men in general will have denied the creative power of the Lord God. This is the good news that because God is the creator of all things, He should be worshiped.

My Gospel

> "Now to him that is of power to stablish you according to my gospel, and the preaching of Jesus Christ, according to the revelation of the mystery, which was kept secret since the world began..." (Rom. 16: 25).

The fifth gospel of this multifaceted truth of God is called "my gospel." The apostle Paul first used the term *my gospel* in his letter to the Roman church. Seemingly, he was the only one of the apostles commissioned by God to fully understand its message; therefore, he called it "my gospel." Later, we will see that Peter, James and Jude also received special wisdom from God that was to enhance Paul's gospel. This wisdom was known as the "salvation of the soul." However, they were not given the additional wisdom that Paul had received and, therefore, could not preach it. Peter mentions this wisdom of Paul's in 2 Peter 3:15b-16, saying that Paul's wisdom was in all his epistles and that some things of his gospel were hard to understand.

Paul's gospel, stated simply, tells us that those of the Gentile church age (saved Jews and Gentiles) will have the right to enter the kingdom, become the bride of Christ and, as a result, become co-heirs with Him when He comes to establish His kingdom over the earth. Those who attain to this high position must earn the right to do so by producing righteous works.

This gospel is contrary to traditional theology, which teaches that all who are saved will automatically become the bride of Christ. However, as one studies the epistles of Paul, especially his prison epistles, it will become evident that this future position is not reserved for those who are just saved, but for those who are "overcomers"; overcomers of the power of sin in their lives, which results in the producing of righteous acts (spiritual works, or fruit); overcomers at the judgment seat of Christ because of the "salvation of their souls."

Paul tells us that the "overcomers" (the bride of Christ and the wedding guests) will be selected from all the saved at the judgment seat of Christ. They will be those who have allowed the Holy Spirit, during this lifetime, to control their lives and produce His works (symbolized by gold, silver, precious stones) through them, saving their souls. On the other hand, those who produce unrighteous works, i.e., works of self (symbolized by wood, hay, stubble), will suffer loss. This loss is the loss of the kingdom and the loss of their souls for one-thousand years (2 Cor. 5:10; 1 Cor. 3:11-15). Paul's "my gospel" divides the "gift" (Rom. 5:15-17), which is salvation, from the "prize" (Phil. 3:13-14), which is reward. The gift of grace is free to every one who believes on the Lord Jesus Christ (taught by the gospel of grace); the prize (taught by Paul's "my gospel") must be attained by righteous works (the works of Christ *through* us), which save our souls and grant us entrance into the kingdom of heaven (reward) at the judgment seat of Christ.

According to our text, Paul's "my gospel" was a mystery from the beginning of the world. This means that it was not known in Old Testament times, nor revealed to the prophets. Jesus was the first one to preach it (Heb. 2:3), and the writer of Hebrews called it "so great salvation." Hence, the "great salvation" of Hebrews is the same as Paul's "my gospel," and speaks of a future salvation that will be given to those who are privileged to enter the kingdom as the bride of Christ to rule and reign with Him. A further exhortation of our Lord, in Heb. 2:1-3, about this great salvation is that we, as Christians, ought to more earnestly heed this gospel and not let it slip away. If we do, there will be no escape at the judgment seat of Christ — the place where all Christians will receive exactly what they deserve (because of good or bad works produced in their bodies after they were saved). This is called a "just recompence of reward" (Heb. 2:2; 2 Cor. 5:10).

Some have argued that what Jesus preached, according to Heb. 2:3, was the gospel of grace. But this cannot be so. The gospel of grace was known in the Old Testament. Adam, Noah, Abraham, David and countless others were saved by grace. The prophets understood grace. Isaiah prophesied of the grace that should come upon us. He wrote of Jesus' death on the cross. But in Heb. 2:3, the Word of God tells us that this great salvation was first preached by Jesus Christ. Never before had it been preached by anyone. Therefore, this secret had been well kept until Jesus revealed it. Later, the apostle Paul was commissioned to explain it; which he did in all of his epistles, especially his prison epistles of Ephesians, Philippians, Colossians and First and Second Timothy. The writer believes that Paul also wrote the book of Hebrews, since it, too, contains the truths of "my gospel."

When Paul first came to the Corthinthian church, they were

babes in the Lord and carnal in their lives (1 Cor. 3:1-2). Since they could not receive meat ("my gospel"), Paul could only give them milk (the gospel of grace)."**For I determined not to know any thing among you, save Jesus Christ, and him crucified**" (1 Cor. 2:2). Howbeit, there were some who were spiritually mature (perfect) in that church, and Paul gave meat ("my gospel") to them; the gospel that had been hidden from the beginning of the world. "**Howbeit we speak wisdom among them that are perfect: yet not the wisdom of this world, nor of the princes of this world, that come to nought: But we speak the wisdom of God in a mystery, {even} the hidden {wisdom}, which God ordained before the world unto our glory.**"(1 Cor. 2:6-7). It is this gospel that gives us wisdom that we might understand the prize; i.e., the rewards of entering into the coming "great salvation."

These rewards reveal what God has prepared for them that love Him — not for those who are just saved, but for those who continually, i.e., are continually endeavoring to (Gr. present active participle), love Him. For "**...it is written, Eye hath not seen, nor ear heard, neither have entered into the heart of man, the things which God hath prepared [the prize, or reward, or inheritance] for them that love him. But God hath revealed {them} unto us by his Spirit [the Word of God that teaches Paul's 'my gospel']**"(1 Cor. 2:9-10a).

The Three Mysteries of My Gospel:

Paul's "my gospel" is made up of three different mysteries, each of which was hidden from the Old Testament prophets. Only as they are revealed in Paul's epistles can we understand how they collectively describe the "my gospel" of Paul.

(1) The first mystery revealed:

"How that by revelation he made known unto me the mystery; (as I wrote afore in few words, (4) Whereby, when ye read, ye may understand my knowledge in the mystery of Christ) (5) Which in other ages was not made known unto the sons of men, as it is now revealed unto his holy apostles and prophets by the Spirit; (6) That the Gentiles should be fellowheirs, and of the same body, and partakers of his promise in Christ by the gospel" (Eph 3:3-6):

Here, Paul reveals the first mystery: that the Gentiles would be fellowheirs with the Jews, and of the same body, and also partakers of the same promises that Israel thought were exclusively theirs. He mentions this again in Eph. 2:14, when he tells us that Christ has broken down the middle wall of partition between the Jews and the Gentiles. This expression comes from the middle wall that was erected to separate the worship area in the temple from the court of the Gentiles. Only the Jews were allowed to partake in the ordinances, promises and covenants of God. The Gentiles could only approach as far as the court of the Gentiles and were shut out by the wall that was erected there. When Christ died and grace was ushered in, Paul used this figure (the middle wall of partition broken down) to teach that a new dispensation had begun and grace was to be for all men, Jew and Gentile. It must be noted that Paul is not speaking about mixing the Gentiles with Israel, but with individual Jews. Hence, this union would form the church — a new people of God; a people whom God would be dealing with for two thousand years after He had rejected national Israel (His earthly people) and set them aside. Thereafter, when any man, Jew or Gentile, would become a member of the church, he would no longer be considered by God to be a Gentile or a Jew, but a member of the church of God (1 Cor. 10:32; 12:12-13). Therefore, in God's eyes, there is no Christian Jew or Christian Gentile, but a Christian with a Jewish or Gentile culture.

This mystery has been interpreted in various ways by those of the church throughout the church age. Some have taught erroneously that Israel has been completeley rejected by God and, as a result, lost all of God's promises to them to the church. Seemingly, these teachers have failed to read Rom. 11, which tells us that **"God hath not cast away his people which he foreknew [elected],"** but that one day all of Israel will be saved (Rom. 11:26a). They do not understand that the covenant that God gave to Israel is unconditional; for one day (during the millennium), all the saved of Israel will dwell safely in their promised land. At the present, the nation of Israel has only been set aside while God deals with His heavenly people (the church). After the rapture, God will again begin dealing with Israel, His "first born son" among the nations.

Another erroneous view that is widely taught by traditional theology is that the church (representing all the saved during the church period) will automatically become the bride of Christ and receive all rewards, no matter how they lived their lives after they were saved. The truth will be seen when we consider the two mysteries that support Paul's gospel. These mysteries teach that only those individuals who receive rewards at the judgment seat of Christ will be called-out of the body of Christ (Gr. *eklektos,* meaning called-out of the called) to become members of a higher body, identified as the "bride of Christ". Opposed to this, those who fail to gain rewards will remain members of only the body of Christ (Gr. *kletos,* meaning called, or saved) (Matt 22:14).

(2) The second mystery revealed:

> "{Even} the mystery which hath been hid from ages and from generations, but now is made manifest to his saints: (27) To whom God would make known what {is} the riches of the glory of this mystery among the Gentiles; which is Christ in you, the hope of glory" (Col.1: 26-27).

The second mystery further helps in defining Paul's "my gospel." The verses in Col. 1:26-27 have remained a mystery to most Christians; for they tell of the reward to be given to the bride (the riches of glory) and what qualifies the bride to receive the reward (Christ in you, the hope of glory).

What are the riches of glory? What is the hope of glory? The Old Testament prophets could not answer these questions, since these secrets were hidden from them. However, during the church age, these answers should be obvious; yet, only a few have discovered them.

The riches of glory is the reward, which is also described as the "prize". In winning, or attaining to, this prize, Paul compared his life, in Phil. 3:14, to an athlete pressing on in order to win this prize. The path that he was running was the path of good works (or the producing of spiritual fruit), which God has ordained we all should walk in (Eph. 2:10). The prize is the high calling of God in Christ Jesus. Notice that in Phil. 3:14, Paul did not say the prize was the "calling" (Gr. *kletos*), but the "high calling". The calling is the free "gift" by grace (Rom. 5:15) and is received the moment one believes on the Lord Jesus Christ. It is through faith and not works. The "prize" is a different thing. It must be attained to, or worked for, since it is the "high calling" of God (a calling out of the called, i.e., the saved).

The apostle Paul again compares this contest to an athlete in 1 Cor. 9:24-27. He tells us that if we win the race, we will win a crown (the incorruptible crown); and if we lose the race, we are in danger of becoming a castaway (Gr. *adokimos*, meaning disapproved, or rejected). This does not mean that a saved person can become a castaway from salvation, for that was purchased by Christ and can never be lost; but a castaway from the "riches of glory," i.e., the prize, or the inheritance, of the kingdom. Hence, the "riches of glory" are not attained by just receiving the free "gift" by grace (salvation), but by attaining, or winning, the "prize" through spiritual works after one is saved.

The text explaining this second mystery also tells us that the only way we can live our lives, i.e., run the race, in such a manner as to produce spiritual fruit is to have the "hope of glory" operating in us. But what is the "hope"? Contrary to traditional theology, it is not faith. Faith looks into the hand of God and sees there what is already his. Then, he reaches out and claims it on the basis of what Christ has already done on the cross. Hope, on the other hand, sees in the hand of God what can be his (the reward, or the prize). Then, he runs the race, in faith, hoping that he can win the prize. The word *hope*, then, means anticipation (Gr. *elpis*). However, this anticipation does not rest as faith does. It knows that it is possible to lose the crown. Therefore, it continues to produce fruit in the race of life, its eye fixed on the prize, anticipating winning it. This hope is established in a believer by the Holy Spirit (Christ in you) as He shows him the "prize" of the kingdom through the scriptures. This hope has been a mystery to most of those of the church age. They have understood that Christ is sealed in every believer at salvation, giving him security and offering him power, but have never understood that to have the hope of glory they must further accept, through faith, His offer of the kingdom. Consequently, they have missed the hope and, without this hope continuously operating in a Christian's life, he cannot produce the spiritual fruit necessary to attain to the prize.

(3) The third mystery revealed:

> "Husbands, love your wives, even as Christ also loved the church, and gave himself for it; (26) That he might sanctify and cleanse it with the washing of water by the word, (27) That he might present it to himself a glorious church, not having spot, or wrinkle, or any such thing; but that it should be holy and without blemish.(28) So ought men to love their wives as their own bodies. He that loveth his wife loveth himself. (29) For no man ever yet hated his own flesh; but nourisheth and cherisheth it, even as the Lord the church: (30) For we are members of his body, of his flesh, and of his bones. (31) For this cause shall a man leave his father and mother, and shall be joined unto his wife, and they two shall be one flesh. (32) This is a great mystery: but I speak concerning Christ and the church" (Eph. 5: 25-32).

In our above text, we examine the great mystery of the bride of Christ, which traditional theology has attempted to claim for all the saved, no matter how they live their lives. As we regard these verses more closely, we will come to see that the bride of Christ is something more than those who are just saved. In teaching these truths, the Holy Spirit employs typology as a method of this declaration.

Consider these points of truth in our text: First, the relationship of the bride to Christ is compared to the relationship of the wife to the husband. Our Lord calls this the great mystery (verses

31-32), for the bride is bone of His bones and flesh of His flesh (verse 30). To understand this more fully, we need to look at Adam and Eve. Adam is a type of Jesus Christ, who is called the last Adam (1 Cor. 15:45). In Gen. 2:21-22, we are told that God took a portion of Adam's body to make him a second body. This second body was also called Adam (Gen 5:2), for Adam said, "This is now bone of my bones and flesh of my flesh" (Gen. 2: 23). Hence, Adam had two bodies. In like manner, the last Adam (Christ) also has two bodies. The first body represents all those who are saved by His work on the cross, while the second represents those who will be called-out of the first body to be His bride (Gr. *eklektos,* meaning outcalled). Therefore, at the judgment seat of Christ, a second body, made up of the "wedding guests along with a higher selection — the bride of Christ," will be taken out of the first body, called the "body of Christ." Those who remain in the first body will be those who are only saved (received the free *gift* of grace); whereas those who become members of the second body will be members of the bride or bridal party (will receive the *prize*). After one is saved, he must attain to the prize, or membership in the bride. This calls for the producing of righteous works and a clean life after he is saved. Only the Holy Spirit can accomplish this work through our lives as we submit to Him through the Word.

The second point of truth in our text speaks of the cleansing of those who will be members of the bride. Before the wedding can take place in heaven, the bride must be presented to Christ (the Bridegroom) without **"spot or wrinkle or any such thing"** and **"be holy and without blemish."** Only the **"washing of water by the Word"** can accomplish this. Nevertheless, not all the saved are constantly being cleansed by the Word of God. Most do not know what the Bible teaches beyond salvation and popular devotional studies. Most are not convicted of their sins when they read the Word and see no need to confess them. Hence, many will be ashamed when they arrive at the judgment seat of Christ (1 John 2:28); they will be saved by the blood of the Lamb, but that is all. Only those who have seen the prize that is set before them and proclaimed by the Word of God will hope and strive for the mastery (of their life) (2 Tim. 2:5). And because of this hope, they will be continually (day by day) cleansed by the Holy Spirit by the washing of the Word (1 John 1:9).

THE SALVATION OF THE SOUL

There is a thin line that separates the doctrine of the "salvation of the soul" and the doctrine of Paul's "my gospel." One tells us how a believer can win the prize, while the other tells us what the prize is. While both are needed to fully understand Paul's "my gospel," the "salvation of the soul" is not necessarily a part of "my gospel." We see there is a difference, because Peter and James preached the doctrine of the "salvation of the soul," but were not permitted to preach Paul's "my gospel."

The apostle Peter tells us that both the "salvation of the soul" and "my gospel" were hidden from the Old Testament prophets; hidden so well that the prophets did not know their meaning or for whom they were intended. He also tells us that even the angels desired to look into this salvation and "my gospel" and to learn more about it. **"Of which salvation [salvation of the soul] the prophets have inquired and searched diligently, who prophesied of the grace {that should come} unto you ['gospel of grace']: Searching what, or what manner of time the spirit of Christ which was in them did signify, when it testified beforehand the sufferings of Christ, and the glory that should follow. Unto whom it was revealed, that not unto themselves, but unto us they did minister the things, which are now reported unto you by them that have preached the gospel ['my gospel'] unto you with the Holy Ghost sent down from heaven; which things the angels desire to look into"** (1 Pet. 1:10-12).

Peter was allowed to see the difference between "salvation of the soul" (to which he refers in 1 Pet. 1:6-9) and "salvation of the spirit." He knew that the "salvation of the spirit" (Gr. perfect tense) was the salvation a lost person must acquire by faith to receive the gift of eternal life. He knew also (according to his writing) that "salvation of the soul" (Gr. present tense) must be won by the believer at the judgment seat of Christ to receive the prize of inheriting the kingdom. However, Peter was not allowed to write on what the "prize" was. Only Paul was commissioned to teach this truth.

Peter apparently knew of the millennial kingdom and the rewards that will be given to the church at Christ's revelation (1 Pet. 1:13), but he was not allowed to write on Paul's "my gospel." Hence, the rewards that Peter wrote about for the church are not those of the millennial kingdom, but the "everlasting kingdom" (2 Pet. 1:11) and the "kingdom of the new heavens and the new earth" (2 Pet 3:13). Therefore, the kingdom in Peter's epistles appears to be the "kingdom of the Father," referred to in Matt. 13:43, which does not come into being until after the one thousand year millennial kingdom has been completed and the earth is destroyed by fire (2 Pet. 3:11-14).

Those Christians who will have an entrance ministered unto them abundantly into the everlasting kingdom (2 Pet. 1:11) will be the same ones who will have attained to an inheritance in the millennial kingdom one thousand years earlier (revealed by Paul's "my gospel"). In light of this, it is the writer's opinion that the prize won at the judgment seat of Christ by the faithful Christian will not only exist for one thousand years (through the millennial kingdom), but forever (throughout the everlasting kingdom).

A Comparison of Peter's and James' Wisdom

"Whom having not seen, ye love; in whom, though now ye see {him} not, yet believing, ye rejoice with joy unspeakable and full of glory: (9) Receiving the end of your faith, {even} the salvation of your {souls}" (1 Pet. 1:8-9).

"Wherefore lay apart all filthiness and superfluity of naughtiness, and receive with meekness the engrafted word, which is able to save your souls" (James 1:21).

Both Peter and James wrote on the "salvation of the soul." Peter tells us when the soul is saved and James tells us how the soul is saved.

In Peter, we are told that the salvation of the soul is a continuing salvation, which begins at the new birth and ends at the judgment seat of Christ. The phrase *receiving the end of your faith*, in the Greek, means "increasing, or maturing (Gr. present tense) your faith until it reaches its goal." The end, or goal, of our maturing faith will not be reached until we arrive at the judgment seat of Christ after the rapture of the church. It is only then that we will begin to walk by sight and not by faith. All believers will not automatically have their souls (Gr. lives) saved at the judgment seat; only those who have, through a maturing faith, produced spiritual fruit. Those who fail to present spiritual fruit will lose their souls (lives in the kingdom); and, because their souls are not saved, they will fail to inherit the kingdom and will be excluded for the entire one thousand years.

In James, we are told how our soul is saved: by laying apart all filthiness (sin) and with meekness receiving the engrafted Word (the Word that is already in the Christian). Hence, to the degree that a Christian grows in the Word, to that same degree is his faith matured (Rom. 10:17). To the degree that his faith, in this life, is matured, to that same degree is his soul saved at the judgment seat of Christ. If his faith is not matured and, as a result, he produced no fruit, he will lose his soul (life) and receive no reward, **"but he himself shall be saved; yet so as by fire"** (1 Cor. 3:15b).

CLOSING THOUGHTS

The purpose of this chapter is to show the mission and message of Jesus in the book of Matthew. He came to preach the good news of the kingdom to the lost sheep of the house of Israel. And only as we see Israel rejecting Him, will we come to understand His prophecies of the coming Gentile church through His parables.

To get a firm grasp of what the gospel of the kingdom is, we must contrast it with the four other gospels of the Bible. Thus, we see the multifaceted good news of God's Word, of which the "gospel of the kingdom" is a part.

NOTES

CHAPTER FOUR

THE CREDENTIALS OF THE KINGDOM

> "These twelve Jesus sent forth, and commanded them, saying, Go not into the way of the Gentiles, and into {any} city of the Samaritans enter ye not: (6) But go rather to the lost sheep of the house of Israel. (7) And as ye go, preach, saying, The kingdom of heaven is at hand. (8) Heal the sick, cleanse the lepers, raise the dead, cast out devils: freely ye have received, freely give" (Matt. 10:5-8).

Many ministers and their churches today sincerely believe that they are performing the signs and wonders of the first century church when they attempt to speak in tongues and heal the sick. I say "attempt," because, according to God's Word, all signs and wonders were terminated at the dispensational boundary line of Acts 28:28, when the preaching of the "gospel of the kingdom" was set aside. This occurred about A.D. 63. In light of this truth, the reader will see that not one legitimate sign or wonder has been performed by the church in the past nineteen hundred and thirty years.

The purpose of this chapter is to reveal the "credentials of the kingdom" and the errors of the charismatic movement in these last days; a movement that is based on emotionalism rather than the Word; a movement that has crossed all denominational and religious lines in an attempt to counterfeit the credentials of the kingdom.

In the above text, our Lord sent His twelve apostles out to preach. As they went, they were to (1) preach only to the "lost sheep of the house of Israel," (2) preach the good news that the kingdom of heaven was at hand and (3) perform certain signs and wonders as credentials to authenticate this gospel. These credentials were the healing of the sick, cleansing of the lepers, raising of the dead and casting out of devils. They were in force until about A.D. 63, when they ceased to exist. Since then, there have been no legitimate signs and wonders given by God and performed by men.

In the writer's opinion, there are three types of individuals who are caught up in the charismatic movement of today. These are (1) those sincere Christians who are seeking to speak in tongues and be physically healed, but cannot, (2) those Christians who believe they have the faith to be healed and the ability to speak in unknown tongues by deliberately making indiscernible sounds and (3) those who are either apostate Christians or counterfeit Christians.

FAITH HEALERS

It is difficult to discern the difference between the apostate Christian and the counterfeit, since the motive for both is the same, self-glory and riches. When either the apostate Christian or the charlatan makes a decision to go into the full time faith healing business, they both will fill great auditoriums with people wanting to be healed. Both will be viewed on Christian television by millions. Both will be in the entertainment business, with one being a lost counterfeit and the other a saved counterfeit. Both will be seeking millions of tax free dollars from their duped followers. The fake divine healing business is big business. It is the largest legal confidence game in the world, since it is classified as a religious exercise. One such faith healer, according to investigative reporting, took in over eighty-million dollars in 1992 alone.

The counterfeit faith healer mainly promotes his healing services by looking for people who have hypochondria (imaginary illnesses) and/or for people who are just caught up in the belief, excitement and expectation of his ability to perform miracles. The faith healer will never allow a person who is blind or who has withered limbs on the stage. They are usually screened out by being told by his associates that there is not enough room for them in that session and for them to come back to the next meeting. Some faith healers have even used actors in wheel chairs to create an atmosphere of credibility for their healing services.

The faith healer must be a combination psychologist, magician and entertainer to be rich and successful in his chosen profession. However, when he leaves this world, he will stand before God Almighty at his judgment. While the charlatan will have his just desserts in the lake of fire forever (Rev. 20:13b-15), the apostate Christian will suffer the fiery indignation of God before the judgment seat of Christ and be thoroughly and dreadfully punished outside of the kingdom of heaven for one thousand years (2 Pet. 2:1-3; Heb. 10:30-31).

Psychic Healers

The reader is particularly cautioned not to follow men who perform psychic healings; for they are not of God. Satan has his own counterfeits in these last days who are deceiving millions through these miracle healings. These so-called signs and wonders from God are satanic deceptions, and they belong to the kingdom of the cult and occult. It would be well for us to remember that Satan has power, too. This was demonstrated when he duplicated the first three miracles of Moses in the presence of Pharaoh. He turned their rods into serpents (Exo. 7:10-12); he turned the river into blood, which caused the fish to die (Exo. 7:20-22); and he called frogs to come up out of the river to cover the land (Ex. 8:5-7).

Do not fall into this satanic trap of psychic healing!

Objections and Observations

There are occasions when the bodies of the afflicted are divinely healed. However, God no longer gives the gift of healing to men. In our present dispensation of the Gentile church (beginning in A.D. 63), God heals men directly by hearing and responding to the prayers of the afflicted and the church. The one condition for divine healings is that it must be within His will. Therefore, since it is always impossible to tell God's specific will for an individual, we can only make our request subject to His will. The one thing that we cannot do is command God to heal! God is sovereign. He is not obligated to act upon anything outside of Himself. Hence, we cannot command the sovereign God of the universe to do our will. However, anything that is within His will, we can ask and receive through faith (1 John 5:14-15). One caution must be observed, however. You cannot expect an answer from God if you are out of fellowship with Him. Hence, all known sin must first be confessed (1 John 1:9).

To summarize this subject, it would be correct to say that there is divine healing that comes directly from God if it is within His will. However, there are no divine healers.

The Charismatic Doctrine Concerning Healing

The major error in the charismatic movement concerning healing is the teaching that when one is saved, he will be automatically healed; and if he cannot be healed, then he has not been saved. They get this misconception from Isa. 53:5, which states the following: **"But he {was} wounded for our transgressions, {he was} bruised for our iniquities: the chastisement of our peace {was} upon him; and with his stripes we are *healed.*"** A closer look at this verse of scripture will reveal that it is not promising physical healing, as they would have you believe, but spiritual healing (salvation of the spirit). The automatic redemption of the body is reserved for a future time at the rapture of the church and cannot be mixed with spirit salvation.

In spite of this clear teaching, the charismatics who believe this error often attempt to bolster their claim by saying that Matthew referred to this physical healing in Matt. 8:16-17 when he quoted Isa. 53:4 (with His stripes we are healed). Nevertheless, Isa. 53:4 does not say that. Instead, it tells us of the healings of Jesus *before* He went to the cross. Matthew quotes only these words, **"he has borne our griefs [sickness] and carried our**

sorrows [pains]," and then He quoted no further. Isa. 53:5, on the other hand, was quoted by Peter in his first epistle (1 Pet. 2:24) to show that we are spiritually healed by Christ's work on the cross (**"with his stripes we are healed"**). Consequently, Isa. 53:4, quoted by Matthew, deals with Jesus' healing ministry *before* the cross; whereas Isa. 53:5, quoted by Peter, deals with Jesus' fulfilled work *on* the cross for our salvation.

THE SINCERE AND UNKNOWING CHRISTIAN

> "And these signs shall follow them that believe; In my name shall they cast out devils; they shall speak with new tongues; (18) They shall take up serpents; and if they drink any deadly thing, it shall not hurt them; they shall lay hands on the sick, and they shall recover" (Mark 16:17-18).

These two verses of scripture have always been a mystery to most of the church. Consequently, many scholars have wanted them removed from Mark's gospel. As a result, one such version (Revised Version) of the Bible was actually printed with these verses deleted from its text. However, the writer believes that the Textus Receptus (the received text) should not be tampered with, but accepted and believed.

Why is it so difficult for some people to believe that these two verses of scripture were written by God? It is because they literally tell us that everyone who is a believer (a Christian) automatically has the power to perform miraculous signs and wonders. Yet, no believer that I know has this power. Certainly the writer does not have it, nor do I believe that the reader has it. Therefore, since these verses seem to be in error, their critics argue that they obviously are in error, and God never wrote them.

Nevertheless, God did write them; and, as we shall see, to those who understand them, a formidable message has been given. On the other hand, many of those who haven't understood their meaning have set about to establish denominations founded upon their false interpretation of these verses. These denominations, of course, represent the charismatic church movement, which has gathered within its folds millions of sincere and well-meaning Christian people who believe they can perform miracles.

The Key of Understanding

Our charismatic brethren are to be commended for their steadfastness in believing God's Word. Nevertheless, they have not seen the key to understanding this scripture; for these verses were written and spoken only to those believers of the first century; those who lived under the preaching of the "gospel of the kingdom," not the "gospel of grace."

The gospel of the kingdom was preached from the time of John the Baptist and extended in time beyond the crucifixion of Jesus to about A.D. 63. During this time, those of the early church had the power to cast out devils, speak in tongues, handle serpents without harm, drink poison without harm and heal the sick. When one adds to these the signs and wonders of the apostles (Matt. 10:5-8), we see that they could also raise the dead. However, scripture teaches that when the early church crossed, in time, the dispensational boundary line of Acts 28:28 (about A.D. 63), ALL SIGNS AND WONDERS CEASED! Keep in mind that after the cross and up to this time, two gospels were being preached simultaneously to the early church, the "gospel of the kingdom" to the Jew and the "gospel of grace" to the Gentile. It was during the overlap of these two gospels, for thirty-three years, that signs and wonders existed in the early church. And while individual Christians of this period of the church had various and miraculous gifts, it seems that only the apostles could raise the dead.

Today, almost two thousand years later, we have denominations of the church that still attempt to perform these signs and wonders when, in reality, they do not have this power. If, for instance, one could speak in legitimate tongues, there should be others walking through the thousands of hospitals and healing the sick. Since the sick cannot be healed in this dispensation by a believer, then neither can a believer speak in tongues. It is a Biblical fact that those who attempt these things are either sincerely wrong, or are counterfeits seeking a way to gain riches or self-glory.

Notice Mark 16:16 that precedes our text (Mark 16: 17-18).

> "He that believeth and is baptized shall be saved; but he that believeth not shall be damned."

This is one of the scriptures that is used by some churches to teach the false doctrine that one must be baptized to be saved. They reach this conclusion by accepting the first part of the verse (though misinterpreted) and ignoring the second part.

The true meaning of this verse is found, first, in recognizing to whom it was written. A close look will show that Mark was writing to those of the early church who were Jews. Hence, his gospel is the "gospel of the kingdom" and not the "gospel of grace." As a matter of fact, the word *believeth* here, in the Greek, is an aorist participle, which refers to one who has believed at some time in the past; and the word *baptized* is an aorist participle in the passive voice, which refers to an outward act of obedience. Therefore, a clear translation would be, "He who believed and was baptized shall be saved" (saved into the kingdom).

Second, the word *saved* in this verse means more then just salvation from hell; it also includes salvation into the kingdom. We see this when we consider the second part of the verse, which leaves out the word *baptized,* "**...but he that believeth not shall be damned**"(eternal damnation, i.e., the lake of fire). Consequently, we understand that one only needs to believe on the Lord Jesus Christ to be saved from the penalty of sin; but to enter the kingdom, he must believe and be baptized. This corresponds to Paul's preaching to the Gentiles. First, he preached the "gospel of grace" for the salvation of the spirit (salvation from the penalty of sin [Eph. 2:8-9]). This salvation was by grace plus nothing, i.e., without works. Then, to those who were saved by grace, he preached "my gospel," which includes the "salvation of the soul." It was this gospel that revealed the prize in the kingdom, which is reserved for those who attain it by works through faith; and the first work of obedience (for entrance into the kingdom) is to be identified with Christ in baptism (John 3:5).

TONGUES IN THE BIBLE

While many charismatic believers strive to achieve the gift of unknown tongues, many other noncharismatic believers remain baffled over this phenomenon. This section will show the correct doctrine of tongues as well as expose the errors of its practice.

The Error of Unknown Tongues

The false doctrine of tongues teaches that there is an unknown tongue known only to God that can be spoken by man. While some charismatic brethren believe that you must strive to obtain this gift of unknown tongues, others, to the extreme, believe that you have not been saved if you cannot speak in this tongue.

According to scripture, there is no such thing as an "unknown" tongue. This is soon discovered in the light of 1 Cor. 14. The word *unknown*, used in this chapter and in other places of the Bible (the KJV), is printed in italics, which means that it was not in the original Greek manuscript and was added by the translators. The translators added many words to the King James Version of the Bible (italicizing them to show they were added); words they thought would clarify the text — and in some places they do. However, just as in some scriptures italicized words help us see the true meaning of the text, in others it confuses the meaning. The translators, like all men, were not without error; and in translating, they, many times, translated in light of their own understanding. Thus, without realizing it, they interpreted scripture at the same time. It has been said that it is impossible to translate without interpreting to one degree or another.

Consequently, in this case, the translators did a disservice to the Word by trying to clarify the word *tongues* in their translation. They should not have added the word *unknown*. Armed with this truth, we can be assured that there is no such expression in the original Greek as an unknown tongue, only tongue. The word *tongue* (Gr. *glossa*) simply means language. And wherever it is found in the scriptures, it means just that — a language; a language that someone is speaking for the purpose of someone else who knows that language to hear its message.

Tongues Are for a Sign:

Contrary to what most charismatic Christians believe, those of the church today do not require a miraculous sign to be saved, to prove they have been saved, or to grow in grace; because the church, since A.D. 63, has been made up of mostly Gentile converts. We can see in our first text below a truth which tells us that the very nature of the Gentile does not require a sign, but wisdom. Only the nature of the Jew requires a sign.

> "For the Jews require a sign, and the Greeks [Gentiles] seek after wisdom" (1 Cor. 1:22).

If we add to these truths what the scripture below teaches, we will find that tongues are for a sign to lost Jews.

> "Wherefore tongues are for a sign, not to them that believe, but to them that believe not: but prophesying {serveth} not for them that believe not, but for them which believe" (1 Cor. 14:22).

Collectively, we see that tongues were for the lost Jew who lived prior to A.D. 63 while the "gospel of the kingdom" was still being preached. Apparently, there were those in certain churches of this period who could, without previous knowledge, speak known tongues (foreign languages) to lost Jews who came into their midst; lost Jews who could understand them in their own tongue. To comprehend this, all we need to do is study what happened at Pentecost. The disciples spoke in known foreign languages to lost Jews who had come from all over the known world to celebrate the feast days at Jerusalem; Jews who heard the "gospel of the kingdom" for the first time; a gospel that told them, as God's people, to repent for crucifying their Christ and to believe and be baptized.

Contrary to the truths of 1 Cor. 14:22, the charismatic movement of today attempts to (1) speak in unknowable tongues (gibberish) (2) to Gentile believers (3) for the purpose of giving them messages that are not in the Word of God. As a result, they unwittingly place themselves under God's curse for practicing extra-Biblical revelation. Compare this with Rev. 22:18.

It is extremely important for the reader to remember that we are living in a different segment of the dispensation of grace from that of the early church period. We have the complete Bible; they did not. God reveals all things to us through His Word; they had only the Old Testament and the gift of knowledge given to certain men, who passed it on to others, to rely on. Therefore, when the church today willingly attempts to reveal a message (supposedly from God) from outside of the Bible, they are then committing a grievous sin of extra-Biblical revelation. Hence, speaking in an unknowable tongue today (if there was such a thing) would fall into this category. It is an attempt to reveal information that is not in the Bible, else they would have quoted scripture.

The Corinthian Church

The phenomenon of speaking in tongues was a practice only reported to have occurred in the Corinthian church. This is not to say that others in other churches, during that period of time, did not have this gift, but only that there was never an occasion to report it. Some Bible teachers believe that the Corinthian church members actually exhibited two different kinds of legitimate tongues — unknown foreign tongues and an unknowable tongue. This theory would give credence to those of today's charismatic movement who attempt to speak in an unknowable tongue by making unintelligible sounds.

However, the writer believes that God gave only one legitimate kind of tongue to early first century Christians (those living under the preaching of the gospel of the kingdom). This tongue constituted the speaking in different foreign languages by those who had not previously learned them. Hence, those of the Corinthian church who attempted to speak in unknowable tongues were probably the chief culprits who generated all of the confusion in this church, since God is not the author of confusion (1 Cor. 14:33).

The Geography and Customs of Corinth:

The city of Corinth was in a strategic place in the spreading of the early gospel. It was located about fifty miles from Athens on the isthmus that connected the Peloponnesus with the mainland. It was situated in a beautiful plain with a view of the Acrocorinthus mountain on the north side rising some two thousand feet above sea level. It was on this mountain that the pagan temple of Aphrodite and its thousand consecrated prostitutes greatly influenced the culture of Corinth and touched every aspect of life in it. In a way, they were like the Hollywood stars of our day, and they particularly enjoyed the popularity and fame accorded to them by the Corinthian women. These prostitutes plied their trade mainly to the commercial travelers and sailors while their ships were being hauled over the narrow neck of the isthmus by slaves using great rollers. By transporting the ships in this manner, from the Aegean sea to the Adriatic sea, more than a week of sailing time could be saved by not having to sail around the entire peninsula. In the meantime, its passengers and crew could spend their time in Corinth being, as the saying went, "Corinthianized" by the pagan temple prostitutes in worshiping Aphrodite. This worship consisted of sexual orgies, since Aphrodite was the Greek goddess of love and beauty (Latin, *Venus*). The temple prostitutes through emotional frenzies and ecstatic utterances, worked themselves up for these immoral rituals.

This sinful culture of Corinth became the root problem of the church; a church identified by scripture as probably the most carnal of all the churches of the first century (1 Cor. 3:3). The temple prostitutes became the fashion setters for all the women of the city. This included dress designs and hair styles (very short). When many of these women became Christians under Paul's preaching, they carried into the church the clothing fashions, the hair styles and the mannerisms of these prostitutes. In view of this, in 1 Cor. 11 and 14 the apostle Paul exhorted the women in the church to let their hair grow long and to keep silent in church; and if they desired to know anything, they were to wait and ask their husbands at home. This command to be silent is particularly important when we note that it is given at the end of the context that deals with confusion in the church over tongues. This is an excellent proof text which shows that women were apparently never given the gift of tongues. Nevertheless, they must have involved themselves in practicing some form of ecstatic utterances in the church (a popular activity) in an attempt to copy the practices of the temple prostitutes. They had not yet learned to turn from the flesh's desire for popularity and admiration for being in "style."

Ecstatic utterances, or speaking in unknowable tongues, is a practice that all pagans have been involved in during their worship of pagan gods. From the Asian and European pagans to the African natives, to the American Indians during their war dance, it is a climax of emotional frenzy promoted by and used by Satan. In spite of this clear teaching from the Word of God, some of those of the modern charismatic movement insist on allowing their women to speak in an unknowable tongue (ecstatic utterances) to saved Gentiles who require no sign.

Paul's Apparent Problem:

The speaking in tongues became a major problem in the Corinthian church; so much so, that outsiders might have thought that the church had become a colony of Aphrodites. To control this, the apostle Paul not only told the women to remain silent in church, but also gave many restrictions against the men who spoke in tongues. In studying 1 Cor. 14: 1-40, we see, first, that he did not encourage those who participated in tongue speaking and tried to dissuade them from doing so. Second, he counseled with them to exercise those spiritual gifts that edified the church and not themselves (1 Cor. 14:4). Third, he pointed out that tongues were the least of all the gifts and that prophesying was the greatest (1 Cor. 14:5,39). Fourth, he said that he would rather speak in five words with understanding than ten thousand words in an unknown tongue (1 Cor. 14:19). We might ask, "Why did Paul not totally forbid the speaking of tongues in the church?" The answer could be twofold.

First, we know that there was the gift of speaking in legitimate foreign languages. Apparently, God had given an abundance of this gift to the church because of their geographical location. They were at the crossroads of the then-known world, the great commercial routes between the Orient and the Occident. Corinth was a growing city of culture and trade; it was a hub for travel to all places in Asia or Europe, and the city was continually filled with travelers during the sailing seasons. What better place for a missionary outpost; for a church that could preach the gospel of the kingdom in the native language of every lost Jew who passed through? This was the gift that Paul did not forbid the church to use, but encouraged them to practice in an orderly fashion.

Second, there was the disorderly conduct of those members who spoke in an unknowable tongue and the confusion they caused. This practice motivated Paul to suppress tongues, though he did not forbid them. The reason for this could be one of several. (1) It may have been that Paul was not able to distinguish between the genuine (unknown) tongue and the counterfeit (unknowable) tongue. Hence, he could not forbid them all to speak. (2) It may have been that he wanted to deal with them in an encouraging way until they could grow spiritual enough to see for themselves the error of unknowable tongues. (3) It could have been that he considered it a remote possibility, which he had no knowledge of, that a legitimate unknowable tongue had been given by God to the Corinthian church. Whatever the reason, Paul's attempt to suppress tongues, though not forbiding them, was because of the confusion and disorderly conduct that this practice fostered in the Corinthian church.

Of the possibility of legitimate unknowable tongues, the writer will make a few comments. It seems highly unlikely, in light of the scriptures, that the unknowable tongues of the Corinthian church were legitimate. This phenomenon is not found in the Old Testament, nor is it found in any of the gospels, nor in any of Paul's other epistles, nor in any of the general epistles of James and Peter. Neither do we have any record of Jesus or His apostles ever speaking in tongues. Furthermore, of all the great Christians that lived in the past, there is no evidence whatsoever that they had ever received the gift of tongues, whether they were missionaries, evangelists, preachers, translators or theologians; none has ever claimed that they spoke in tongues.

With this to consider, we must ask ourselves why God would give to the most carnal of all the churches a gift by which they could personally edify themselves (1 Cor. 14:4a). Would this gift not serve better for a spiritual Christian than a carnal one? Nevertheless, even if it were true that only a few Christians in all of Christendom were ever given this gift, then we can safely say that it, along with the tongues of Pentecost (speaking in foreign languages), CEASED TO EXIST AT THE DISPENSATIONAL BOUNDARY LINE OF A.D. 63. Hence, throughout church history from this time forward, no tongues of any kind were ever known.

THE MODERN TONGUE MOVEMENT

The modern tongue movement was begun in England in 1831 by Edward Irving, who presented himself as a prophet and began to speak in unknowable tongues. His followers, the Irvingites, passed this practice down until it reached the church of today. Of Irving and his movement, old saintly Thomas Carlyle, after hearing

Irving's ecstatic utterances, facetiously remarked, "God is evidently working miracles by hysteria."

Confusing Scriptures Used by the Modern Charismatics

As early as the fourth century, Paul's 14th chapter of First Corinthians was confusing to the church. Even John (the Golden-mouth) Chrysostom, who was born in A.D. 345 and was pastor of the churches at Antioch and Constantinople, was puzzled at Paul's account of the tongue speaking in the Corinthian church. He said, "The whole passage [1 Cor. 14:1-40] is exceedingly obscure and the obscurity is occasioned by our ignorance of the facts and the cessation of happenings which were common in those days but unexampled in our own" (W.A. Criswell, *The Holy Spirit in Today's World*, p. 179, Zondervan Publishing House, Grand Rapids, Michigan, 1966). Note that this great Christian of the fourth century stated that he was not sure what the tongues of the Corinthian church were because of two things: (1) not having enough facts, and (2) because these tongues in his day HAD ALREADY CEASED.

The opinion of the writer, living over seventeen hundred years after John Chrysostom lived, is that the most obscure portions of Paul's writing in this chapter of God's Word are contained in the following verses:

> "For if I pray in an {unknown} tongue, my spirit prayeth, but my understanding is unfruitful" (1 Cor. 14:14).

> "For he that speaketh in an {unknown} tongue speaketh not unto men, but unto God: for no man understandeth {him}; howbeit in the spirit he speaketh mysteries" (1 Cor. 14:2).

The modern charismatic movement, according to some of its leaders, base their belief on speaking in an unknowable tongue on these two verses of scripture. They maintain that they can speak to God in some kind of heavenly tongue that no man can know. However, upon a closer examination of these verses, another plausible explanation of their meaning can be offered, which does not teach of an unknowable tongue. Here are the facts: (1) It seems that those who could speak in legitimate tongues (various foreign languages without previous knowledge of them) did not know what they were saying until an interpreter translated it for them and for all the church to hear (1 Cor. 14:27-28). This must be so, else the tongue speaker could have translated it himself. It could be that whenever a Jew who spoke another language came into their midst, one or more in the church would preach to him the "gospel of the kingdom" in his own language. And since none of the church knew what he was saying, an interpreter would translate the meaning to the church for their understanding and edification. (2) It also seems to me that this chapter teaches that those who could speak in legitimate tongues could control their tongues. That is, they had the power to speak or not to speak at any given time. Thus, by adding these two facts together, we see that some had the power to speak when they desired to, but when they spoke, the meaning of their speech was not known to them without an interpreter (1 Cor. 14:27-28).

Armed with this truth, we can easily see how Paul could intentionally pray in an unknown tongue (not an unknowable tongue) if he so desired, for he had this gift, too. However, he was not able to understand his own prayer, since there were no interpreters at his private prayer time (1 Cor. 14:14). Therefore, since he had the option to pray in the spirit with a foreign tongue that he did not know, or in the spirit with his own tongue, which he could understand, he naturally elected to pray in his own language.

This same truth is seen in 1 Cor. 14:2, which simply says that when anyone in the Corinthian church who had the gift elected to speak in a foreign language, and there was no man present who could understand it, then he would be speaking to God. The things that were said would be mysterious things, since there would be no interpreter; for even the one who spoke could not know what he said in the spirit.

Modern Charismatics and the Corruption of the Word

Some modern Charismatics believe that you are not saved until you can speak in an unknowable tongue. Others, however, believe that you can be saved without speaking in an unknowable tongue, but speaking in an unknowable tongue is evidence that you have received the "second blessing" or the "baptism of the Holy Spirit" In this section, we will examine both of these false views.

Dr. W.A. Criswell said: "The program of the glossolaliast to teach us how to speak in tongues is something new for the books. A few days ago I received through the mail a tract concerning how to receive the 'baptism' of the Holy Ghost and how to speak in unknown tongues. I quote from the tract: 'How can I receive the Holy Ghost? All you have to do to be saved is to raise your hands up toward heaven and turn your head up toward heaven and begin praising God just as fast as you can and let your tongue go and let the Holy Ghost come in. Thousands of people receive the Holy Ghost this way. You can receive it too, if you will just let the Holy Ghost speak through your tongue.' A book that I read from a famous glossolaliast, gave specific instructions how anyone could receive the 'baptism' of the Holy Ghost. 'Raise up your hands and your eyes to heaven,' he said 'and begin speaking words, sounds, syllables, and keep it up, faster, faster, faster, louder, words, more words, faster, faster, and it has happened! You have received the baptism of the Holy Ghost!' Seekers after the 'baptism' are encouraged to remain in 'tarrying meetings' in which they are taught to loosen the tongue by imitations of the leader in saying 'ah-bah, ah-bab, beta, beta' etc. The leader will shake the lower jaw of the seeker to loosen it so that the gift will come. What am I to think about all of this? Is the Holy Third Person of The Trinity, the moving, mighty Spirit of God, thus controlled and directed by the loosening of the joints of the jaw? By the gibberish of senseless sounds? I am bewildered by the suggestion." (W.A. Criswell, *The Holy Spirit in Today's World*, p.

180, Zondervan Publishing House, Grand Rapids, Michigan, 1966).

The False Teaching of the Baptism of the Holy Spirit:

The following is one of the favorite verses of scripture used by the charismatic movement:

> "For by one Spirit are we all baptized into one body, whether {we be} Jews or Gentiles, whether {we be} bond or free; and have been all made to drink into one Spirit" (1 Cor. 12:13).

By using this verse, many charismatics have built their own doctrine concerning the "baptism of the Holy Spirit"; a doctrine of error that teaches that after one has been saved, he must receive a "second blessing," the "baptism of the Holy Spirit," to speak in tongues. Simply put, they believe that the Holy Spirit is the baptizer who baptizes a believer into the body, which is composed of all those who can speak in tongues.

However, the Greek text says something different. This is understood when we examine the word *by* in the Greek text; for it is the word *en* and should have been translated *in*. Hence, this verse is not saying that one is baptized "by" the Holy Spirit (the baptizer), but "in" the Holy Spirit (the element). It is not the Holy Spirit who is baptizing the believer, but Jesus Christ. Therefore, the moment one is saved, he is baptized by Jesus Christ into the Holy Spirit. This immersion into the Holy Spirit places him in the body, which is the body of Christ. We have a better understanding of this baptism when we examine the following verse:

> "I indeed baptize you with water unto repentance: but he that cometh after me is mightier than I, whose shoes I am not worthy to bear: he shall baptize you with the Holy Ghost, and {with} fire" (Matt. 3:11).

In this verse, John the Baptist uses the same Greek word *en* (meaning *in*) that is found in 1 Cor. 12:13, but the translators of the KJV translated it here as the word *with* (three times). With this in view, the reader should see that Greek grammar will not permit the word *with* to be used here in the place of *in*, since one cannot immerse something with water. Hence, the meaning of the verse is that as John immersed repentant Jews in water, so Jesus Christ would immerse every newborn Christian in the Holy Ghost the moment he believes and, at a future time, would also immerse every believer in fire (at the judgment seat of Christ) (1 Cor. 3:13-15).

To sum up these thoughts: Scripture does not teach of the second blessing, the baptism of the Holy Spirit; nor does it teach of the speaking in tongues as a result. When one is saved through faith, he is instantaneously baptized (immersed) by Jesus Christ into the Holy Spirit, which makes him a part of the body of Christ (the church). At this moment of baptism, the believer will obtain all of the Holy Spirit. As he grows in the Word and begins walking by faith, he will begin experiencing the filling of the Holy Spirit. What is this filling? It is not the second blessing of the charismatics, but the continuous yielding of the believer's life to the control of Christ. This yielding, which brings the filling, can only come through the faith of the believer, which is attained as he studies and understands God's Word (Rom. 10:17). This filling of the Holy Spirit, then, is in direct proportion to how much one is filled with the Word of God (compare Eph. 5:19 with Col. 3:16). Consequently, as the result of a believer growing in the Word and yielding his life, the fullness of the Holy Spirit will occur many times in his life. This will, in turn, accomplish the salvation of his soul (Gr. salvation in the present tense). However, concerning the receiving of the Holy Spirit into a believer's life, this can only happen once — when he first believes for the salvation of his spirit (Gr. salvation in the perfect tense).

The Interpreter of Tongues:

Getting back to our text (1 Cor. 14:1-40), there were those in the early Corinthian church who were given the gift of interpreting (translating) legitimate foreign tongues spoken by other church members. We also read in this chapter of those who apparently attempted to counterfeit this gift of interpreting tongues. How do we arrive at such a conclusion? The apostle Paul would allow only one interpreter at a time to interpret, since they did not always agree. Does it not make good spiritual sense to believe that if they were all genuine interpreters from God, they would all come up with the same interpretation? Yet, in 14:26, we see the disorderly conduct that was probably caused by the interpreters not agreeing with one another. Hence, in 14:27, Paul's remedy was to allow only one person to interpret. If there were no interpreters present, they were all to be silent.

How could one know if he was hearing the truth when the interpreter translated the language? Who could tell whether he was right or wrong? For Paul said, "For no man understandeth him" (14:2). In light of this, it is reasonable to believe that there were genuine interpreters in the Corinthian church and also counterfeit interpreters. This was due to their carnality, the opportunity for personal glory and the impossibility of being detected. This same thing holds true for the modern charismatic movement with one exception. There are no genuine interpreters in the church of today, since THIS GIFT, ALONG WITH SPEAKING IN TONGUES, CEASED IN A.D. 63. Consequently, it must be that all so called interpreters of tongues in the church today are counterfeiters.

A carbon copy of the disorderly conduct in the Corinthian church can be seen in the modern charismatic movement. As an example: "A seminary graduate who had majored in Hebrew attended a tongues meeting in California. In the midst of the meeting he stood up and quoted by memory the first Psalm in the original language. After he had finished, the interpreter arose and solemnly, piously made known in plain English what the brother had spoken in an unknown tongue. The interpreter made it an utterance, Spirit-inspired, about women prophesying in the church. When the seminarian made known what he had done and what he had said, pandemonium [disorderly conduct] broke loose." (Dr. W.A. Criswell, *The Holy Spirit in Today's World*, p.

176, Zondervan Publishing House, Grand Rapids, Michigan, 1966).

To summarize this section, the doctrine of the charismatic movement of today is in gross error. (1) They maintain that speaking in tongues is evidence of the baptism of the Holy Spirit. Contrary to this, the apostle Paul tells us that all the Christians that were at Corinth had already been baptized by (in) the Holy Spirit, though not all could speak in tongues (1 Cor.12:13; 12:28-30). (2) After A.D. 63, speaking in tongues was not known for centuries in church history. Only in the nineteenth and twentieth centuries have they appeared; the centuries of the last days, the days during which our Lord warned us against the counterfeits of Satan; the centuries of the multitudes of cults and occults set up by Satan to dilute the truth just before the coming of the Lord. we might add this warning to the reader. Be careful (Rom. 16:17-18). Search the scriptures to prove every doctrine, whether it be from God or man. (3) In every place where unknowable tongues are spoken in these last days; there is also great confusion. And since God is not the author of confusion (1 Cor. 14:33), then He must not be the author of unknowable tongues. (4) The reader should beware of any doctrine that contradicts the scripture by willfully magnifying the Holy Spirit above Christ in its teachings: **"Howbeit when he, the Spirit of truth, is come, he will guide you into all truth: for he shall not speak of himself; but whatsoever he shall hear, {that} shall he speak: and he will shew you things to come. (14) He shall glorify me: for he shall receive of mine, and shall shew {it} unto you"**(John 16:13-14). This error is the foundation stone that is used to legitimize all of the faith healers and tongue speakers in the charismatic movement. As an example, one well known faith healer recently wrote a book and entitled it "Good Morning, Holy Spirit." By this very title, the author suggested that Christians ought to pray to the Holy Spirit. This, of course, is in conflict with the teachings of the Word, which instruct us to pray to the Father in the Name of Jesus. Also, in the writer's opinion, the author of this same book approached heresy when he wrote, "If it were not for the Holy Spirit, Jesus could have sinned." An overall review of the teachers in the charismatic movement today reveals that many seem to teach the magnifying of the Holy Spirit above Jesus Christ in worship, as well as limiting, or doing away with, the Lordship of Jesus Christ. The reader should flee those who teach such.

CLOSING THOUGHTS

Not all who are connected to the charismatic movement are guilty of the errors we have discussed; and we are sure that there are many who love the Lord. In this chapter, the writer has attempted to reveal the error of this movement while at the same time, not to judge the hearts of its individuals, for only God knows the heart. However, He has given the church the right and privilege to judge all doctrine in the light of scripture (2 Tim. 3:16; Rom. 16:17-18; Phil.3:17-18).

Finally, keep in mind that scripture teaches that ALL SIGNS AND WONDERS CEASED AT THE BOUNDARY LINE of Acts 28:28 (about A.D. 63). Hence, there are no genuine performances of signs and wonders today, such as "healing ministries" (healing of the body), speaking in unknowable tongues, drinking poison without harm, being bitten by a deadly serpent without harm, casting out devils (demons) or raising the dead. These were the credentials of those who preached the "gospel of the kingdom" in the early part of the first century, and it has not been preached since that time.

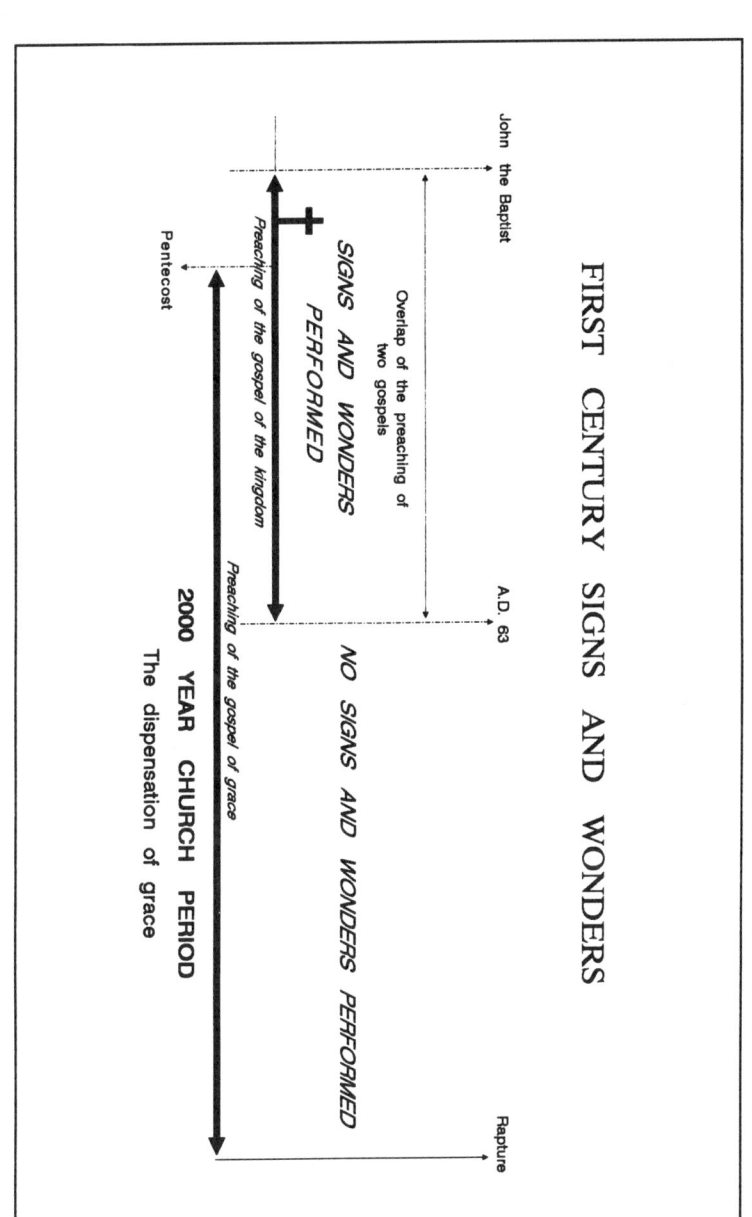

NOTES

CHAPTER FIVE

INVITATIONAL BOUNDARY LINE OF THE KINGDOM

In the last chapter, we revealed the credentials of authority that accompanied the preaching of the "gospel of the kingdom" in the first century. These credentials were the performing of signs and wonders by those who personally heard Jesus (Heb. 2:4), as well as other members of the early church, including those who spoke in tongues at Corinth. This chapter will show that all of these credentials were taken away when the preaching of this gospel ceased; when Israel, as a nation, was set aside by God; when salvation was sent to the Gentiles (Acts 28:28); and when the gospel of grace began to be preached to every nation (including the individual Jew).

In this chapter, the church will be viewed through its historical change from its beginning to what it is today. Within this view, three major phases will be revealed and expounded upon; the early church period, the transitional church period, and the Biblical church period.

THE EARLY CHURCH PERIOD

This period of church history began at Pentecost and abruptly ended about A.D. 63. As we have already seen, the church during this period was composed mainly of Jewish believers who were saved under the preaching of the "gospel of the kingdom." God had proffered the kingdom of heaven to Israel on the basis of their national repentance; a repentance, first, for their disobeying of God's commands and, second, for their crucifying of the Messiah. Those individual Jews that repented and believed became a part of the early church. Those of Judaism who did not repent had opportunity to do so up until the time that Paul preached to the last outpost of Jewish leaders in Rome. Chronologically, this occurred at the same time that Paul pronounced the consequences prophesied in Isaiah 6:9-10 upon Israel and sent this salvation to the Gentiles (Acts 28:28). Hence, the Gentiles, who are the wild olive branches spoken of in Rom. 11:17, were historically grafted into the natural olive tree at this place in history.

In view of this, someone will ask the question, "Is this where the church started?" No; the church started at Pentecost and was composed totally of Jewish believers. As time went on, the Samaritans, who were half-Jew and half-Gentile, were saved under the preaching of Philip. After that, Cornelius (a full-blooded Gentile) was saved under the preaching of Peter. Then the apostle Paul was sent to the Gentiles and, as a result, established churches composed of mostly Gentiles throughout Asia Minor and into Europe. During this time, the kingdom was still proffered to Israel on the basis of a national repentance. But when they said no to God for the last time (when Paul was in Rome), His patience finally ran out. Consequently, He broke them off (as branches) from the natural olive tree to graft in the Gentiles (branches) who were of the wild olive tree (Rom. 11:17).

Again, someone may ask, "Since this is the official beginning of the Gentile portion of the church, are scriptures written before this time written to us?" All teachings and commandments of Christ to the church are for all the church, no matter whether it be mostly a Jewish church or a Gentile church. For the scriptures declare that **"there is neither Jew nor Greek, there is neither bond nor free, there is neither male nor female: for ye are all one in Christ Jesus"**(Gal. 3:28). Therefore, the commandments to the believers of the early Jewish church by Jesus through the gospels, the Acts of the Apostles, and the epistles are for all the church.

The List of Gifts

During this probationary period of about thirty-three years after the time of the cross, while the "gospel of the kingdom" was still being preached, the apostle Paul enumerated the gifts that were given by Christ to the early church. This list of gifts is found in the following verse of scripture.

> "And God hath set some in the church, first apostles, secondarily prophets, thirdly teachers, after that miracles, then gifts of healings, helps, governments, diversities of tongues" (1 Cor. 12:28).

It is important for the reader to understand that this verse of scripture does not speak of the church of today. For of the eight gifts listed here, only one, teachers, is still a valid gift. All the other gifts either ceased or faded away.

The first gift mentioned in this list, apostles, faded away as the apostles died. Contrary to what many teach, there were only twelve apostles, including Paul, who took the place of Judas; because only twelve men met the qualifications for apostleship. First, they had to be personally selected by Christ; and second, they had to have personally seen Christ (Acts 1:22b). The apostle Paul met both of these requirements when he was saved on the road to Damascus; for he not only saw the resurrected Christ, but he was personally selected by Christ to be His apostle to the Gentiles (Acts 9:15). Since Paul was the last person to have met these qualifications, it follows that there were only twelve apostles. As each died, the gift of apostleship then faded away. Some may become confused with this truth when they read in the scripture that Paul and all of his traveling companions were called apostles. However, even though Barnabas and, later, Silas were sent by God as Paul's companions, they were not apostles, but were called apostles while in the company of the apostle Paul.

The second gift mentioned in the above verse is the gift of prophecy. This gift gave certain men in the church the authority to prophesy, i.e., to give to the church spiritual communications from God. This gift was given to the church by the Holy Spirit because the New Testament, at that time, had not been completely written. Therefore, to the same degree that the canon of the New Testament scriptures was being written and formed into twenty-seven books, the gifts of prophecy and knowledge were at the same time vanishing away. Hence, from the fourth century (forming of the canon) until now, there has been no need for the continuance of the gifts of prophecy and special knowledge. Now we have the completed Bible, which is God's complete revelation to us.

It can be said, then, that these special gifts of prophecy and knowledge disappeared sometime during or before the fourth century. Perceptively, the reader should beware of those in these last days who claim to be prophets, since their prophesying constitutes extra-Biblical revelation, which has a curse upon it (Rev. 22:18). All knowledge and revelation that God wants us to have has already been written in His Word. Further, those who claim to be prophets, not by fore-telling, but by forth-telling out of the Word of God are also in error. Forth-telling out of the Word does not make one a prophet, but a teacher.

The remaining gifts in the above verse, except for teachers, were abolished after A.D. 63. In 1 Cor 13:8, Paul tells us that tongues would cease. In the Greek text, "cease" means to come to a sudden stop. In light of this, I have often wondered how this verse is explained away by those who insist on speaking in unknowable tongues.

THE TRANSITIONAL CHURCH PERIOD

The transition of the early church period into the Biblical church period began about A.D. 63 and continued until the fourth century. It was sometime during the fourth century that the canon of the scriptures was completed and the church was fully established in scripture. Therefore, during the transition period (over two hundred years), all signs and wonders ceased or faded away.

The Revised List of Gifts

As we have previously seen in 1 Cor. 12:28, the apostle Paul enumerated the gifts that were given by the Holy Spirit to the early church. This list included gifts of miracles, healings and diversities of tongues. Most Bible scholars agree that this epistle was written by Paul at the close of his three years' residence in Ephesus in A.D. 59 (Acts 20:31; 1 Cor. 16:5-8). About five years later (A.D. 64), Paul effectively canceled the authority of this Corinthian list by giving a new one in his epistle to the Ephesians. This second list excluded all signs and wonders (gifts of tongues, healing, etc.) enumerated in the Corinthian list and added the gifts of evangelist and pastor-teacher. It was written while Paul was in Rome in A.D. 64, one year after the dispensational boundary line of Acts 28:28. Here is the new list:

> "And he gave some, apostles; and some, prophets; and some, evangelists; and some, pastors and teachers; (12) For the perfecting of the saints, for the work of the ministry, for the edifying of the body of Christ: (13) Till we all come in the unity of the faith, and of the knowledge of the Son of God, unto a perfect man, unto the measure of the stature of the fulness of Christ" (Eph. 4:11-13).

Only four gifts are mentioned in this new list: apostles, prophets, evangelists and pastors and teachers (note: pastors and teachers are the same gift). Moreover, verses 12 and 13 tell us that these gifts to the church are all that are necessary for the perfecting (maturing) of the saints and the work of the ministry and the edifying, or building up, of the church. In other words, no signs and wonders will be needed for the future Gentile church, since they do not require a sign (1 Cor. 1:22). It was the Jews in the early church that required a sign. After Israel was set aside by God and the church changed to a mostly Gentile church, all signs and wonders CEASED. The church from this time forward sought after wisdom, not signs; wisdom from God through the apostles, the prophets, and the pastor-teachers; and later, wisdom through the complete canon of the scriptures (all sixty-six books). Notice in the second list that no provision is made for any future signs and wonders to be placed back into the list. For, verse 13 tells us that these gifts would be sufficient to bring the believer to stand one day at the judgment seat of Christ, mature and with all that is necessary for him to inherit the millennial kingdom.

As we consider the second list, the reader will recall that we addressed the fact that the apostles and prophets would fade away during the transitional period (from A.D. 63 to the fourth century). Apparently, the apostles all died before the close of the first century — John being the last to die. The prophets probably all died during the same period. There is no evidence that the Holy Spirit commissioned prophets for the church after the first century. Apparently, enough of the Word had been written and passed around to the various churches during this time that prophets were not needed. This left only two valid gifts on the list that was given to the church. These were evangelists and pastor-teachers. Hence, with these two gifts, the Biblical church period began; the period we are presently living in, which extends from the fourth century and is known for having the complete canon of scripture.

The canon of scripture (our Bible) came into existence by a process rather than an event. The 27 books of the New Testament were not decided on at the council of Nicea in A.D. 325, as some believe. As a matter of fact, the council did not even discuss the matter. It was at Carthage, in A.D. 397, that this list of 27 books (the canon) was proclaimed to be the only books that could be read in church as divine scripture. Notwithstanding, there is some traditional evidence that this list of 27 books was accepted as the complete scriptures as early as A.D. 367 — and possibly much earlier. In light of this, we can only say that God directed the coming together of these 27 books to form our New Testament, and excluded many other books that were not inspired by Him. This, then, was a process rather then an event, which was finalized in the fourth century.

When That Which Is Perfect Is Come

"Charity never faileth: but whether {there be} prophecies, they shall fail; whether {there be} tongues, they shall cease; whether {there be} knowledge, it shall vanish away. (9) For we know in part, and we prophesy in part. (10) But when that which is perfect is come, then that which is in part shall be done away. (11) When I was a child, I spake as a child, I understood as a child, I thought as a child: but when I became a man, I put away childish things. (12) For now we see through a glass, darkly; but then face to face: now I know in part; but then shall I know even as also I am known" (1 Cor. 13:8-12).

This passage is a portion of the great love chapter written by the apostle Paul to the Corinthian church. It was here that he clearly told them that the time would come when the gift of tongues would cease, i.e., come to a sudden stop. As we have seen, this occurred about four years later while he was in prison in Rome (A.D. 63). Also, the gift of healing ceased. This can be clearly seen in Paul's own life. Before A.D. 63, he had the power to heal, and did so many times while he was in Ephesus (Acts 19:12), Lystra (Acts 14:9-10) and the isle of Meleta (Acts 28: 8-9). However, after A.D. 63, while he was in Rome, he could not heal Epaphroditus, who almost died of an illness (Phil. 2: 25-27). Neither could he later heal Timothy; instead, he wrote a letter advising him to take a little wine (medicinal) for his stomach's sake (1 Tim.5:23).

Additionally, he told them that all special knowledge through the prophets would fade away, i.e., vanish, or be abolished. We know now that this prophecy was fulfilled in a process of time. For, as the prophets with special knowledge died, i.e., faded away, the New Testament canon of scriptures was in the process of being written and accepted into one book as divine scripture.

In verses nine and ten of this great chapter, Paul describes the contrasts between the early church period and the Biblical church period, in which we are now living. Since the early church did not have the New Testament scriptures as we have, Paul could only say: **"For we know in part and we prophesy in part..."** However, as he was allowed by God to look forward into time, he saw all of the Bible; the complete canon of scriptures that would be given to the church. Hence, he continued to write, **"...but when that which is perfect is come [the complete Bible], then that which is in part [the gift of prophets] shall be done away [abolished]."**

Continuing to show us this contrast, Paul, in verse eleven of this passage, shows us that God likened the early church period to a small growing child: "**...When I was a child, I understood as a child, I thought as a child....**" This was natural, since they did not yet have all of the New Testament scriptures. As a result, all of their gifts (tongues, healing, prophecy, casting out demons, etc.) were counted only as part of the characteristics and qualities of children. This same truth can be seen in the actions of some in the charismatic movement of today. They are as children, still playing with children's toys of the first century (tongues, healings etc.) and refusing to grow up. Paul continues: "**...but when I became a man, I put away childish things.**" Today, the church has more than just the fourteenth chapter of First Corinthians. We are living in the Biblical church period. We now have all of the Bible. Those who study it are growing into spiritual manhood; spiritual men who have learned how to rightly divide its doctrines, dispensations, etc. As a result, they are feeding on the meat of the Word — not just its milk.

Paul continues his analogy: "**For now we see through a glass [mirror of the Word] darkly [as in a riddle].**" Paul first likens the early church to a child who could not understand the puzzle he was seeing in the incomplete canon of scripture of his day. This incomplete portion probably contained no more then the Old Testament scriptures and the Corinthian epistles, which Paul had written to them. "**...but then face to face: now I know in part; but then shall I know even as also I am known**" (13:12). As Paul continues this verse, he reveals the early church's grand future beyond the rapture, where all riddles will be solved and they will see Jesus face to face. He seems to make a giant sweep from one extreme to the other, as if there was nothing in between. But there is something between. There is another mirror that must be looked into; a clear mirror that has no riddles. This is the mirror of God's complete Word, which the Biblical church is privileged to gaze into continuously (2 Cor. 3:18).

THE BIBLICAL CHURCH

The church of the child apparently became the church of the man sometime in the fourth century when the canon of scriptures was completed. From this time forward, the Biblical church would not have to know in part, for that which is perfect had come, the complete Word of God. It was by the Word that God would reveal how the church was to grow from a child into a spiritual man; by constantly studying the Word (beholding the glory of Christ in it) and being changed.

> "But we all, with open face beholding as in a glass [mirror] the glory of the Lord, are changed into the same image from glory to glory, {even} as by the Spirit of the Lord" (2 Cor. 3:18).

This further revelation of scripture tells the Biblical church of today, that, as we study the Bible, it becomes like a mirror that reflects to us the glory of Christ (truths of the kingdom) from glory to glory. It reveals all of God's truth and dispels all riddles. It completely matures us and prepares us to stand unashamed before the judgment seat of Christ. In a spiritual sense, we can now see Jesus face to face in the Word. We need not know in part; for we have all of the Word, all sixty-six books of the complete canon of scripture. That which is perfect has come.

CLOSING THOUGHTS

One of the greatest problems of the church of today is its attempt to reproduce the "credentials of the kingdom." These were the signs and wonders which were given only to the early church. Most Christians of today do not know that these signs have ceased, and were exercised only during the time of the preaching of the "gospel of the kingdom" (for Jews only). Being mainly Gentile, the church today should seek after wisdom, not signs; wisdom that comes from gazing into the mirror of the Word of God; a complete and clear mirror that lets us see the face of Jesus apon whom, as we gaze, will change us from glory to glory.

The time will come when signs and wonders will again make their appearance on earth. This will be when antichrist makes his presence known to Israel after the rapture of the church. His main goals will be to deceive and to destroy Israel. Knowing the requirements of a Jew (1 Cor. 1:22a), the antichrist will cause signs and lying wonders to appear to convince the Jews to follow a false Messiah (2 Thess. 2:9).

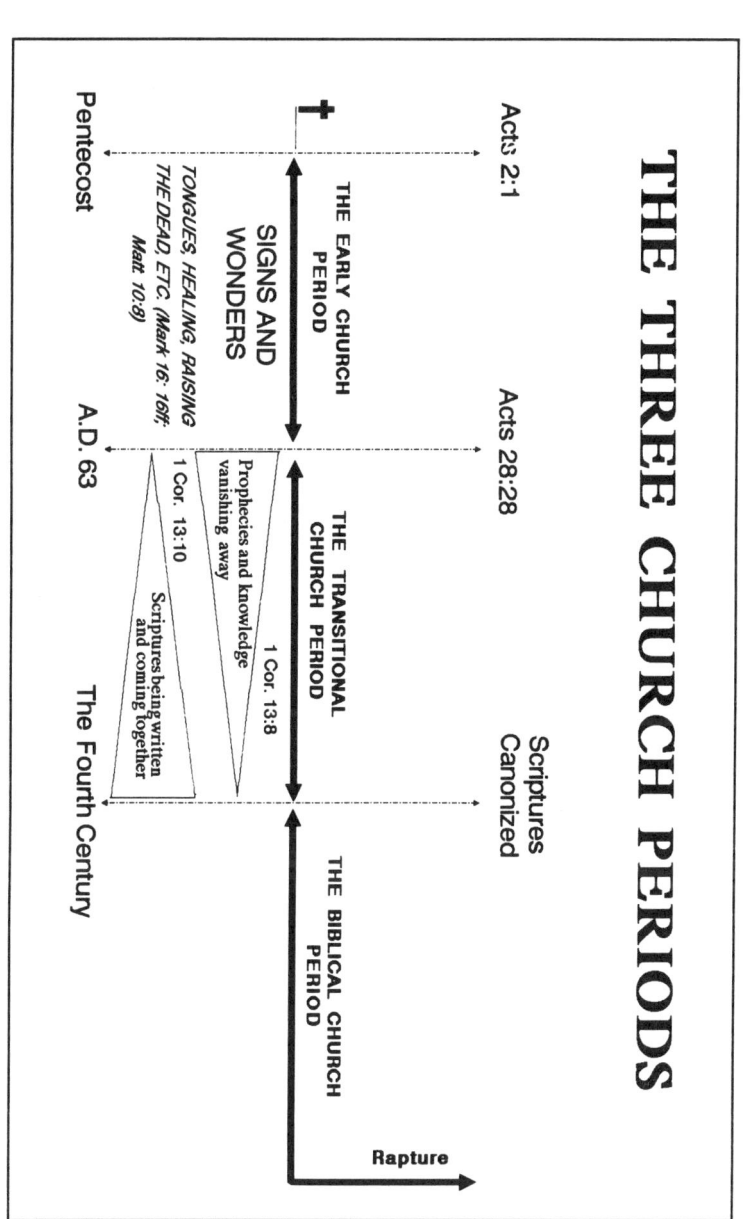

NOTES

CHAPTER SIX

QUALIFICATIONS FOR THE KINGDOM

This chapter will clearly define that needed for every believer to enter the coming kingdom of heaven to rule and reign with Jesus Christ.

In Matthew's third chapter, when John the Baptizer began preaching, "Repent, for the kingdom of heaven is at hand," he gave, through this message, the first prerequisite that was needed for all Jews to enter into the earthly portion of this kingdom; a kingdom that had been promised by God to Abraham and his national seed. This prerequisite was to forsake their sins of disobedience and turn back to God in repentance. During Jesus Christ's ministry, He added to this prerequisite the full requirements for entrance into the heavenly portion of the kingdom. These are found in His sermon on the mount and are recorded in chapters five through seven of Matthew's gospel.

Contrary to what some teach today, the sermon on the mount was not written to Israel, but to all believers, whether Jews or Gentiles. Though it is true that all scripture is not written to the church, it is, nonetheless, written for the church. The book of Matthew is a good example of this truth, for while most of its message was given by Jesus to Israel, it was, at the same time, for the church. However, not one portion of the sermon on the mount was addressed to Israel, i.e., the multitudes, though they heard it. It was, instead, preached to our Lord's disciples (those who believed in Him). Notice how it begins: **"And seeing the multitudes, he went up into a mountain: and when he was set, his disciples came unto him: And he opened his**

mouth, and taught them, saying..." (Matt. 5:1-2). It follows that since this sermon was preached to His disciples, it was also to the church and for the church.

Some will say, "How could this be, when the church did not begin until Pentecost, fifty days after the crucifixion?" The apostles became the first members of the church. Hence, their teachings, and those of the prophets, became the foundation of the church. Consider this verse of scripture: **"Now therefore ye are no more strangers and foreigners, but fellowcitizens with the saints, and of the household of God; (20) And are built upon the foundation of the apostles and prophets, Jesus Christ himself being the chief corner {stone}"** (Eph. 2:19-20). The foundation of the apostles and prophets speaks of the doctrine that was taught by them and became the foundation on which the church is built. To deny the church that taught to the apostles by Jesus, is to deny the church the New Testament scriptures that the apostles wrote; for the Bible is the source of all doctrine. Summarily, the Bible is our foundation, which is made up of the writings of the apostles to us and the writings of the prophets for us.

To further prove this, we need to look closely at what Jesus said to His apostles just before He ascended into heaven:

> "Go ye therefore, and teach all nations, baptizing them in the name of the Father, and of the Son, and of the Holy Ghost: (20) **Teaching them to observe all things whatsoever I have commanded you:** and, lo, I am with you alway, {even} unto the end of the world" (Matt. 28:19- 20).

According to this scripture, the sermon on the mount must be counted as part of the "all things" that Jesus taught and commanded his disciples to observe. Subsequently, they were to go and teach all nations (the future Gentile church) these same commandments (including the sermon on the mount) after they had, first, been saved (verse 19) and, then, baptized (verse 20).

THE DUAL DISPENSATION

In view of this, someone may ask, "But what about those Jews who believed John's message and repented; were they not of Israel and not the church? Didn't they believe before the time of the crucifixion; were they not under the law?" To help the reader understand this, he needs to realize that the law ended at the preaching of John the Baptizer, not at the time of the crucifixion, though it was at the crucifixion that the law was fulfilled. We see this in Luke 16:16, **"The law and the prophets {were} until John: since that time the kingdom of God is preached, and every man presseth into it."** In light of this, those who believed the gospel of the kingdom before the crucifixion and lived unto the day of Pentecost became a member of the church. Like the apostles, these disciples lived in a dual dispensation. The first was the dispensation of the law; the second, the dispensation of grace. Between these two dispensations was the preaching of the kingdom of God, the "gospel of the kingdom," which was extended into the dispensation of grace and ended only when Israel, as a nation, was set aside in about A.D. 63 (Acts 28:28). This was about thirty-three years after Pentecost. How, then, can one say that the sermon on the mount was only for Israel?

Still another question that could be asked is, "What happened to those who believed before the crucifixion and died before reaching the dispensation of grace?" The same thing that happened to all the Old Testament saints who died; their souls went to the paradise section of sheol, which was located in the heart of the earth. The Jews called this place "Abraham's bosom" (Luke 16:22). They remained in paradise until their sins had been paid for by Jesus' death on the cross (up to that time, their sins had only been covered). After His death, the soul of Jesus Christ went down to this same place for three days and three nights (Luke 23:43) to claim those whom He had purchased with His own blood. It was then that He consummated their salvation by moving all of them to the new paradise located in the third heaven (Eph. 4:8; 2 Cor.12:4). The thief on the cross was the last known person to have entered paradise in the heart of the earth before it was moved to the new location far above the universe (Luke 23:43).

The souls of all the saints who have died since the time of the cross have gone directly to paradise in the third heaven; because all their sins were paid for by Christ on the cross before they died.

THE SERMON ON THE MOUNT

When Jesus preached the sermon on the mount, it was not directed to those who were lost, but to those who were saved; it was not a plan of salvation, but a plan by which one could inherit the kingdom. This sermon, then, tells a saved person during the church period what he must do to enter the coming kingdom of heaven to rule with Christ over the earth. Contrary to this, some have taught that this sermon is the constitution of the kingdom; that its commandments will make up the laws and by laws that will govern those who live in the kingdom. However, this is not true. The sermon on the mount is not for the millennium, but for the present. It is not a constitution for those living in the kingdom, but a set of commandments to be kept to enter the kingdom.

As we begin to analyze the sermon on the mount, it is not the intention of the writer to present an entire exposition of it. To do so would cover many volumes of work, which others have already adequately done. Instead, we will briefly survey the sermon and then major only on what is considered the keys to its message. To help the reader more easily understand the sermon's message, the writer will take license to divide its three chapters into five major points: the beatitudes, the similitudes, the commandments, the keys, and the warning.

(1) The Beatitudes

As the reader has already discovered, the Christian must have his soul saved when he reaches the judgment seat of Christ to enter (inherit) the coming kingdom; and the measure of that salvation is seen in the first twelve verses of the sermon on the mount (Matt. 5:1-12). They are known as the beatitudes. They act as a mirror to reflect the continuous and changing attitudes of a Christian in his spiritual growth. Hence, when a Christian is saved by trusting Jesus as his Saviour (Gr. perfect tense), he begins to take on the spiritual character and attitudes of Christ. As he grows spiritually through the Word, he continues to change by growing into the likeness of Christ. This continuing change reflects the continuing salvation of the soul, or life, of the Christian (Gr. present tense), which can only end at the judgment seat of Christ. At this future place, the Christian will receive a "just recompense of reward" (Heb. 2:2) in accordance with how he lived his life in his body (2 Cor. 5:10). He will either receive a reward or he will suffer loss for one thousand years during the kingdom age (1 Cor. 3:11-15).

The Poor in Spirit:

"Blessed are the poor in spirit: for theirs is the kingdom of heaven." The first beatitude shows the attitude of a growing baby Christian, i.e., his first realization after salvation. This realization shows him how poor he is in the spirit; how inadequate he is when compared to what he thought he was before he trusted Christ; how spiritually emptied he is; emptied of self-importance, self-righteousness and self-assurance. To be poor in spirit is to realize that one has nothing and has need of all things. With this awakening, one can see that his own best efforts are totally unacceptable to God and he needs to let Christ reign in his life. The first beatitude, then, is foundational for every newborn Christian. Everyone who is poor in spirit has the evidence that he is saved; that the Holy Spirit is sealed within. Because of this, the Lord calls him "blessed." However, not every Christian has this attitude prevailing in his life. This attitude can be lost when a Christian gets out of fellowship with God and leaves the Word for the world and the flesh. When this happens, he is falling away from this blessed newborn attitude and is seeking once again his own self-importance. For those Christians who do not confess their sins and turn back to God, theirs is not the kingdom of heaven.

They That Mourn:

"Blessed are they that mourn: for they shall be comforted." The second beatitude is the next experience of spiritual growth for the Christian. It is the next rung on the ladder of a maturing faith.

The world would ask, "If one is blessed, why does he mourn? If he mourns, why is he called blessed?" Only the growing Christian can understand this paradox, for his mourning is spiritual and continual. Our Lord did not say blessed are they who have mourned, but they that mourn (Gr. present continuous tense). Until the day at the judgment seat of Christ when we find out our souls are saved, we will spiritually mourn if we are spiritually growing. Mourning is an experience that springs from a sense of sin, a sensitive conscience and a heart broken over our rebellion against God. The closer we grow to the Lord, the more we will mourn. The more we grow into experiencing the remaining beatitudes, the more we will mourn. It will be an ever-deepening discovery of the depravity of our old sin nature that corrupts all that we attempt to do for Christ; our lack of faith, our coldness of love and pride in our own self-righteous works.

But "they shall be comforted." Those who mourn are closely associated with those who are poor in spirit. One cannot come to mourn until he is conscious of his spiritual poverty. As the Spirit shows him his sins and worthlessness, He does not leave him there, but causes him to look away to Christ. It is only then that the sensitive and broken Christian is comforted. For **"if we confess our sins, he is faithful and just to forgive us {our} sins, and to cleanse us from all unrighteousness"** (1 John 1:9). Victoriously then, as a growing, repenting Christian continually mourns for his sins, he is continually comforted and forgiven of those sins that he confesses.

The Meek:

"Blessed are the meek: for they shall inherit the earth." The third step in the spiritual maturing process of a Christian is the beatitude of meekness. Meekness is the sum total of many spiritual attributes gained by a Christian who is growing in Christ through the Word of God. It is, first, associated with lowliness (Matt. 11:29; Eph. 4:1-2), then gentleness (2 Cor. 10:1; Titus 3:2). It is teachable (Psa. 25:9) and opposite to wrath (James 1:20-21). But the main attribute of "meekness" is the patience of one suffering unjustly. We see the fullness of this manifested in Jesus Christ when He was unjustly accused and put on the cross. Yet, He did not utter one word of defense or threat, even though He had the power to avenge Himself. He was meek.

In His meekness of suffering on the cross, Jesus was teaching us the "principle of the cross." This principle of not defending ourselves, resulting in suffering though we are innocent, is the only course of action that is acceptable to God (1 Pet. 2:20). Thus, **"..it is given in the behalf of Christ, not only to believe on him, but also to suffer for his sake"** (Phil. 1:29). Consequently, a Christian cannot progress spiritually until he learns to become meek. Unless he can learn this spiritual lesson of life, he will not inherit the earth (the millennial earth). Those who do are "blessed"; blessed here in this life and in the coming kingdom.

Hunger and Thirst after Righteousness:

"Blessed are they that hunger and thirst after righteousness; for they shall be filled." Righteousness is a term denoting all spiritual blessings; and the hungering and thirsting reveals a deep yearning of those who seek God's favor and image in their lives. Righteousness is both an imputed righteousness and an imparted one; an initial righteousness and a continuing righteousness. It begins the moment one trusts Jesus Christ as his Saviour (salvation of the spirit) and continues throughout the Christian's life as long as he hungers and thirsts for it (salvation of the soul). However, not all believers who once hungered and thirsted after righteousness will necessarily continue to receive it. It is one thing to receive imputed righteousness when you are saved; but it is quite another thing to continue to receive imparted righteousness after you are saved. To do this, the believer must continue to hunger and thirst after it.

God uses His Word to fill a hungering and thirsting Christian. Through His Word, He continuously reveals Himself and the truths of His higher wisdom; the wisdom that teaches of the coming kingdom and of Jesus Christ and His bride, who will rule and reign over the earth.

While it is true that the worldly Christian cannot understand these truths, because he has no spiritual hungering or thirsting, it is equally true that every Christian who has experienced these truths had to first hunger and thirst after righteousness before he could be filled. Nevertheless, while in this world, a Christian cannot reach total fulfillment of righteousness, because he still has his old nature.

The Merciful:

"Blessed are the merciful: for they shall obtain mercy." This is the first of the beatitudes that speaks of the fruit of a Christian and not just the exercises of the heart. Mercifulness is a gracious characterization toward other men. It is the spirit of kindness and favor that exhibits sympathy for the sufferings of others. This sympathy is a spiritual fruit and is not rooted in the old nature of man. It is the operation of the Holy Spirit through the Christian who renders help to those in need. It is not limited to the material needs of men, but also applies to the spiritual needs.

"For they shall obtain mercy." The Christian who shares this spiritual fruit with others will reap happiness (Prov. 14:21), will be dealt with in mercy by others and will receive mercy from God (Psa. 18:25).

The Pure in Heart:

"Blessed are the pure in heart: for they shall see God." This beatitude speaks of truth in the inward parts of man, and is attained three ways: first, by the imputed nature of Christ at the new birth; second, by the continuous sprinkling of him by the precious blood of Christ to purge his conscience (Heb. 10:19-22a); third, by a continuous and protracted spiritual growth, so that through His power, he can mortify the sins of the flesh and live unto God. As a result of this, he can grow to become the pure in heart, who has a sincere desire and resolve not to sin against God. For only the "pure in heart" will ascend into the hill of the Lord (the government of Christ in the millennial kingdom) and stand in His holy place (Psa. 24:3-6).

The Peacemakers:

"Blessed are the peacemakers: for they shall be called the children [Gr.*sons*] of God." One does not automatically become a peacemaker when he becomes a child of God as the KJV would suggest; rather (as the Greek bears out), he becomes a peacemaker when he becomes a son of God. The term *son of God* in the scripture is always used by God to identify mature Christians; those who will be manifested at the judgment seat of Christ as the "church of the firstborn," who will gain the reward (Heb 12:23). Who are the sons of God? The peacemakers; those who bring warring factors, or parties who are offended at one another, together. This is not the task of the children of God; but of those who have spiritually grown to sonship through the preceding levels of beatitudes. This beatitude, then, has more to do with conduct than character; conduct that was forged through many levels of spiritual growth; conduct that not only strives to heal the wounds of others, but also strives to live peaceably with all men (Rom 12:18).

The Persecuted:

"Blessed are they which are persecuted for righteousness' sake: for theirs is the kingdom of heaven." If a Christian was satisfied to live a just and merciful life in this world, but not a Godly life with Christ, he could gain all the plaudits of this world and still have his salvation. However, Christ is not speaking in this beatitude of eternal life in heaven, but of millennial life in the coming kingdom of heaven.

Therefore, this beatitude informs us that it takes more then just salvation to become joint-heirs with Christ and to share His glory in His kingdom. To become a joint-heir with Christ, a Christian must suffer with Him by living a righteous life (Rom. 8:17). A Christian, according to the scriptures, has the choice of suffering with Him here and gaining his life there, or denying Him here and losing his life there. If he suffers here, he will reign with Him there. If he denies Him here, Christ will deny him at the judgment seat of Christ (2 Tim. 2:12). It follows that to enter the kingdom of heaven, a Christian must live a Godly life, which automatically brings persecution from the world (2 Tim. 3:12). If the world hated Christ, the Head, so will they hate the manifested body of Christ.

The Reviled and Persecuted:

"Blessed are ye, when {men} shall revile you, and persecute {you}, and shall say all manner of evil against you falsely, for my sake. (12) Rejoice, and be exceeding glad: for great {is} your reward in heaven: for so persecuted they the prophets which were before you." This is the first of the beatitudes that is spoken directly to and for the disciples. Notice the words *blessed are ye* as opposed to *blessed are they* which are written in the other beatitudes. Also notice that the persecution described here that the disciples were to suffer is compared to the persecution of the Old Testament prophets. It follows that Christ is speaking to all who have been personally called by God into the ministry of the Word. Their lot will be to suffer while doing God's will; for all who wish to live for Christ will suffer persecution from men's tongues and men's hands (1 Pet. 2:21; 2 Tim. 3:12).

The reward that will be given to the faithful teacher for his suffering is described as a "great reward"; a reward far above that mentioned in the other beatitudes. There, only the promise of the kingdom was given, but here, the kingdom, plus a great reward, is promised. This beatitude compares to the faithful and wise servant of Luke 12:42, who gives meat (teaches kingdom truths) in due season (last days of the church) and, as a result, is made ruler over all that Christ has (the great reward). Looking forward to the great reward, the faithful and wise teacher in these last days should rejoice and be exceedingly glad when he is persecuted for his faithfulness to the Word.

(2) The Similitudes

> "Ye are the salt of the earth: but if the salt have lost his savour, wherewith shall it be salted? it is thenceforth good for nothing, but to be cast out, and to be trodden under foot of men" (Matt. 5:13).

The similitudes of salt and light speak specifically to the ministers of God. Notice again that this section begins with the word *ye;* a word which shows a connection to the last beatitude given by Christ and directed to His disciples. Thus, a minister of the Word is to be like salt in his preaching of the Word. Salt is incorruptible and is opposite to leaven, which corrupts easily and arouses fermentation. Salt is a figure of the "truth," which sanctifies the soul. As salt stops natural corruption, so the Word of God works against moral corruption. Thus, the servant of Christ is an anti-corruptionist to this world as salt is to meat. Only when the rapture of the church occurs will the salt of the earth disappear into heaven. After the removal of the church (the salt), the world will be totally corrupted in sin for the space of seven years, (the tribulation period). At the end of this period the Lord will return to judge them.

Salt is also used medicinally to heal wounds. This speaks of the minister of the Word whose life, testimony and teaching from the Word can heal sin sick souls. Again, salt tastes good on food and it makes one thirsty. In like manner, the Word of God is pleasant to men and makes them thirsty for the water of life.

The apostles were called the salt of the earth. This leads us to believe that anyone who has been set apart for the ministry is called the salt of the earth. However, they are not literal salt, but only resemble salt in their labors. And though they are the primary salt source of the earth, they are not the only source. All believers should be dispensing salt by living the truth of God's Word.

> "Ye are the light of the world. A city that is set on an hill cannot be hid. (15) Neither do men light a candle, and put it under a bushel, but on a candlestick; and it giveth light unto all that are in the house. (16) Let your light so shine before men, that they may see your good works, and glorify your Father which is in heaven" (Matt. 5:14-16).

The second emblem used for the minister of the Word is light. Those who are called and who preach the Word are like a city set on a hill. Their ministry is not a secret one, but a ministry that everyone should see; for being set on a hill not only draws men to the truth, but also draws the persecution of the world. The man that is called to this glorious task is like a light that cannot be hid. Yet, many are placing their ministry under a bushel in these last days and allowing darkness to fill the whole house (church). Since they are not preaching the Word of God, they rely upon the word of man to tickle the ears of their hearers.

The order of the salt and the light used in these similitudes is significant. Salt speaks of humbleness and is common, inexpensive and trivial to the world. Light, on the other hand, speaks of illumination, obviousness and elevation. Where the first speaks of the servant who is called, the second speaks of his message.

However, there is a warning to those who resemble salt and light. If salt loses its savour, it is no good except to be cast out to be trodden by men. This casting out as worthless will occur at the judgment seat of Christ, where all the church will be judged. Its meaning is clear. The one who is called and hides his light in this life, loses his savour. Hence, at the judgment seat, he will be cast out of the kingdom for one thousand years.

We find, in Luke 14:33-35, these words, **"So likewise, whosoever he be of you that forsaketh not all that he hath, he cannot be my disciple. (34) Salt {is} good: but if the salt have lost his savour, wherewith shall it be** seasoned? (35) **It is neither fit for the land, nor yet for the dunghill; {but} men cast it out. He that hath ears to hear, let him hear.**" Here, the use of salt is a similitude of the disciple of Christ. What does it take to be a disciple, i.e., a learner, of Christ? Verse 33 tells us it takes all; all that we have and all that we own; or we cannot be His disciple. One may ask, "Does this passage of scripture speak of salvation and eternal life?" No, for that is by grace plus nothing. It speaks, rather, of the salvation of the soul and millennial life. For all believers who, as salt, lose their savour (their usefulness to Christ) in this life will be cast out at the judgment seat of Christ.

(3) The Commandments

The third section of the sermon on the mount is the longest of the four sections (chapters 5 through 7). Its purpose is to give to all believers the commandments of Christ, so that by keeping them, they may enter the coming kingdom of heaven. These commandments are also known as the law of Christ (Gal. 6:2).

To rightly understand this section, the reader must know the difference between the "law of God" and the "law of Christ." In the opening verse of this section (verse 17), our Lord tells us that He came to fulfill the law of God. This was accomplished on the cross when He died; for in His death, He fulfilled the claims of the law and paid its penalty of eternal death for all who would believe on Him. Hence, this salvation can be termed the salvation of the spirit; a salvation completed in the past with results that extend into the present in a *finished* state (Gr. perfect tense), saving every one who believes on Him from the penalty of sin; i.e., the penalty of breaking the law.

Once a Christian has experienced this salvation, he is placed under a new set of commandments known as the "law of Christ." These commandments are personally given by Jesus Himself in this third section of the sermon on the mount. The believers who keep them, and teach others to keep them, will be called great (have great reward) in the kingdom of heaven. The believers who break only the least of these commandments, and teach others to do so, will be called the least in the kingdom (loss of all reward). It follows that those who keep them will have their souls saved. Those who fail to keep them will suffer ruin and destruction outside the glory of the kingdom for one thousand years.

After reading the commandments in this section, the believer may ask, "How can this be? How can I keep a new set of laws?" You cannot; only Christ can. How does He accomplish this? While He was on the cross, He fulfilled the demands of the law for you by taking its penalty upon Himself. Then, when you trusted in Christ, two things happened. First, you were declared by the law itself as being judicially dead in Christ and outside of its power to condemn. Second, Christ took up His personal residence in your life (the sealing of the Holy Spirit), where He now stands ready to personally fulfill His own laws in and through your life (Eph. 1:13).

The fulfillment of His commandments will become automatic for a believer as he yields his life to Him through a continuing faith; a faith that comes from a daily growth by studying and obeying the Word of God (Rom. 10:17). When one first believes in Christ, righteousness is imputed. Then, when he yields his life through a continuing belief, righteousness is imparted. The first is judicial; the second is experiential. The first is objective; the second is subjective. The first is salvation of the spirit; the second is salvation of the soul (James 1:18-21). The first gives eternal life; the second gives millennial life.

Christ gave all believers a warning in verse 20 when He said, **"...for I say unto you, That except your righteousness shall exceed {the righteousness} of the scribes and Pharisees, ye shall in no case enter into the kingdom of heaven."** In view of this, only the imparted righteousness of Christ, as He lives through us, can exceed the righteousness of self. In New Testament theology, this is called the "Lordship of Christ"; it is the believer allowing Christ to have continuous rule over his life. The Lordship of Christ in a believer's life results in the salvation of his soul at the judgment seat of Christ and gives to him a position of rulership in the kingdom of heaven.

The commandments of Christ that Christians must keep to enter the kingdom of heaven are listed in the remaining portion of chapters five, six and seven of Matthew. Since most are self-explanatory, the writer will not expound upon them. A few of these include relationships with others, such as: do not kill, do not get angry without a cause, do not commit adultery, do not take revenge, do not hate your enemies, do not take oaths, do not act self-righteously, do not seek for riches in this life, do not worry over or seek the necessities of life, do not judge others, do not give spiritual truths to those who will trample them, and beware of false prophets. While many of these commandments are given in the negative, still others are in the positive, such as give to him that asketh thee, love your enemies and pray to your Father in secret.

The Mystery Commandment:

In view of the kingdom, the reader would do well to continually study these commandments for his own life. Generally speaking, there should be no confusion about what they are saying. However, the meaning of one of these commandments may be complicated and perplexing to the reader. This commandment is found in verses 29-30, and is part of the section that deals with adultery and immorality (see verse 28). "**...and if thy right eye offend thee, pluck it out, and cast {it} from thee: for it is profitable for thee that one of thy members should perish, and not {that} thy whole body should be cast into hell. (30) And if thy right hand offend thee, cut it off, and cast {it} from thee: for it is profitable for thee that one of thy members should perish, and not {that} thy whole body should be cast into hell"** (Matt. 5:29-30). The warning of the consequence of hell by our Lord to those Christians who practice the sin of adultery and immorality has been an enigma for Bible teachers and preachers for centuries. This is particularly true in light of the scripture that teaches eternal security for believers, as well as the fact that His disciples whom He was addressing were saved.

The answer to this enigma will become increasingly clear as the reader begins to understand the consequences of losing the kingdom. Many parables teach of the loss of the kingdom and of the places where the non-overcoming believers of the church period will spend the millennial age. Contrary to what others have taught, Gehenna, one of those places, is not the lake of fire (although it is translated "hell" here and in other places in the KJV), but is the place of the severest judgment of God upon His own people. This can first be seen in the Old Testament when Israel (God's covenant people) sinned against God by sacrificing their children to a pagan god in the "valley of the son of Hinnom." As a result, God judged them by slaying them and burying their bodies in this same valley (2 Chron: 28:1-3; Jer. 7:30-33; 19:5-6). When Jesus came, He used the valley of the son of Hinnom as a type to teach of another valley of judgment in the spiritual world, where the apostates (the Christians who fall away from God) will be punished for one thousand years. It is of Gehenna that Christ, in the above commandment, warns every immoral and adulterous Christian. (Note: for details on the outer darkness and Gehenna, see author's book *Shock and Surprise Beyond the Rapture*.)

(4) The Keys to the Sermon

The following two verses comprise the keys to understanding the sermon on the mount. They give the secret of happiness for the Christian while here on earth, and the secret of how to rule and reign with Christ in the coming kingdom of heaven.

The First Key:

> "Not every one that saith unto me, Lord, Lord, shall enter into the kingdom of heaven; but he that doeth the will of my Father which is in heaven" (Matt. 7:21).

Contrary to the teaching of many, not all believers will automatically inherit the kingdom of heaven. This spiritual truth is revealed in our above text, which teaches that it will be given only to those believers who do His will. This verse speaks to Christians concerning reward, not eternal life.

Many Christians in that day (at the judgment seat of Christ) will attempt to prove that they are worthy of the kingdom. They will cry, "Lord, Lord, did we not prophesy in your name, and cast out devils in your name, and do many wonderful works in your name?" But the Lord will say, **"Depart from me, ye that work iniquity, I never knew you"** (verses 22 and 23). As the reader ponders this indictment, he will see that those whom Jesus will address in that day are not the lost, but the saved (the body of Christ). Consider this clear scriptural evidence: first, those of this verse will be at the judgment seat of Christ where no lost man will appear; second, they will call Him Lord, thus showing that they possess the Holy Spirit (1 Cor. 12:3); third, they will have done what they will consider as many wonderful works. However, these works will not be the works of Christ through them, but the religious efforts of the flesh, symbolized in 1 Cor. 3:12 as wood, hay, and stubble. Consequently, since this group will be of the body of Christ, the indictment of Jesus upon them will not be to depart into hell, i.e., everlasting hell fire (as it will be to the lost nations in Matt. 25:41,46), but to depart from His presence (outside of the kingdom).

There will also be a favored group of believers at the judgment seat whom He will choose out of the body of Christ; they will be privileged to go into the marriage. They will be made up of the "wedding guests" (Matt. 22:10) and the bride of Christ. (Matt. 25:10). Consequently, those who are saved and are not members of the bride or the wedding guests will not be allowed to enter the wedding (inherit the kingdom). Hence, the word *know*, or *knew*, as it is connected to the judgment seat of Christ, means that He will not recognize this group as being a part of the bride of Christ. To "know," here, means intimate knowledge, as in marriage (Matt. 1:25). Therefore, the bride of Christ will be those who are known by Christ as a special and submissive people who allowed the Holy Spirit to rule over their lives and to produce spiritual fruit through them. This will be accomplished by obedience to the Word of God and by "doing" His commandments.

The Striving of the Bride:

A companion passage of scripture that will direct more light on this teaching is found in Luke 13:23-28, where we read:

> "Then said one unto him, Lord, are there few that be saved? And he said unto them, (24) Strive to enter in at the strait gate: for many, I say unto you, will seek to enter in, and shall not be able. (25) When once the master of the house is risen up, and hath shut to the door, and ye begin to stand without, and to knock at the door, saying, Lord, Lord, open unto us; and he shall answer and say unto you, I know you not whence ye are: (26) Then shall ye begin to say, We have eaten and drunk in thy presence, and thou hast taught in our streets. (27) But he shall say, I tell you, I know you not whence ye are; depart from me, all {ye} workers of iniquity. (28) There shall be weeping and gnashing of teeth, when ye shall see Abraham, and Isaac, and Jacob, and all the prophets, in the kingdom of God, and you {yourselves} thrust out."

Like our main text, this section of scripture is not referring to the salvation of the spirit and eternal life, but to the salvation of the soul and millennial life (the kingdom). We see this in Jesus' answer to the one who asked if there would only be a few saved (into the kingdom). His answer was to "strive" to enter in at the strait gate (entrance to the kingdom). The word *strive*, in the Greek, means to agonize as an athlete would in his attempt to win an athletic contest. It means to work unreservably in accomplishing a task. The lost do not strive by works to be saved; for salvation of the spirit is **"not of works lest any man should boast"** (Eph. 2:9). Perceptively, then, our Lord in this passage is speaking to every Christian who has a desire to enter the coming kingdom. To do this, he must strive to do the will of the Father and to keep the faith and to finish the race (2 Tim. 4:7-8).

Paul used "strive" in 1 Cor. 9:25 to describe his own spiritual race when he said, "**And every man that striveth for the mastery is temperate in all things. Now they {do it} to obtain a corruptible crown; but we an incorruptible.**" In 2 Tim. 2:5, he said, "**And if a man also strive for masteries, {yet} is he not crowned, except he strive lawfully.**" Lawful striving (striving against the flesh) causes one to submit to the rulership of Christ over his life.

This passage (Luke 13:26-28) also discloses what will happen at the judgment seat of Christ to those Christians who failed to strive in this lifetime for spiritual masteries; those who did not allow the Holy Spirit to rule over their lives to produce spiritual fruit through them; those who were not concerned in doing the will of the Father; those whose only interest was in this world, seeking the pleasures of money, power, popularity and accolades of this world system. They, too, will knock at the door (to the kingdom) at the judgment seat and say, "**Lord, Lord, open unto us.**" But Jesus will answer, "**I know you not whence you are**" (I do not recognize you as being a part of this group — the bride). Then they will try to prove that they should be allowed to enter the kingdom by saying "**We have eaten and drunk in thy presence, and thou hast taught in our streets**" (We are saved members of the church). But the Lord will say in that day that He does not recognize them as members of the bride, and to depart because of their works of iniquity (religious works of the flesh). "**There will be weeping and gnashing of teeth....**" The expression *weeping and gnashing of teeth* is never found in the Word of God describing those who will be in eternal hell; instead, it is always found in the context of the judgment seat of Christ or "the outer darkness" (obscurity outside of the kingdom for one thousand years)(Matt. 22:13;24:51;25:30).

Two Foundations:

> "Therefore whosoever heareth these sayings of mine, and doeth them, I will liken him unto a wise man, which built his house upon a rock: (25) And the rain descended, and the floods came, and the winds blew, and beat upon that house; and it fell not: for it was founded upon a rock.

(26) And every one that heareth these sayings of mine, and doeth them not, shall be likened unto a foolish man, which built his house upon the sand: (27) And the rain descended, and the floods came, and the winds blew, and beat upon that house; and it fell: and great was the fall of it" (Matt. 7:24-27).

Our Lord, at the judgment seat of Christ, will liken every Christian to one who has chosen either a rock foundation or a sand foundation on which to build his life. If a Christian hears the sayings of Jesus in the "sermon on the mount" and does them, he will have a life founded upon the doctrines of the "rock." If he hears these sayings and does them not, his foundation will be as sand.

The rock in this passage is a Biblical emblem of Christ. It comprises the "smitten rock" (typified in Ex. 17:1-6 as Jesus being crucified), the "stumbling stone" of the Jews (1 Cor. 1:23), the "foundation stone" of the church (Eph. 2:20), and the "smiting stone" of His coming judgment on the world (Dan. 2:34-35). This passage does not teach the contrast between the lost and the saved; it teaches the contrast in the foundation of Christians who hear the sayings of the sermon on the mount and obey them, as opposed to those Christians who hear and obey them not. It is work (doing the will of the Father) that is taught here, not salvation, which is by grace through faith (Eph. 2:8-9). Hence, those Christians who hear and do its sayings will have lives founded upon Bible doctrines of the rock, which teach the Saviorship of Jesus (the smitten stone), the Lordship of Christ over the life (the foundation stone), and the coming Kingship of Christ to set up His kingdom (the smiting stone).

Rock Christians are those who believe in the kingdom truths; truths that teach that to enter the coming kingdom, one must have works; i.e., doing the will of the Father by keeping the commandments of Jesus Christ. Sand Christians are those who build their lives on sand, which stands for legalism (works of self). They see nothing beyond salvation; they believe that since they are saved and cannot lose their salvation, they can live in any way they choose (no Lordship of Christ in their lives). These two different Christian lives are characterized as lives that the storms of life will either destroy or not destroy. The rain, floods and winds are emblems of the trials of this world. Those lives built upon the legalism of sand (efforts of self) will utterly fail when trials and tribulations occur. Those lives built upon the rock (the full doctrine of Christ) will survive all the trials and temptations of this world. Those whose lives are built upon the rock of Christ will be the wedding guests or the bride of Christ; the ones chosen out of all the saved at the judgment seat of Christ to enter the kingdom. Those lives built upon the sand will not only fall in this lifetime, but also at the judgment seat of Christ. And "great" will be that fall.

In its historical setting, the sermon on the mount spoke to the disciples of Jesus of that day. They could either continue in their efforts to anchor their lives in the shifting sands of Judaism (works of self), or anchor their lives in the rock of Jesus Christ; they could futilely try to enter the kingdom by their own works, or they could strive to allow Christ to produce the needed works through them. In its contemporary setting, it speaks the same truth to the church. Those Christians who have founded their lives upon the rock of Jesus Christ are likened unto "wise men"; those who have founded their lives upon the sands of the religious works of self are likened unto "foolish men."

To understand the Biblical meaning of a "wise man" versus a "foolish man," the reader should study the parable of the "ten virgins" (Matt. 25:1-13). This parable teaches that the five foolish virgins had only one portion of oil in their lamps (oil, a symbol of the Holy Spirit), thus revealing that they possessed salvation. The five wise virgins had two portions of oil; the first, which is an emblem of the sealing of the Holy Spirit that every believer receives the moment he is saved (Eph. 1:13), and a second, which is emblematic of the Holy Spirit in our learning and applying the higher knowledge of the kingdom. It was this second portion that the five wise virgins carried with them in vessels, thus showing that they were not only saved, but also had a double portion of the Spirit of God that gives knowledge of the kingdom, i.e., the "above knowledge" (Gr. *epignosis*) of the kingdom. Hence, their lives were founded upon a rock.

This parable informs us that at the judgment seat, the wise will go into the marriage, while the foolish will try in vain to obtain the extra oil that will be needed to enter. The door will be shut to the heavenly marriage and they will be left outside crying for the Lord to open the door to them. The foolish in this parable represent most of Christendom, who will fail to inherit the kingdom. The wise represent a very small portion of Christendom, who, at the judgment seat of Christ, will enter the kingdom. These two groups are the same as those characterized in Matt. 7:21-23. To understand this is to understand the first key to the sermon on the mount.

The Second Key:

"But seek ye first the kingdom of God, and his righteousness; and all these things shall be added unto you" (Matt. 6:33).

The second key to understanding the sermon on the mount teaches that the believer is to "seek first the kingdom of God (the coming millennial kingdom) and His righteousness." When this becomes his first priority, then obedience to all the other commandments of Christ will follow.

The Heavenly Blessing:

What truths does this text hold for us who are Christians? It speaks of excitement; the excitement of something new! A new place for the heart to be; a new understanding and excitement for His Word; a new outlook on life; a new commitment to the Lord; a new rest and peace; a new focus for living; a new hope for the glorious future. All this can be ours if we meet one condition: **"Seek ye first the kingdom of God and His righteousness..."**

What is the kingdom of God in this verse? It is not heaven, or eternal life, as some teach; for the saved are not told to seek the things they already have. It is the coming millennial kingdom of our Lord, and only those who hope for it have the opportunity to attain it.

What is hope? The word *hope*, for a believer, means to live his life in anticipation of the coming kingdom. As used in the scriptures, it conveys the idea that one may, or may not, attain what is hoped for. Hope does not mean the same as faith. Faith claims something that God says is already ours. Hope, on the other hand, shows us what can be ours if we can achieve it. We see this in Paul's prayer for the Ephesian church, when he prayed that they might receive the "hope of God's calling," which was an invitation to the "riches of the glory of His inheritance [the coming kingdom]" (Eph. 1:17-18).

In light of this, our hope is for the inheritance laid up in heaven (Col. 1:5). However, it does not automatically become ours when we reach heaven; for we must first be presented at the judgment seat of Christ as holy and unblamable to inherit these eternal riches. For this to happen, we must continue (Gr. present indicative active) to live now in a grounded and settled faith and not be moved away from the hope (anticipation) of the good news of the inheritance (Col. 1:21-23). This blessed hope (anticipation) is the looking for the glorious appearing (not the rapture, but the revelation) of the great God and our Saviour Jesus Christ to set up His kingdom (Tit. 2:13). Hope becomes the helmet of our spiritual armor, which protects us from the forces of Satan, the flesh and the world (1 Thess. 5:8). Christians who have the helmet of hope will purify themselves (1 John 3:3).

"Seek ye first the kingdom of God and His righteousness." What is "righteousness"? Righteousness is right living. As the coming kingdom should be the goal for every Christian, righteousness, or right living, is the spiritual method to reach that goal. Every believer has two natures; the old nature living in the soul of man and the new nature (Holy Spirit) living in the spirit. When a believer allows the old nature in the soul to rule over his life, he produces works of unrighteousness. When he submits to the

Holy Spirit to rule over his life through his spirit, he produces works of righteousness. To seek righteousness, the Christian must seek to give all control of his life to Christ, who lives in him. This submission will cause him to be obedient to His commandments, which is the standard of righteousness needed to inherit the kingdom. The turning away from the desires of this world to the hope of the next world is that which causes us to strive against our old nature and allows Jesus to be the Lord of our life; and only by striving can we enter into the strait gate (Luke 13:24).

At the judgment seat of Christ, every Christian will have his works tested in the fires of God. If he has works of gold, silver and precious stones (the righteous works of Christ through him), his works will not burn up and he will receive a reward (will inherit and enter the kingdom). If he has works of wood, hay and stubble (the unrighteous works of the flesh), they will burn up and he will suffer loss (of the kingdom); yet, he shall be saved (1 Cor. 3:11-15). **"For we must all appear before the judgment seat of Christ; that every one may receive the things {done} in {his} body, according to that he hath done, whether {it be} good or bad"** (2 Cor. 5:10).

The Earthly Blessing:

The Bible speaks of the two kinds of Christians in our text as the "spiritual" Christian and the "carnal" Christian (1 Cor. 2:15-3:3). It is the spiritual Christian whose life is anchored on the rock, and who can assimilate spiritual meat (the kingdom truths) of the Word. It is the carnal Christian whose life is built upon the shifting sands of self effort, and who can only assimilate the milk of the Word. The spiritual Christian's hope is in the coming kingdom; the carnal Christian's hope is in his success in this present world. The spiritual Christian has a reverential fear of God, who, he knows, will judge all his works at the judgment seat of Christ (2 Cor. 5:10). Because of this fear, he is able to receive wisdom, "for the fear of the Lord is the beginning of wisdom" (Prov. 9:10; 15:33); thus, as he receives wisdom (the double portion of the oil), he becomes a wise man. The carnal Christian has no fear of God. He correctly believes that he is saved and cannot lose his salvation; but he incorrectly believes that since he is saved, he will automatically gain all rewards in heaven, no matter how he lives here on earth.

Our text tells us that there is an earthly promise (in addition to the coming kingdom), which is given by God to every spiritual rock Christian seeking after the kingdom. He promises us that He will add (Gr. *prostithemi*, meaning to add additionally) all of the necessities of life (food, shelter, clothing, etc.). Because of this, the Christian is told not to worry (take no thought for the morrow), but to live each day one at a time (Matt. 6:31,34). He is to continue in steadfastness to hope for the coming glory, believing that God will super-supply all of his needs. With this truth in mind, it is no wonder that the rain, floods, and winds of this world will have no effect upon his life. For while his hope is anchored in heaven beyond the veil (Heb. 6:19), all the needs of this life are being "super-added" to him.

(5) The Warning:

"Enter ye in at the strait gate: for wide {is} the gate, and broad {is} the way, that leadeth to destruction, and many there be which go in thereat: (14) Because strait {is} the gate, and narrow {is} the way, which leadeth unto life, and few there be that find it" (Matt. 7:13- 14).

In this warning passage, our Lord is showing us the two paths that can be walked by Christians. The strait gate and narrow path speak of the life choice of the spiritual rock Christian, who anticipates the kingdom. The wide gate and broad way speak of the life choice of the carnal sand Christian, who hopes for the success of this world.

The strait (narrow) gate to this narrow path is restrictive, showing that the Christian must enter empty handed and yielded. Along the narrow path itself, he must learn the spiritual disciplines of tribulation, patience, hope and love (Rom. 5: 2-5). Those who enter its gate and walk its path to the end will find life (millennial life). Those who choose the wide gate and the unrestrictive broad way of popularity, power and money of this world will find at the end (the judgment seat of Christ) destruction (loss of the kingdom in the outer darkness or the blackness of darkness) for one thousand years.

CLOSING THOUGHTS

For hundreds of years, the popular pulpit has erroneously taught at least four different interpretations of the sermon on the mount: that (1) it is the way of salvation for the lost world; (2) it was the way of salvation for lost Israel; (3) it is a moral code for all men to live by; (4) it is the constitution of all who will live in the coming kingdom. We have presented what we believe to be the correct interpretation; a standard of righteousness demanded by our Lord of all believers in this life if they are to inherit the kingdom.

We have shown to the "wise" Christian that the beatitudes of the sermon reveal the maturing process of Christians who will inherit the kingdom; and that the similitudes manifest the spiritual qualities to be reached by all Christian disciples and teachers.

We have shown that the exclusive commandments of Christ are specific rules of conduct for those who aspire to be in the kingdom. Each of these commandments must be seriously considered, because the ignorant or willful violation of any one could disqualify the believer for his inheritance in the kingdom.

Finally, we have shown that the wise Christian should be impressed with the truth of the sermon; a truth which verifiably teaches that it is utterly impossible for a believer, in his own strength and self-effort, to keep any one of these commandments. Only as he becomes a mature and spiritual rock Christian by feeding on the Word can he trust Christ to perform these commandments through him (Phil. 2:12-13). The foremost of His commandments is, "**...seek ye first the kingdom of God and his righteousness, and all these things shall be added [super added] unto you**" (Matt. 6:33), since it embodies all of the other commandments.

THE MOVING OF PARADISE

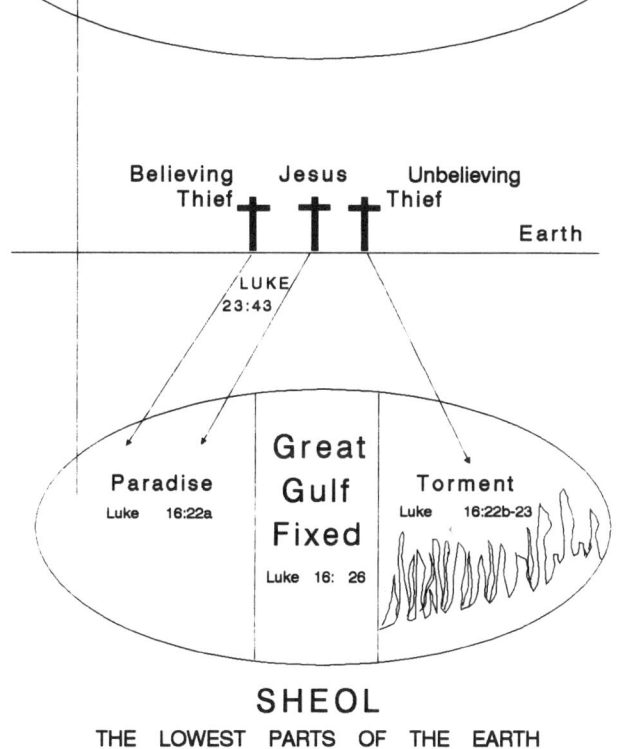

NOTES

CHAPTER SEVEN

THE REJECTION OF THE KINGDOM

This chapter will cover Matthew's chapters eight through twelve and will show the deteriorating relationship between Israel and Jesus during His Galilean ministry. This relationship will be broken in the twelfth chapter of Matthew when Israel will obstinately refuse to repent and thus, will reject the preaching of the "gospel of the kingdom."

To teach the major truths of this section of scripture, the writer has chosen six topical subjects: (1) Israel's lack of faith; (2) the calling and instructing of the apostles; (3) the upbraiding of Israel; (4) the personal invitation of Jesus; (5) the unpardonable sin; and (6) the one sign of Jonah.

ISRAEL'S LACK OF FAITH

Israel's lack of faith is first seen in the eighth chapter of Matthew and is revealed in spite of the miracles that Jesus performed in their sight. Because of their lack of faith, Jesus began prophesying that they would be cast out of the kingdom.

The First Mention of Outer Darkness

And I say unto you, That many shall come from the east and west, and shall sit down with Abraham, and Isaac, and Jacob, in the kingdom of heaven. (12) But the children of the kingdom shall be cast out into outer darkness: there shall be weeping and gnashing of teeth" (Matt. 8:11-12).

Prior to this verse of scripture, a Gentile Roman centurion had demonstrated his faith in Jesus Christ by asking Him to heal his servant by long distance; i.e., without the necessity of Him coming to his house. His faith was so great that Jesus marveled and said,

"I have not found so great faith, no, not in Israel."

In comparing the faith of the centurion to Israel's lack of faith, Jesus informed that generation of Israel (the children [Gr. *sons*] of the kingdom) that they would not enter the kingdom of heaven. Instead, they would be cast into the darkness outside of the kingdom. We may liken the kingdom to a great banquet hall lit for the honored guests, those who were originally invited to the festivities (Israel) would not be allowed to enter, but would be cast out into the darkened rooms and halls outside. Other saints of Israel, however, would come from the east and the west and would be allowed to sit down with Abraham, Isaac and Jacob in the kingdom.

This is the first time that the term *the outer darkness* appears in Matthew and the only time it is ever mentioned in connection with Israel. It is recorded two more times in later chapters in connection with the church. Contrary to popular teaching, the outer darkness is not the place of everlasting hell where the lost go, but a place of obscurity outside the kingdom where those who lose their inheritance will go for one thousand years.

To have a clear assessment of this, the reader must understand the scope of Jesus' ministry to Israel. The book of Matthew does not teach that He came to tell them how to be saved by the preaching of the cross, since He had not yet been rejected and crucified; the scope of His message to Israel was the kingdom. Seemingly, Gentile believers have a hard time understanding that Israel, as a nation, already belonged to God, though individually they had to believe. In the Old Testament, God calls them His "firstborn son" (Ex. 4:22). Therefore, being the national seed of Abraham and, as such, under the Abrahamic covenant (salvation by grace, see Rom. 4:1-4), the scope of Jesus' message was not how to be saved from eternal death, but how to be saved into the "kingdom of heaven." Those who repented and followed Him (brought forth fruit) would be in the kingdom; but those who failed to repent would be cast out into the darkness, i.e., obscurity outside of the kingdom, for one thousand years.

Nevertheless, a new dispensation would begin after the cross, making it necessary for the Jews to repent for their crucifixion of Jesus (under Judaism) and to believe that He was their Messiah (the Son of God) to be saved. Under this new dispensation of grace, believing Jews would be members of the early church; a new people; a new creation of God. Moreover, under the teaching of the New Testament to the church, all believers (Jew and Gentile) who would fail to have their souls (Gr. *psuche,* meaning life) saved at the judgment seat of Christ, would be cast out into the outer darkness (outside of the kingdom) in total ruin for one thousand years. See the parables of the "wedding feast" and the "talents" (Matt. 22:1-14; 25:14-30).

Israel's Birthright in the Kingdom

"And Jesus said unto them, Can the children of the bridechamber mourn, as long as the bridegroom is with them? but the days will come, when the bridegroom shall be taken from them, and then shall they fast. (16) No man putteth a piece of new cloth unto an old garment, for that which is put in to fill it up taketh from the garment, and the rent is made worse. (17) Neither do men put new wine into old bottles: else the bottles break, and the wine runneth out, and the bottles perish: but they put new wine into new bottles, and both are preserved" (Matt. 9:15-17).

This passage informs us of Israel's right to the kingdom as the "children (Gr. *huios,* meaning sons) of the bridal chamber." The revelation of this truth comes to us in response to Jesus' answer to the Pharisees who wanted to know why His disciples did not fast. He informed them that there was no reason to fast when there was no mourning. Jesus had come to Israel and all who would recognize Him as the Messiah (the Bridegroom) would be counted as the children (sons) of the bridal chamber; i.e. the wedding guests. This new relationship could be nothing but joy. However, one day He would be taken away (crucified). Then, the children (sons) of the bridal chamber would mourn. The sons of the bridal chamber are not the church (at this time), but clearly the believers of Israel. As a believing people under a covenant relationship with God, they were to be the "wedding guests" (Matt. 22:2-7), while the prophets of Israel were to be the "friends of the bridegroom" (John 3:29).

Another reason why the believers of Israel were not the bride is that the Bridegroom does not come to earth to choose His bride and then, afterward, leave them. Instead, the bride will be taken from the earth and chosen at the judgment seat of Christ and thereafter will always be with Christ.

Who, then, is the bride? The answer is the church; a new nation of people made up of Jews and Gentiles; a body of baptized believers who are bringing forth *much* spiritual fruit. In Old Testament typology, the bride of Christ is always a Gentile bride, thus speaking of the mostly Gentile church. By comparing the brides of Isaac, Jacob, Joseph and Moses (types of Christ), the reader will quickly recognize that these brides were not Jewish, but Gentile.

In Matt 9:15-17, Jesus continues to inform the Pharisees, through a parable, that the dispensation of law had ended. This was evidenced by the fact that the Bridegroom, i.e., the Promised Seed of Gal. 3:19, had come, and a new dispensation would begin that would be different. He illustrated this by saying that you would not sew a new patch of cloth to an old garment that is tearing with age, because it would make it tear more. Hence, the church (the new dispensation of grace) would not be united with Judaism.

This cloth is clearly a type of the righteous acts of Christ that would be produced through the lives of believers totally yielded to Him during the church period. It would be sewed to other pieces of new cloth and would constitute the wedding garments of the bride and the wedding guests at the judgment seat of Christ (Matt. 22:11-13; Rev. 19:7-8). It is inconceivable that the old garments of Israel (a type of the law) could become the wedding garments for the bride of Christ, or even that pieces of the wedding garment could be sewed to them.

Jesus also told the Pharisees that you would not put new wine (a type of the joy experienced at weddings) into old wineskins (a type of bondage under law), for the two are incompatible and the wineskins would break. New wine is to be placed in the skins of grace and preserved (aged as wine is aged) until that day of great joy when the wedding guests, the friends of the bridegroom and the bride will all sit down together in the heavenly wedding feast at the end of this age.

Despite these teachings, the Pharisees could not understand this parable, since its meaning could only be revealed by the Holy Spirit (Matt. 13:10-11). Therefore, all parables spoken to Israel in the New Testament are, in reality, spoken to the church and for the church.

THE CALLING AND INSTRUCTING OF THE APOSTLES

The tenth chapter of Matthew concerns itself with Jesus selecting His apostles out from among His disciples and instructing them in their mission. They were to go only to the lost sheep of the house of Israel to preach the gospel of the kingdom. They were given the power to perform signs and wonders as credentials of their authority. Most of this chapter will be easily understood by the reader as long as he keeps in mind to whom the apostles were to go and what they were to preach. The reader must also remember that it is erroneous teaching if any one attempts to make the instructions of this chapter (under the preaching of the gospel of the kingdom) speak to the pastors and evangelists of the church age (under the preaching of the gospel of grace). The only exception to this is the faithfulness and obedience that Christ expects from all whom He sends to preach either gospel.

As examples of error that can be taught, preachers today are not instructed anywhere in the epistles of the New Testament to go from city to city preaching the gospel without shoes, or two coats, or without money. Neither are they instructed to shake the dust off their feet when they depart from those who would not receive them.

The Warning of Gehenna

"And fear not them which kill the body, but are not able to kill the soul:

but rather fear him which is able to destroy both soul and body in hell" (Matt. 10:28).

In the continuing instructions to the apostles given in this chapter, we encounter another mystery verse like that of Matt. 5:29. The difficulty, here, is that Jesus is instructing His apostles, who are saved and cannot lose their salvation. Yet, He warns them of the possibility of having their soul and body destroyed in hell (Gehenna) if they fail to preach (because of fear) the message He has given to them. The word *hell* in this verse is not everlasting hell as some preach, but "Gehenna"; a special place of punishment for God's own people who fall away (apostatize) from him.

As previously stated about Matt. 5:29, Gehenna gets its name from its earthly counterpart in the "valley of the son of Hinnom," located south of Jerusalem. It was there that the sons of Judah worshiped another god and sacrificed their children in the practice of this idolatry. As a result, God swore that He would call that valley the "valley of slaughter," where He would bury the bodies of His own apostate (fallen away) people of Israel (Jer. 7:32-34; 19:6-15). Historically, this likely occurred when God allowed Israel to be invaded by the Chaldeans in about 606 B.C. and taken into captivity and, again, when the Romans decimated Jerusalem in A.D. 70. Many were slain and their bodies probably thrown into this valley south of Jerusalem. It is important to notice that God never slew or buried any lost person there — only His own apostate people of Israel. Even the lost nations, who will be slain by the Lord Himself at His second coming, will not be slain or buried in this valley, but in the valley of Jehoshaphat (Joel 3: 12-16). This makes the valley of the son of Hinnom (Heb. *ge Hinnom*, short for *ge ben Hinnom*, translated Gehenna) a type of the spiritual place where God will judge His own apostate believers of the church period for one thousand years.

This punishment will be for all pastors and teachers who willfully and deliberately fall away from the revealed truth that they are to preach (in many cases commercializing their ministry), and stubbornly remain in the sins of the flesh and of the world unto the coming of the Lord (Matt. 24:48-51). Gehenna will also be for all Christians (not necessarily teachers or leaders) who willfully and obstinately refuse the Lordship of Christ over their lives and knowingly fall back into the sins of the flesh and of the world, becoming enemies of Christ unto the end (the rapture) (Luke 19:14,27). According to scripture, this punishment, i.e., the slaying of the apostates, will occur at the judgment seat of Christ where the apostates will lose their redeemed bodies to Gehenna and their souls to the blackness of darkness (Psa. 88) during the kingdom age. This blackness of darkness is described in Jude 1:13 as lasting one thousand years (note: the Greek word *aion* in this verse, translated *forever* in the KJV, should have been translated *for the age,* i.e., the millennial age).

The reader may ask, "How can a spiritual body be slain?" The scripture answers this by inferring that the believers at the judgment seat of Christ will not have spiritual bodies, but will have redeemed bodies; for they must first (before receiving their spiritual bodies) be judged for the things done in their earthly bodies (2 Cor. 5:10). The term *redemption of the body* (Rom. 8:23b) means a body has been purchased back by the redemptive work of Christ on the cross and restored at the time of the rapture to the same state that it was in Adam before Adam sinned.

At the judgment seat of Christ, all believers, in their redeemed bodies, will be judged according to the things done in their bodies, whether good or bad (2 Cor. 5:10). As a result of this judgment, many will either be cast into the outer darkness or slain and cast into Gehenna. The "overcomers," however, will receive their spiritual bodies (bodies animated by the Spirit) through the out-resurrection (a higher resurrection) (Phil. 3:11), and will inherit the kingdom. They will have bodies of the resurrection, likened unto our Lord's body. Notwithstanding, after one thousand years have passed, all those who have been punished in the outer darkness and Gehenna will be resurrected into their spiritual bodies at the close of the kingdom age (1 Cor. 15:51-58) and will live forever in heaven, but without the inheritance. They will have eternal salvation through the redemptive work of Jesus Christ on the cross; yet, they will have lost all rewards during the kingdom age and for the ages to follow.

The doctrine of Gehenna has not been seen by modern or traditional theology. To the writer's knowledge, only three other expositors have ever mentioned punishment of a believer in Gehenna during the kingdom age; Robert Govette, G.H. Pember and Watchman Nee. A profound message of warning is given through this doctrine to all Christian teachers and preachers who fail (through fear) to preach what Christ has commissioned them to teach, preach, or write. (In *Shock and Surprise Beyond the Rapture*, the writer has devoted an entire chapter to teach its details).

In summary to the doctrine of losing the inheritance of the kingdom, the apostles were not only instructed not to fear what men would do to them, but also to confess Christ in their lifestyle. These same instructions are valid for all Christians as a condition for entrance into the kingdom. If a believer confesses Christ in his life here, Christ will confess him before His Father in heaven. If he denies Him here, Christ will deny him before His Father in heaven (Matt. 10:32-33). This will occur at the judgment seat of Christ.

One's love for Christ must be greater than his love for any earthly possession, including father or mother, to gain the inheritance. This is the quality of love that motivates the believer to follow Christ no matter what the world may do to him; a love that demands that he carry his own cross; a devotion that requires him to lose his life here for Christ's sake, so that he may find it there (inherit the kingdom). If a believer seeks to gain his life here (loving the world), the scriptures declare that he will lose his life there for one thousand years and ultimately lose the inheritance forever (Matt. 10:32,33,37-39).

THE UPBRAIDING OF ISRAEL

"Then began he to upbraid the cities wherein most of his mighty works were done, because they repented not" (Matt 11:20).

In chapter eleven, we begin to see a marked difference in the relationship between Jesus and Israel. The cities of Galilee would not repent despite all the mighty works that Jesus did. For this reason our Lord begins to pronounce woes (judgments) on them. First, He upbraids Chorazin and Bethsaida by telling them that if He had done the same wonderful works in Tyre and Sidon (pagan cities of Phoenicia), they would have repented. Then speaking to Capernaum, He informs them that if these same mighty works that were done in Capernaum had been done in Sodom, Sodom would have repented and not been destroyed (vs. 21-24). In both cases, Jesus says that the punishment for those cities of Israel, in the day of judgment, will be much greater than for those cities of the pagans.

It is difficult to understand why the people of Israel, who belonged to God and saw the great miracles of healing by Jesus, rejected Him and His message. According to our text, Jesus' mighty works (miracles) must have been awe-inspiring. The scriptures tell us that His fame for healing people spread throughout the land. This was especially true in Capernaum, the headquarters for His ministry, where the people lined up to be healed. Yet, they refused to repent. Their idea of the coming kingdom was that their Messiah would come from heaven in a flame of fire and cast out their Roman masters. Even those who submitted to the idea that Jesus could be the Messiah wanted Him to first raise up an army and overthrow the Romans. They had no concept of His first coming as the suffering servant who would be their sin offering. They had a mind-set.

John tells of the occasion when Jesus fed five thousand men with five loaves and two fishes. This miracle of multiplication only made the people more determined to make Him a "bread king"; one who could give them welfare by magically making bread appear for them every day. Jesus later explained to them in John, chapter six, that He was not sent to be a welfare king and there would be no more bread given except the bread of life (Himself), who had come down from heaven (antitype of the manna in the wilderness). He explained that for a man to be saved, he must eat of this bread, i.e., spiritually appropriate (take to and for oneself) His flesh and His blood (meaning to believe on Him). But when many heard that, they went back and followed Him no more (John 6:66).

Before we leave this section of scripture, it is important to notice the difference in the scope of Jesus' message in John and that in Matthew. In Matthew, the message was on the national level; in John, it is on the personal level. In Matthew, the message was to Israel, as a nation, to **"repent, for the kingdom of heaven is at hand"**(Matt. 4:17); in John, it was to the individual who thirsted to **"come unto me and drink** [Gr. perfect tense denoting salvation of the spirit]" (John 7:37b).

In John 7:38, Jesus said, **"He that believeth** [Gr. present continuous tense, denoting salvation of the soul] **on me as the scripture hath said, out of his belly shall flow rivers of living water."** It is clear that the book of John was written to all men who would form the church; for the next verse (John 7:39) explains that the water that would flow out of the belly (innermost part) of the believers who would continue to believe would be the Holy Spirit in power. And this could not occur until the day of Pentecost (the beginning of the church), after Jesus had ascended and was glorified in heaven. The entrance at Pentecost of the Holy Spirit into the church was for the purpose of giving power to all believers of the church period to produce spiritual fruit; fruit that would be necessary to pass the fiery tests of the judgment seat of Christ (1 Cor. 3:11-15).

THE PERSONAL INVITATION

"Come unto me, all {ye} that labor and are heavy laden, and I will give you rest. (29) Take my yoke upon you, and learn of me; for I am meek and lowly in heart: and ye shall find rest unto your souls. (30) For my yoke {is} easy, and my burden is light" (Matt. 11:28-30).

At the close of the eleventh chapter of Matthew, the message of Jesus began to change. Instead of preaching exclusively to the lost sheep of the house of Israel to **"repent, for the kingdom of heaven is at hand,"** He began preaching to the individual lost sheep of Israel who would believe and become the first members of the early church. This message, then, is to the church and for the church, which would soon be revealed in the sixteenth chapter of Matthew.

The Two Rests

The message of Christ in our text is comprised of two rests; one given and one found. The first rest is given by Christ to all those who labor and are heavy laden (recognizing their need for Christ) and accept His invitation to come to Him. This is the salvation of the spirit of man, which gives eternal life.

The second rest is found by the believer when he yields his life to the Holy Spirit so that Christ may live through him. This Christ-controlled life then willingly takes on the yoke (work and commandments) of Christ and grows spiritually by learning of Him through the Word. Hence, with Christ in control of every surrendered aspect of the believer's life, he will find (experience) the second rest. The second rest is the continuing salvation of the soul.

Before leaving this invitation of Christ to all men, we must recognize in scripture a third rest found in Heb. 3:18. This is called "His rest" and represents the millennial rest in the coming kingdom for one thousand years. Our Lord teaches of this rest by referring to Israel as a type of the Christian. During Israel's wilderness wonderings after they left Egypt, many lacked faith and, consequently, failed to enter the promised land (a type of the coming kingdom). Our Lord warns the Christian through this type to: (1) hold fast the confidence and the rejoicing of the hope firm unto the end, and (2) not to harden his heart by unbelief departing from the living God (Heb. 3:6-19). Notice that this generation of Israelites did not lose their salvation, but their reward. They had already been saved out of Egypt (type of salvation of the spirit) through faith in the blood of the passover lamb (type of Jesus Christ) and had been baptized unto Moses in the cloud and in the sea (1 Cor. 10:2). However, in the wilderness (a type of where the Christian is now), they failed to continue to believe to the saving of their lives (souls) and, consequently, failed to enter the promised land (type of the kingdom); because of their lack of faith, they could not enter in (Heb. 3:19).

Summarily, this type (foreshadow) in Hebrews teaches that those of the church period who will be allowed to enter the third rest must have the first rest of Matt. 11:28 (salvation of the spirit) and continue to experience the second rest of Matt. 11:29 (salvation of the soul).

THE UNPARDONABLE SIN

"But when the Pharisees heard {it}, they said, This {fellow} doth not cast out devils, but by Beelzebub the prince of the devils... (32) And whosoever speaketh a word against the Son of man, it shall be forgiven him: but whosoever speaketh against the Holy Ghost, it shall not be forgiven him, neither in this world, neither in the {world} to come" (Matt. 12:24,32).

These verses are among the most misunderstood verses in the New Testament. Pastors and teachers alike have done irrevocable damage to the saints of the church by their misinterpretation of them. Unlike what they have taught, our text does not declare that a believer of the church period will go to eternal hell, without any hope, if he utters a word against the Holy Ghost. If this were true, then it would be necessary to do away with many other verses of the Bible that teach the opposite; verses that assert that a believer cannot lose his salvation. Jesus said, **"All** that the Father giveth me shall come to me; and him that cometh to me I will in no wise cast out" (John 6:37). John said, "If we confess our sins, he is faithful and just to forgive us our sins, and to cleanse us from all unrighteousness" (1 John 1:9).

What does the scripture say the unpardonable sin is? It is a sin that Israel could commit only while Jesus was here in His earthly body. Notice that the leaders of Israel said, "**This fellow,**" i.e., this man, Jesus, "**doth not cast out devils but by Beelzebub, the prince of the devils [Satan].**" Hence, no one of the church age can commit this sin. The "whosoever" in verse 32, then, speaks of the whosoever of Israel who committed this sin. Since only the leaders of national Israel committed this sin, only national Israel (represented by its leaders) would have to suffer its consequences, *which would be the loss of God's favor for one age and the loss of the kingdom for the second. In the Greek, Jesus did not say that they would not be forgiven forever, but that they would not be forgiven in this world (Gr. age) or in the world (age) to come. This means that Israel would not be forgiven in that age (the present age) or in the age to come (the millennial age).* After that, they would bring forth fruit.

In closing this chapter, we see Israel rejecting Christ and thus rejecting the kingdom. Because of this willful rejection of Jesus as the Christ, verses 43 through 45 liken Israel to a house that has a demon. When the demon goes out of the house to find rest, Israel cleans itself (through reformation; i.e., works of the law). When the demon returns and finds the house empty (Christ not living in it) and it swept and garnished (under legalism), he goes out and invites seven more demons worse than himself to come and live with him. The result is that the house (Israel) was much worse in the last state than it was in the first. So it was with the house of Israel at the close of the twelfth chapter of Matthew.

ONLY ONE SIGN

Isa. 53:1 asks the question, "**Who hath believed our report** [message]? and to whom is the arm of the Lord revealed?"** Jesus had come **"to his own and his own received him not"** (John 1:11). Jesus the Christ, who was the arm of God, had been personally and bodily present with Israel; yet, they had refused to believe in Him. Instead, Israel was looking for a Messiah to accomplish their own agenda; to cast out the Romans and return them to the golden days of David. They expected a great sign from God to authenticate these expectations; perhaps, the sign of a fiery entrance of the Messiah from heaven; or, maybe, the sign of an immediate and miraculous raising up of an invincible army of Jews. With this in mind, they asked Jesus to show them a sign.

> "But he answered and said unto them, An evil and adulterous generation seeketh after a sign; and there shall no sign be given to it, but the sign of the prophet Jonas: (40) For as Jonas was three days and three nights in the whale's belly; so shall the Son of man be three days and three nights in the heart of the earth" (Matt. 12:39-40).

The leaders of Israel had apparently been studying only the portions of the Old Testament that prophesied of the signs of His second coming, the same signs they had been seeking after. When they asked Jesus for a sign of this nature (possibly a great celestial sign), Jesus told them that because of their unbelief, there would be no sign given except the sign of Jonah; a sign that speaks of His death, burial and resurrection. **"For as Jonas [Jonah] was three days and three nights in the whale's belly; so shall the Son of man be three days and three nights in the heart of the earth."**

The Ridicule of the Book of Jonah

There are three books of the Bible that are persistently attacked by Satan more than any of the others; Genesis (especially the first three chapters), Revelation and Jonah. Satan's hatred for the first two books comes from the fact that while the book of Genesis teaches the Christian that Satan will be destroyed by the Seed of the woman (Jesus Christ), Revelation clearly shows him the details of this coming destruction. As a result, Satan has been trying to discredit these two books by convincing the world's liberal theologians to teach and preach that Genesis is mostly a collection of myths, while Revelation is a book of confusion that no one can understand.

Along with this deception, Satan has also been quick to attack the book of Jonah in an attempt to discredit it on the basis that it is unscientific. Satan knows that Jonah is an accurate prophecy of the death and resurrection of Jesus Christ; the one act that he hates the most; the one act that sounded the death knell for his coming complete destruction.

Satan's attempt to discredit Jonah has been carried out by a two-pronged attack upon its accuracy. First, he has used the skeptics and infidels to make sport of its literality; to laugh at the notion that a man could be swallowed by a whale and live in its belly for three days. Second, he has used the liberal theologians of the early Roman church to show that Jesus had to be wrong about Jonah being in the belly of the whale for three days and three nights. They have taught instead that His death occurred on Friday afternoon, which caused Him to be in the tomb only one day and two nights. This false teaching has so permeated the entire Christian church that even many fundamental Bible scholars of today readily accept it and stand ready to defend it against anyone who would teach otherwise. To make this sound more palatable, the proponents of this false doctrine have asserted that the ancient rabbis counted part of a day as a whole day. This would have made us have a couple of hours on Friday (possibly only one hour or a part of one), all day Saturday, and a few hours on Sunday, and that is supposed to be three days and three nights.

Jonah's Death

To thwart Satan's attack upon Jonah that says it is unscientific for a man to remain alive in the belly of a whale (actually a great fish) for three days and three nights, we would ask, "Who said that Jonah remained alive in the belly of the whale?" We must not forget that Jonah is a type of the death, burial and resurrection of the Lord Jesus Christ. Therefore, as Jonah's body went into the whale's belly, so Jesus' body went into the tomb. As Jonah died and went to sheol, so Jesus died and went to the heart of the earth (paradise section of sheol). As Jonah was resurrected into his body and spit up by the whale onto dry ground, so Jesus was resurrected into His body and came out of the tomb.

The Bible is very clear that Jonah died in the belly of the whale; for he **"prayed unto the Lord out of the fish's belly,"** and then, after he died, **"...he heard me; out of the belly of hell [sheol]"** (Jonah 2:1-2).

In verse one, Jonah is in the belly of the fish; but in verse two, he is in the belly of hell. The two Hebrew words for "belly" are different. In verse one (belly of the fish), it is *me-ah*, which literally means "an abdomen"; in verse two (belly of hell), it is *betan*, which means a "hollow place." This tells us that in verse one, Jonah cried out of the abdomen of the fish; but in verse two, he cried out and was heard in a hollow place of the heart of the earth (hell; *sheol*).

"When the prophet Jonah was cast into the sea and was swallowed by the great fish, he became a clear type of the death and resurrection of the Lord Jesus Christ. The miracle in Jonah is not that he remained alive in the belly of the fish for three days, but the miracle in Jonah is far greater; namely, that Jonah *died,* and after three days and three nights arose from his grave in the belly of the fish, and became preacher of the gospel to the Gentiles. All of the efforts, therefore, to prove the possibility of a man surviving Jonah's ordeal without dying are entirely without point or purpose, and a waste of valuable time and effort. There is not one single hint in the entire record that Jonah remained alive in the belly of the fish. This has been carried over by sheer tradition" (M.R. De Haan, *Jonah,* p. 80, Zondervan Publishing House, Grand Rapids, Michigan, 1961).

The Friday Crucifixion Myth

To thwart the second attack of Satan on the book of Jonah, we assert that Jesus did not die on Friday afternoon as most of the Christian church believes and celebrates, but on Wednesday afternoon. Here are the scriptural reasons why:

(1) It is impossible to have three complete days without having three complete nights. Our text says, "**...three days and three nights.**" This immediately rules out the partial day theory.

(2) It is a fact that a day in scripture (the light portion of a day) is counted by God as being twelve hours long, as the night (the dark portion of a day) is twelve hours long (John 11:9; Ex. 13:21). When placed together they make one twenty-four hour period of time, or one complete day. In view of scripture, the Jews always began their new day (a twenty four hour period of time) at sundown (6:00 P.M.); for Gen. 1:5 tells us, "**...the evening and the morning were the first day.**" Hence, each of the Jewish days began with the evening.

In keeping with this, the body of Jesus was placed in the tomb on Wednesday afternoon of the passion week, sometime after He died (3:00 P.M.) and before the beginning of a new day at sundown (6:00 P.M.). Scripturally speaking then, He was in the tomb for three days (three light portions of twelve hours each) and three nights (three dark portions of twelve hours each) and arose sometime after sundown Saturday (the beginning of the Jews' Sunday). In summation to these truths, we have no authority from the Word of God to make a portion of a day a whole day.

(3) The error of the Friday crucifixion began by a misunderstanding of the sabbath. As an example, Mark 15:42 tells us that the day after the crucifixion was the sabbath. By using scripture, it was easy for Satan to convince people to believe that the next day had to be Saturday. But this is not so, as we will see, for the Jews had more than one sabbath. There were weekly sabbaths, which always fell on Saturday, and there were ceremonial sabbaths,

which fell on set calendar days. This is borne out in Leviticus 23, which teaches of the "passover sabbath," which always fell on the 14th day of the Hebrew month *Abib* (approximating our March) (verse 5), and, the "unleavened bread sabbath," which always began on the day following the passover, the 15th day of the same month (verse 6). Then there was the "feast of the first fruits sabbath" and the "feast of Pentecost sabbath." Every one of these are sabbaths of rest and are called so in the Bible.

Which sabbath, then, was on the next day after the crucifixion? John informs us that it was the passover sabbath, for it was called a "high" sabbath day (John 19:31). John, apparently, used this term to show us that this sabbath was not a normal weekly one, but one that was special. This sabbath just happened to fall on Thursday that year, with its preparation day on Wednesday (day of the crucifixion). Having this information, we can now know that on the day after the passover, there was still another sabbath day of rest called the "feast of unleavened bread." This sabbath always followed the passover sabbath and, thus fell on Friday of that week. On the next day, Saturday, came the regular weekly sabbath. Hence, there were three sabbath days, one after the other. There was the passover sabbath on Thursday, the feast of unleavened bread sabbath on Friday, and the weekly sabbath on Saturday.

Jesus' body, then, was resting in the tomb during three sabbaths and did not arise until after sundown on Saturday. This is proven in Matt. 28:1, where the word *sabbath* in the Greek text is plural (*sabbaton*): **"In the end of the sabbath [sabbath days; i.e., three of them], as it began to dawn toward the first day of the week [Sunday] came Mary Magdalene and the other Mary to see the sepulchre."**

(4) Finally, Satan has convinced many in the Christian world to believe that Jesus arose from the grave at sunrise on Sunday morning. This is in contrast to scripture, which teaches that Jesus arose sometime after sundown on Saturday (Sunday evening for

the Jews) and before sunrise the next day. For John tells us that Mary Magdalene first came to the tomb while it was "yet dark" (before sunrise) and discovered that the stone had already been rolled away from the tomb (John 20:1).

Someone may ask, "What about those scriptures that say He arose the third day?" Does this not suggest that Jesus arose on the third day rather than after the third day? Scripture seems to tell us that the expression *the third day* is synonymous with *after the third day*. A good example of this is found in John 2:1: **"And the third day there was a marriage in Cana of Galilee; and the mother of Jesus was there."** Here, scripture records "the third day" as being the day of the marriage; yet, all Jewish marriages took place on a Wednesday (counting three days from the first day), which was a custom of the Jews. How, then, can one be married on Wednesday and call it the third day? The answer must be that the expression "the third day" in this verse means "after the third day."

CONCLUDING THOUGHTS

Someone may ask, "Does it make any difference which day we accept as the crucifixion day?" Yes! If Jesus was not in the tomb for three whole days and three whole nights, then He cannot be the infallible Son of God; for His authority must rest on His Word. He told the Pharisees that they would not be given any signs except one: **as Jonah was in the belly of the fish for three days and three nights, so would the Son of man be in the heart of the earth for three days and three nights.** How can we accept any day but Wednesday as the day of His crucifixion?

In closing this chapter, we see the Jews of Judaism refusing to repent and rejecting Jesus as the Messiah. In the next section, we will see Jesus ministering to the Jews who believed and who would become the first members of a new assembly; an assembly that Jesus would later call the church.

NOTES

CHAPTER EIGHT

THE MYSTERIES OF THE KINGDOM: PART ONE

The seven parables of Matthew 13 contain an accurate and detailed prophecy of the church period and the ages beyond. It begins in the first century and extends for more than three thousand years into the future. Within this time frame, they precisely prophesy the rapture of the church, the judgment seat of Christ, the great tribulation period, the rise and fall of the false church, the tribulation saints, the inheritance of the bride, the millennium and the eternal ages.

Each of these seven parables has a different message, which contributes to the forming of a mosaic of truth, revealing the historic and future destiny of the church. They teach the "mysteries of the kingdom," which were to be received and understood by the saints of the dispensation of grace. They were not for Israel, since Israel could not understand them (Matt. 13:11). This includes the prophets of the Old Testament who caught only a glimpse of them, but did not know whom they were for or what manner of time it would be (1 Pet.1:9-12). Only the New Testament saints could know their complete meaning. But sad as it is, only a few of this dispensation will ever know, or care to know, the wondrous truths of this chapter.

THE POPULAR TEACHING VERSUS THE TRUE

Before beginning our exposition of these parables, we need to examine the popular error that is taught concerning the term *mysteries of the kingdom*. Many say that this term denotes the kingdom of God within the heart of a believer. As a result, they have written books on this unscriptural subject, giving titles to them like *The Secret Kingdom Within* and *The Kingdom of the Heart*. In reality, those who believe and teach such error are liberal and amillennial (meaning they do not believe in the millennial kingdom age) in their theology. "They claim that the kingdom that was 'At Hand' [during the time when Jesus preached] was not an outward visible kingdom, but a spiritual kingdom, and that it was not withdrawn but is seen today in the 'New Born' believers. They base their claim on the fact that the earthly visible Kingdom of Christ could not be set up until after He had suffered and died on the Cross as the Savior of men, and had risen from the dead, and had ascended to the Father and received the kingdom, and that therefore the offer of an outward visible and earthly Kingdom was not a 'bonafide' offer, and that John the Baptist and Jesus must have meant by the 'Kingdom of Heaven' something else than an outward visible and earthly kingdom" (Clarence Larkin, *Dispensational Truth*, p. 86, Rev. Clarence Larkin Est., Philadelphia, Pennsylvania, 1918). To deny a coming, literal, visible kingdom is to deny its coming, literal, visible King (Jesus Christ). Hence, amillennialism teaches that the kingdom is an invisible spiritual kingdom in operation now, and that Jesus will not come again literally, but will come in Spirit only. This is a false teaching that blatantly corrupts the scriptures (Acts 1:11).

What does scripture teach? The Old Testament scriptures teach that there is to be a visible, earthly kingdom over which the Son of man is to rule (Dan. 2:23-35; 7:13-14; Jer. 23:5; Zech. 14:9). In the Hebrew language, this rule over the earthly kingdom is called *malikut schamayim*, or the rule of the heavens (plural) over the kingdom (the kingdom of heaven); and we know that at the time of Jesus' birth, there was a widespread expectation of the coming of the Messiah to set up this kingdom. In the first twelve chapters of Matthew, we saw the kingdom being offered to national Israel, but in the twelfth chapter, we saw them rejecting it. Now, in the thirteeth chapter, we see Jesus prophesying of a new assembly of people; a people who will be called from all nations; a people whom He will call the church. They will constitute the highest portion of the mysteries of the kingdom. While some will have the opportunity to take the place of national Israel as the "wedding guests" in the kingdom, others of their number will become the "bride of Christ," ruling and reigning with Him in the kingdom. Thus, the kingdom was postponed at the time of the cross for two thousand years, until all the chosen of the church have been called out by the Holy Spirit. One day Christ will literally and visibly appear the second time with His literal and visible bride to rule over a literal and visible kingdom here on earth for one thousand years.

While it is true that the Holy Spirit is sealed in every believer and wants to rule over his life, this is not the meaning of the mysteries of the kingdom of heaven spoken of in these parables. The word *mysteries*, here, suggests that it means literal people who will be privileged to enter the spiritual portion of the kingdom of Christ at His return. Two groups will be permitted to enter. The first and uppermost will be the faithful of the church saints who pass the fiery test at the judgment seat of Christ (1 Cor. 3: 11-15), gain the inheritance of the kingdom (2 Tim. 2:12a) and rule and reign with Christ. The second will be made up of faithful Jews who lived before the cross and were called out of the saved of Israel because of their obedience to God. What position they will hold in the kingdom is not clear in the scriptures, though many of them will be called the friends of the bridegroom. Both of these groups will be revealed to us in detail in the fifth and sixth parables of our study.

These Mysteries Are Still a Mystery

The reader will come to see, as he studies these seven parables, that these mysteries are still a mystery to the church today. The reason is twofold. First, most seminaries train their pastors in amillennial theology; they, in turn, teach the same gross error to their churches. Second, since the amillennialists greatly outnumber the premillenialists, they are looked upon as the more theologically correct. Since the amillennial view is becoming the popular view, its proponents are the ones who are invited to write the Sunday school lessons and text books that are used in indoctrinating the churches. As a result, the church today does not understand the higher truths connected to the second coming of Christ and His kingdom, and remain ignorant of its mysteries.

The First Four Parables:

The first four parables of Matthew 13 were given by Jesus "by the seaside" (verses 1-35); the last three were given "in the house" (verses 36-50). The first four speak of the history of the church period; whereas, the last three speak of the kingdom (those believers who will be in both the spiritual and physical portions of the kingdom). In speaking to Israel in the first four parables, Jesus never intended for them to understand their meaning. He only spoke to them to fulfill the prophesy of Isaiah 6:9-13 and to be overheard by His disciples, who represent all the saved. This is made clear by Jesus' answer in Matt. 13:11-17 to His disciples' question in verse 10.

From His explanation, there are at least two truths to be learned. First, in fulfillment of Isaiah's prophecy, Jesus spoke to a people who had rejected Him; a people who, without God, could not understand parables; a people who were destined by their own disbelief to be scattered throughout the world, leaving their cities wasted and their homeland desolate (Isa. 6:11-12). This finally occurred in A.D. 70, when Rome invaded Jerusalem and scattered the Jews throughout the world. For two thousand years, they have been the "wandering Jew," hated and persecuted by all nations. Only in this century, starting in 1948, were they permitted to begin their return to their homeland. This regathering will not be completed until near the close of the great tribulation period. God will gather them all for judgment; a judgment in which two-thirds will perish in the furnace of affliction (Zech. 13:8-9; Isa. 48:10). However, those who pass through alive will be the "remnant" of

Israel who are saved at His coming; they will be refined as silver and tried as gold in the fire; they will be the natural branches of the olive tree who will be grafted back into the natural tree (Rom. 11:23). Hence, this first parable by Jesus tells us the beginning of Israel's coming sorrows. Their sorrows, however, would not begin immediately; but by the patience of God, would be withheld for about forty years. Not until Acts 28:25-28 do we see the inauguration of this prophecy, when God finally sets Israel aside and sends the salvation of God unto the Gentiles.

The second truth that we recognize in Jesus' answer to His disciples' question in Matt. 13:10 is that only the saved can understand parables. Why? Because only the saved have the Holy Spirit to reveal their meaning. Granted that the disciples did not know the meaning of the first parable until Jesus explained it to them; but it must be remembered that they also, at this time, did not have the Holy Spirit in them — only with them. It is different with us. We have the Spirit of Christ (the Holy Spirit) dwelling in us to reveal all truth. Hence, we have spiritual eyes to see with and spiritual ears to hear with — if we will use them.

The Last Three Parables:

The last three parables were given by Jesus in the house to His disciples only. This shows the intimacy of the parables themselves to the saved of the church period, since they were not even told in the presence of Israel. They needed no interpretation to those who had ears to hear and who heard. Their purpose was to identify the two groups of believers who would enter the heavenly portion of the kingdom, as well as an earthly group who would enter the earthly portion.

I. THE PARABLE OF THE SOWER

"The same day went Jesus out of the house, and sat by the sea side. (2) And great multitudes were gathered together unto him, so that he went into a ship, and sat; and the whole multitude stood on the shore. (3) And he spake many things unto them in parables, saying, Behold, a sower went forth to sow; (4) And when he sowed, some {seeds} fell by the way side, and the fowls came and devoured them up: (5) Some fell upon stony places, where they had not much earth: and forthwith they sprung up, because they had no deepness of earth: (6) And when the sun was up, they were scorched; and because they had no root, they withered away. (7) And some fell among thorns; and the thorns sprung up, and choked them: (8) But other fell into good ground, and brought forth fruit, some an hundredfold, some sixtyfold, some thirtyfold. (9) Who hath ears to hear, let him hear" (Matt. 13:1-9).

Jesus' Interpretation of the Parable

"Hear ye therefore the parable of the sower. (19) When any one heareth the word of the kingdom, and understandeth {it} not, then cometh the wicked {one}, and catcheth away that which was sown in his heart. This is he which received seed by the way side. (20) But he that received the seed into stony places, the same is he that heareth the word, and anon with joy receiveth it; (21) Yet hath he not root in himself, but dureth for a while: for when tribulation or persecution ariseth because of the word, by and by he is offended. (22) He also that received seed among the thorns is he that heareth the word; and the care of this world, and the deceitfulness of riches, choke the word, and he becometh unfruitful. (23) But he that received seed into the good ground is he that heareth the word, and understandeth {it}; which also beareth fruit, and bringeth forth, some an hundred fold, some sixty, some thirty" (Matt. 13:18-23).

The first of the seven parables of Matthew 13 shows Jesus Christ as a sower sowing seed, which falls on four different kinds of ground. These different grounds represent four different kinds of believers. Contrary to the popular teaching in the church today, this seed is not the word of salvation; but, according to Christ's own interpretation, is the *word of the kingdom* (Matt. 13:19). Therefore, it is the doctrine of the "kingdom of heaven"; the coming, literal, visible kingdom that will be established by Christ when He returns to rule and reign over the earth. Furthermore, as we continue to unravel the mysteries of these seven parables, we will see that this seed (the word of the kingdom) also includes the doctrine of reward for the faithful Christians and the doctrine of the bride of Christ, who will be co-heirs with Him. This first parable, then, teaches *fruit-bearing,* not initial salvation. The four kinds of ground represent saved people, not lost people. The sower begins His sowing in the first century and continues throughout all the church period, right up to the rapture of the church. His method of sowing has always been through the Bible, the Word of God.

The Wayside Christian

The first kind of ground in our parable is called the "wayside" ground. It typifies those Christians who are not in the way, or the path, where Jesus walks (in the Word). They are saved and that is all. Some are even trying to serve God in the church by their own self-efforts. They represent a great percentage of Christians; those who say to themselves, "There are no other Bible truths that I need. After all, I am saved and cannot lose my salvation. I am going to heaven where all the saved are equal; where there will be no more pain and trials; where everyone will be happy forever. This is enough. Why should I learn more?" With this attitude, the wayside Christian fails to understand the word of the kingdom when he hears it. He has no teachable spirit. As a result, the fowls (verse 4), which are emblems of the agents of Satan (verse 19), come and catch away the seed before it can root itself in his heart. Sadly, he is left void of the truths that could have produced hope and joy in his life and inheritance in the coming kingdom.

This kind of Christian is found not only in the local church, but also on the teaching staff of many theological schools. They are generally "amillennial" in their theology and teach only the "word of salvation" and church and denomination service. Their number is increasing in the pulpit and the pew, where they tend to dismiss anyone who does not agree with them as ignorant and unscholarly.

The Stony Ground Hearer

The second kind of Christian in our parable is called the "stony" ground Christian. He receives with joy the seed of the word of the kingdom; but, because of stones (shallowness of his life), the seed fails to root itself deeply in the soil of his heart. As a result, his sudden growth in the truths of the kingdom withers away and no fruit is brought forth (verses 5-6, 20-21). The stony ground

Christian typifies the average Christian who is excited over the truths concerning the coming kingdom when he hears and understands them; but he is unwilling to pay the price necessary to inherit the kingdom.

In verse 21, Jesus tells us that these stones represent his shallowness, or lack of "root in himself." He hears the word of the kingdom and receives it with joy; but when tribulation and persecution arise (perhaps the loss of his job or friends) because of the Word, he is offended. The word of the kingdom, which once excited him, withers away because the "ground" is shallow and it can form no root, making it impossible for him to be renewed again unto repentance at the judgment seat of Christ (Heb 6:1-6). Saved? Yes! But that is all; a Christian who will arrive at the judgment seat of Christ without any fruit; one who will have no inheritance in the kingdom because he became offended because of tribulation and persecution.

Overcoming the Shallow Heart

According to James 1:2-4, temptation is necessary to try the faith of Christians, for without its trials and perseverance of those trials, the inheritance of the kingdom (the crown) cannot be given. The apostle Peter tells us the same thing when he speaks of the necessity of the "trial of your faith," that it might be found unto praise and honor and glory at the appearing of Jesus Christ (1 Pet. 1:7). The apostle Paul tells us that we ought to glory in our tribulation, knowing that it works patience; and patience, experience; and experience, hope (Rom. 5:3-4).

The writer has pastored many stony ground Christians. In every case, after they heard the word of the kingdom, they would, with great joy, receive the truths of the kingdom and begin to be a great service to the Lord. Then they would fall away like a wilting flower. First, they would stop attending our church's mid-week services; then Sunday evening services. Finally, they were gone from our Sunday morning services. They were not willing to pay the price that the word of the kingdom demanded to rule and reign with Christ in His coming kingdom. We have also known stony ground pastors who were privileged to see these truths, but fearing the tribulation and persecution that would result from preaching them to their congregations, they, too, fell away and preached only simple salvation and self works to their churches and, as a result, produced no fruit.

The Thorny Ground Christian

The third kind of ground in our parable represents the "thorny" ground Christian. Scripture tells us that when the seed (the word of the kingdom) fell on this kind of Christian, he did not receive it, nor did he have any joy over it. He only heard it (verse 22), when it was choked out by the thorns springing up (verse 7). Our Lord informs us that the thorns represent the "care of this world" and the "deceitfulness of riches" (verse 22), showing that this Christian was interested only in this world and not the one to come. He worshiped money and probably all the schemes that could make it for him. He had not yet learned that a believer cannot worship both God and mammon (Matt. 6:24).

The thorny ground Christian is probably the most common of all the Christians in these last days of the church period; one who is just saved and that's all; one who is carnal and totally involved in the world for what he can get in this lifetime. His life is so full of thorns (care of this age) that he cannot, or will not, receive any truths of the word of the kingdom (the age to come). Hence, he becomes unfruitful (verse 22b).

The Word of God gives a strong warning to all pastors who go after the deceitfulness of riches and the care of this world; who make merchandise of their ministry (2 Pet. 2:1-3). James 3:1 tells us that the masters (teachers of the Word of God) will receive a double condemnation if they lose their souls at the judgment seat of Christ; and those who cause others to fall with them will literally be cut asunder (bi-sected) at the judgment seat of Christ (Matt. 24:48-51). The soul will be separated from his redeemed body, and both will be cast into "Gehenna" (the place of fire for the body, and the place of blackness of darkness for the soul) for the millennial age, i.e., one-thousand years.

When examined closely, all three kinds of unfruitful Christians appear to be interested only in having a fire escape from hell, while they profit as much as possible from this present world, at ease and undisturbed.

The Good Ground Christian

The "good" ground of our parable represents the Christian who, after receiving the seed (the word of the kingdom), brings forth spiritual fruit. He has no fear of the tribulation or persecution that could fall on him because of his hope and testimony of the coming kingdom of Christ. He also has no care for this world; and he is generally not involved in environmentalism, protest demonstrations or politics to save the world from its own evil. He recognizes the sovereignty of God, which has decreed the end to all things, including the earth; and he knows that this earth will be redeemed by Christ for a thousand years before it is consigned to flames in, probably, the 31st century.

This Christian is also wise concerning the riches of this world, knowing that they who would be rich fall into **"temptation and a snare, and into many foolish and hurtful lusts, which drown men in destruction and perdition"** (1 Tim. 6:9). He knows that the love of money is the root of all evil, while the love of Christ and hope (anticipation) of the kingdom is the root from which all spiritual fruit springs forth. His hope is to be a member of the "mysteries of the kingdom"; those who will produce spiritual fruit, earning for themselves eternal riches in the kingdom. Hence, he lives by faith; faith that comes from hearing, and hearing by the Word of God (Rom. 10:17).

Our parable, finally, teaches that there are three kinds of good ground Christians; those who produce a hundredfold, those who produce sixty, and those who produce thirty (verse 23b). Apparently, the amount of fruit that each produces is indicative of how much truth of the kingdom that each sees and commits his life to; a commitment that automatically cultivates the stones and the thorns out of his life.

These three amounts of fruit also represent three major levels in the coming kingdom: (1) the highest level, reserved for the Christians bringing forth a hundredfold; (2) the second highest level for the Christians bringing forth sixty and (3) the lowest level for those bringing forth thirty. These three levels of rule are seen in other parables of Matthew that will be briefly covered in later chapters.

Comparing the Parable:

In comparing this parable to itself, recorded in two other gospels, we see a marked difference in its settings, word constructions and meanings. The Holy Spirit has purposely done this to give a complete picture of the three-fold salvation of those who will inherit the kingdom (Luke 8:5-18; Mark 4:3-20; Matt. 13:3-23). Like a transparent spiritual overlay, Luke's parable of the sower shows the fruit-bearing Christian by emphasizing the "salvation of his spirit"; Mark's gospel reveals the fruit-bearing Christian by emphasizing the "salvation of his soul," i.e., his submission to the Lordship of Christ over his life. Finally, Matthew completes the triunity of salvation, revealing the fruit-bearing Christian by emphasizing his submission to the word of the kingdom, i.e., the "great salvation" (Heb. 1:3).

A Few Points of Difference:

(1) Luke's parable is the message of salvation, Mark's is the message of a Christ-controlled life, and Matthew's, the message of the kingdom.

(2) Luke's parable speaks of justification, Mark's speaks of sanctification, and Matthew adds glorification in the kingdom.

(3) Luke's parable reveals a rest that is given (Matt. 11:28), Mark's discloses a rest that is found (Matt. 11:29), and Matthew expresses a rest in the future that must be attained, the millennial

kingdom (Heb.4:9,11).

(4) Luke's seed is called the "word of God," Mark's is called the "word," and Matthew's is called the "word of the kingdom."

(5) In Luke 8, the wayside hearer heard the "word of God" (the word of salvation) and despised it by treading it underfoot (verse 5), where the fowls (agents of Satan) devoured it... lest he should believe and be saved (verse 12). In Mark 4, the wayside hearer, who is already saved, heard the "word" (how to have the fullness of the Holy Spirit in his life) and immediately it was taken away by the fowls (verses 4,15). In Matthew 13, the wayside hearer, who is already saved and possibly has a Christ-controlled life, heard the "word of the kingdom" and it was caught away out of his heart by Satan, because he failed to understand it (verse 19).

(6) In Luke and Matthew, Jesus uses the expression *mysteries of the kingdom,* which emphasizes *believers.* In Mark, Jesus changes this expression to the "mystery" (singular) of the kingdom, which emphasizes the *Holy Spirit in believers* (Mark 4: 11). This subtle change is explained in verse 13, where Jesus tells us that this mystery (the Holy Spirit) is the one who reveals all truth to the believer. Therefore, the seed of Mark, called the "word" speaks of a Christ-controlled life by the "mystery of the kingdom" (the Holy Spirit). This same mystery is seen in Col. 1:26-27, where it is identified as "Christ in you." Here, we see that one of the purposes of the Holy Spirit dwelling in our lives is to "make known the riches of glory" and the "hope of glory" (the coming kingdom of Christ).

In view of these three parables and the different salvations they present, it is the belief of the writer that those who will be a part of the mysteries of the kingdom must first be saved and have a Christ-controlled life (the mystery of the kingdom). Only then will they have a hunger to understand the word of the kingdom. For no one can be filled with this higher knowledge (Gr.*epignosis*) unless he spiritually hungers for it. Even then, he must be permitted by God to see it and to experience it (Heb. 6:3).

Someone may ask, "Can a Christian who has a Christ controlled life, according to Mark's parable, but does not see the word of the kingdom, according to Matthew's parable, enter the kingdom?" We believe he can and will; for we believe that this Christian is identified in Matthew's parable as the fruitbearer who bore only thirtyfold. We also believe that he is represented by the wedding guests of Matthew 22:10b and is the one whom Christ addresses in Luke 19:17,19 as the "good servant."

Apparently, the higher levels of the kingdom are reserved for those who understand the word of the kingdom and, as a result, bring forth sixtyfold or a hundredfold of fruit. The higher of these two positions will be reserved for the "faithful and wise" servants (the hundredfold producers), who will be ruling as the bride of Christ **"over all His goods"** (Luke 12:44; Matt. 24:47), while the lower of these two positions will be reserved for the "good and faithful" (Matt. 25:21-23) (the sixtyfold producers) who will also be a part of the bride of Christ, ruling in the kingdom **"over many things."**

II. THE PARABLE OF THE WHEAT AND TARES

"Another parable put he forth unto them, saying, The kingdom of heaven is likened unto a man which sowed good seed in his field: (25) But while men slept, his enemy came and sowed tares among the wheat, and went his way. (26) But when the blade was sprung up, and brought forth fruit, then appeared the tares also. (27) So the servants of the householder came and said unto him, Sir, didst not thou sow good seed in thy field? from whence then hath it tares? (28) He said unto them, An enemy hath done this. The servants said unto him, Wilt thou then that we go and gather them up? (29) But he said, Nay; lest while ye gather up the tares, ye root up also the wheat with them. (30) Let both grow together until the harvest: and in the time of harvest I will say to the reapers, Gather ye together first the tares, and bind them in bundles to burn them: but gather the wheat into my barn" (Matt. 13:24-30).

Jesus' Interpretation of the Parable

"He answered and said unto them, He that soweth the good seed is the Son of man; (38) The field is the world; the good seed are the children of the kingdom; but the tares are the children of the wicked {one}; (39) The enemy that sowed them is the devil; the harvest is the end of the world; and the reapers are the angels. (40) As therefore the tares are gathered and burned in the fire; so shall it be in the end of this world...

[Second Division]

"The Son of man shall send forth, and they shall gather out of his kingdom all things that offend, and them which do iniquity; (42) And shall cast them into a furnace of fire: there shall be wailing and gnashing of teeth. (43) Then shall the righteous shine forth as the sun in the kingdom of their Father. Who hath ears to hear, let him hear" (Matt. 13 37-43).

The parable before us is composed of two divisions. The first division is revealed in the parable itself and the second, when Jesus interpreted it. Thus, within the interpretation of this parable, some added information is given that was not in the initial disclosure of it. We call this added information the second division.

As we begin, the reader needs to be aware that every word spoken by our Lord in His parables is important; each word is placed there to minutely reveal every aspect of its truth. The error that says a parable teaches only one thing dishonors God. It is frequently used by so-called Bible teachers who need a scholarly sounding justification to cover up their own disregard of the parable's true meaning. Typically, this kind of liberal teacher will dismiss several words of a parable as unimportant to make it say what he wants it to say.

The First Division of the Second Parable

"Another parable put he forth unto them, saying, The kingdom of heaven is likened unto a man which sowed good seed in his field" (Matt. 13: 24). The first division of our parable is not hard to understand by the children of God if we let it speak to us. We should never read into parables what we want them to say, but faithfully read out of them what they are saying.

The parable simply states that the sower is Jesus, the field is the world, the seed are the children of the kingdom, the tares are the seed of the wicked one, the enemy that sowed them is the devil, the harvest is the end of the world (age) and the reapers are the angels. Notice that the seed is not the same as the seed that was sown in the first parable. There it was a *doctrine,* while here it represents *saved individuals.* Notice also that the title given to the seed is the "children [Gr. sons] of the kingdom." This title is indicative of all believers of the church period i.e., all those who are born again (Gr. born from above). They are born again as heirs of God and represent the four hearers in the first parable. They are sown in the beginning of this dispensation for the purpose of producing fruit and, at the close of this dispensation, will be taken out to give an account of that fruit at the judgment seat of Christ.

Only the good ground believers will produce fruit and realize their purpose. The remaining three kinds of believers will fail to produce fruit and, thus, will lose their inheritance of the kingdom. The scriptures tell us that to inherit the kingdom, a believer (heir of God) must become a co-heir with Christ. This can only be attained by suffering (patiently enduring) with Christ in this present life (salvation of the soul), which is indicative of a fruit-bearing Christian (Rom. 8:17).

"But while men slept, his enemy came and sowed tares among the wheat, and went his way" (Matt. 13:25). This parable tells us that the Lord Jesus Christ, at the beginning of this dispensation, began sowing in the world the "children of the kingdom." Their purpose was to bear the fruit of *wheat* so that through them, the *bread of life* (Jesus Christ) would appeal to all who were spiritually hungry. This, again, is proof that fruit-bearing is caused by the personal presence of Jesus Christ living through the believer. After the sowing, **"while men slept,"** the devil came and sowed tares, which are his children. This portion of our parable is now fulfilled prophecy and has become the history of the early church. For the children (sons) of the kingdom went to sleep in the third century under Romanism, and they continued to spiritually sleep throughout the Dark Ages until the time of the reformation. It was during these thirteen centuries of sleep that the devil sowed his tares. It is interesting that before this time, the devil attacked the church from the outside, which resulted in spreading it. But in the fouth century, he joined it and attacked it from the inside. This is clearly seen in history when the church was united with the state under Emperor Constantine, who also gave a "wholesale license" for all the pagans to join the church. It was from this point in history until Martin Luther that the plan of salvation by grace through faith, plus nothing, was lost. The church (the men), spiritually speaking, went to sleep and the devil went to work creating his counterfeit Christianity by sowing tares. Today, sixteen centuries later, we are still in a mixed state of affairs; the false and the true side by side; the tares and wheat growing together. Church history, then, tells us that the tares started in Romanism (the Roman Catholic Church) and have spread in these last days to every denomination and to most churches, even to having their own cults and sects.

Satan has ever been an imitator. He has never been an originator. It is in this parable that a remarkable expose of his methods is revealed. First, he has an imitation gospel whose foundation rests upon the works of men; men who also worship angels and saints. Galations 1:7-9 clearly tells us that this is an abomination to God. **"Though we, or an angel from heaven preach any other gospel to you than that which we have preached unto you, let him be accursed."** Second, Satan has placed imitation ministers in the pulpits of churches. 2 Cor. 11:13-15 reveals that they are called **"false apostles, deceitful workers, transforming themselves into the apostle of Christ. (14) And no marvel; for Satan himself is transformed into an angel of light. (15) Therefore {it is} no great thing if his ministers also be transformed as the ministers of righteousness; whose end shall be according to their works."** Third, he has an imitation righteousness founded on works (Rom. 10:3-4). Fourth, he has an imitation church, so cleverly disguised that much of the world is fooled into thinking and calling it "the Church." Fifth, Satan will produce an imitation

Christ after the true church has been raptured. Known in the scriptures as the antichrist, he will cause most of the people of the world to worship him. This will be Satan's masterpiece of deception.

In this parable, the Lord is revealing the imitation Christian of the church period by using the figure of a tare. Tares, which are weeds, look exactly like wheat and cannot be distinguished from wheat until they come to fruition. Since they were sown while men slept, we believe that the teaching primarily identifies the Roman Catholic Church, whose pagan membership and doctrine was sown by the devil over the course of many centuries. It is not, however, restricted to Romanism. History bears out that the tares moved out into Protestantism and into many and varied sects. Unfulfilled prophecy declares that they will all return and be gathered under the wings of Rome after the rapture, in the latter days.

"But when the blade was sprung up, and brought forth fruit, then appeared the tares also" (Matt. 13:26). The minute accuracy of scripture is demonstrated in this verse. The tares did not make their appearance until after the wheat had sprung up and brought forth fruit. This is a reference to the time after the reformation; for no fruit was brought forth from the whole field until after that time. It is not said that the tares "came up," but that they "appeared"; thus pointing out that they could have already been present, but not recognized as tares until the wheat bore fruit that they could not duplicate. The tare is also known as the "darnel"; a weed that produces a purple flower that, in turn, produces a poisonous substance. This substance is harmful to wheat when spread by the wind. With this revelation of truth, the writer is convinced that our Lord, in this parable, is pointing to the Roman Catholic Church as the fountainhead of all false systems. They purposely draw and deceive millions of people with their external religious trappings, which are symbolized by the purple flower produced by the darnel. They promise the bread of life when, in reality, their fruit is poisonous to the genuine wheat. Even the color of the flower of the darnel is that chosen to represent the papacy. Note that in past coronations of popes, they were all dressed in scarlet and "purple".

"But when the blade was sprung up...." The words *sprung up* refer to the reformation period, which, in the sixteenth century, "sprung up" in the world. Up to this time, the tares, i.e., the Roman church, had enjoyed their imitation Christianity by keeping the people ignorant. But Martin Luther, a Roman priest, rediscovered the Biblical doctrine of salvation by grace through faith, plus nothing. This exciting news sprung up throughout the known world producing the "blade" of the genuine wheat. During the time the blade was springing up, the printing press was invented. This, in turn, ushered in the Renaissance, which was a period of great learning; a period when the world learned how to read books, and particularly, the newly translated scriptures. The Renaissance period served as a vestibule to the reformation under Luther and, later, Zwingli, Calvin, and Knox. Millions read the truth of God's love through faith. **"The blade sprung up,"** thus revealing the tare. It was not long before the ear and then the full corn in the ear appeared.

"So the servants of the householder came and said unto him, Sir, didst not thou sow good seed in thy field? from whence then hath it tares? (28) He said unto them, An enemy hath done this. The servants said unto him, Wilt thou then that we go and gather them up? (29) But he said, Nay; lest while ye gather up the tares, ye root up also the wheat with them"(Matt. 13:27-29). In this portion of the parable, we learn the servants of the Lord have enough spiritual wisdom to recognize that there are tares in the field (world), but not enough wisdom to know who the tares are. Therefore, they are instructed by the Lord to leave them alone lest they root up the wheat. With this clear teaching, it is amazing how many have violated it, from the reformation until now. Servants of the Lord have hunted down and rooted up what they thought were tares, resulting in the hurt of much wheat. We are not to be heresy hunters that murder the physical body or damage the reputation of a person; but we are to be watchdogs standing guard against the wolf and warning the sheep. We, as Christians, do not have enough wisdom to tell, in every instance, the difference between wheat that does not produce fruit and tares, which cannot produce fruit. Even in the harvest, they cannot be separated except by the angels. Thus, the imitation Christians and their imitation church are not to be rooted up by either the Christian or the angel servants.

"Let both grow together until the harvest: and in the time of harvest I will say to the reapers, Gather ye together first the tares, and bind them in bundles to burn them: but gather the wheat into my barn" (Matt. 13:30). There is much prophetic instruction to be gained from this 30th verse. First, the Lord has promised a harvest. This will occur when He removes all the Christians from the earth at the rapture of the church and gathers them to His barn where the wheat will be garnered (judgment seat of Christ). This corresponds with 1 Thess. 4:16-17. However, it is important that before the harvest is come, He will have already had the tares gathered together and bound. In this operation of divine providence, the scripture does not speak of them being rooted up or cut down, but gathered together, bound into bundles, and left standing in the field. Second, the tares will be burned while standing in the field. Even though our Lord resolutely decrees that the final punishment of the tares will be in the "lake of fire," that punishment is not in view here, and is reserved until after the great white throne of judgment, which will occur at least one thousand years later. Here, the burning of the tares represents the wrath of God that is to fall upon the field (world) after the rapture of the church and during the ensuing seven year tribulation period.

The binding also signifies a fourfold purpose in the separation of the tares: first, that they may be separated from the wheat and from those who will be saved during the tribulation; second, that they may be numbered as the children of the antikingdom; third, that they may be burned while standing in the field (world); and fourth, that they may be damned to eternal retribution.

In the first signification, we know that the binding of the tares into bundles is already rapidly proceeding in various directions. In the commercial world, the tares are being bundled into organizations, trusts, co-ops, corporations, syndicates, combines, cartels, consortiums, conglomerates and partnerships. In the social world, the tares are being bundled into clubs, fraternities, guilds, societies, and associations. In the political world, the tares are being bundled into federations, unions, coalitions, united nations and the one world government. In the ecclesiastical world, the tares are being bundled into cults, the occult, the ecumenical movement and the national and world council of churches. All these bundles are being formed so they may return to their fountainhead during the tribulation period. For it is then that the antichrist will come to power and use the false church at Rome, along with the organizations of finance and commerce, and many other kinds of bundles, to further his own kingdom.

In the second signification, the tares are called the **"children of the wicked one"** (verse 38). Apparently, the Holy Spirit used this expression, rather than the word *devil*, for the purpose of connecting it to the counterfeit kingdom, since the antichrist is called "that Wicked" in 2 Thess. 2:8. **"...and then shall that Wicked be revealed."** Therefore, as the Christians are children of the coming visible kingdom, which will be ruled over by that righteous One, the Lord Jesus Christ, so are the tares the children of the coming, visible antikingdom, which will be ruled over by that "wicked one," the *antichrist*. Their gathering and binding, then, represents a separation and preservation into the antikingdom.

In the third and fourth significations, the binding represents the impossibility of their salvation after the rapture. However, this applies only to those who have heard the gospel of grace and have rejected it before the rapture occurred. Those who have never heard the gospel will have an opportunity to believe the "gospel of the kingdom," which will be preached by the 144,000 sealed Jewish evangelists (Rev. 7:4-9) during the first half of the tribulation period (3 1/2 years). These Jewish evangelists will be preaching to all Gentile nations, and their converts will be too numerous to number. Revelation 7:9-14 gives us a glimpse of the souls of their converts in heaven after their lives are lost during the "great" tribulation (the last 3 1/2 years). As for the tares who have heard and have not believed, God arranges it so that it is impossible for them to be saved after the rapture. This is made clear in 2 Thess. 2:11-12. **"And for this cause God shall send them strong delusion, that they should believe a lie [believe the antichrist]: (12) That they all might be damned who believed not the truth, but had pleasure in unrighteousness."** God gives no man a second chance after death or after the rapture.

As we survey current events in light of Matt. 13:24-30, we conclude that the order to bind the tares has already gone forth. All that is left to be done is the harvest.

The Second Division of the Second Parable

"Then Jesus sent the multitude away, and went into the house: and his disciples came unto him, saying, Declare unto us the parable of the tares of the field" (Matt. 13:36). The reader will remember that this parable has two divisions. The first has already been interpreted. Before we can begin the exposition of the second division, a question should be answered. "Why did Jesus tell two other parables between this parable and its interpretation?" The answer will be obvious if we remember that the first four parables (four is the Biblical number for world) speak of the history of the church in this world. They reveal the true church and what will happen to it, and the false church and what will happen to it. The last three parables (three is the Biblical number for manifested Deity) reveal who the mysteries of the kingdom will be (those who belong to Christ and will inherit the kingdom). Hence, the two parables between this parable and its interpretation must be added information concerning the history of the church. Therefore, after we conclude this second division of the parable of the wheat and the tares, we will return to the two parables between and expound the truths that they teach, fitting them into their proper place in church history.

"As therefore the tares are gathered and burned in the fire; so shall it be in the end of this world [age]" (Matt. 13:40). This verse, in harmony with verse 30a, gives us a complete picture of what will happen to the tares. They will be gathered and bound while still standing in the field (the world) (verse 38a) and then burned. We have no Biblical authority to connect verse 40 with verse 41. In verse 40, the Lord made an emphatic statement that was concise and complete. The tares in the world are finished; they died in the fires of God's wrath during the great tribulation period while standing in the field. We have no right to interpret verses 41 through 43 as a repetition of verse 40, or as a commentary on verse 40. The words of verse 40 are final words. All that was to be said about the tares was said. This ends the thought and the subject, and we are not to carry it over into verse 41.

"The Son of man shall send forth his angels, and they shall gather out of his kingdom all things that offend, and them which do iniquity" (Matt. 13:41). This verse marks the true beginning of the second division of our parable. What is to follow is additional information that was not told in the parable itself. With this in mind, we are able to see that the Lord, in this verse, shows us a gathering out. Is it the tares? No, for the tares have already been gathered, bound and burned in verse 40. Is it the lost of the world who never professed Christianity? No, for they are of the world and in the world. These, however, are not of the world, but of the kingdom. Notice that they are gathered out of the kingdom not because of unbelief, but because of their works of iniquity (efforts of the flesh). Since the kingdom has its official beginning when Jesus enters into His Kingship, and a king and judge are one in the same, then the judgment seat of Christ has to be within the boundaries of the kingdom. Here, Jesus will no longer be our High Priest, but our Judge (John 5:22). Not only will the individual be gathered out of the kingdom (at the judgment seat of Christ), but all his works (all things that offend). Summarily, if the angels are the reapers, and they have already gathered and bound the tares in verse 40, then this must be a detailed picture of the rapture and the separation of the wheat before it is stored in the barn (verse 30). This, then, is a picture of the judgment seat of Christ.

"And shall cast them into a furnace of fire: there shall be wailing and gnashing of teeth" (Matt 13:42). This verse is an excellent description of the testing of the Christian's works at the judgment seat of Christ. The furnace of fire is not the "lake of fire," where the lost will go, but is a description of the all consuming fire of God at the judgment seat. "Furnace of fire," in scripture, is always an emblem of a place of refinement and not of hell. When one wants to refine his gold or silver by separating the impurities from it, he places it into a furnace of fire, which burns off the worthless dross and make his precious metal pure (Prov. 17:3; 27:21). The furnace is not only used by God as an emblem of the place of judgment for the Christians in heaven, but also as a place of judgment for the nation of Israel on earth. On earth, it is called the "furnace of affliction." It will be located in Jerusalem during the great tribulation to burn off the dross and to make pure the silver and gold of Israel (Isa. 31:7-9; 48:10; Ezek. 22:19-22). With this earthly judgment of God's earthly people, two thirds will perish in the tribulation fires; fires that will come from the nations of the world when they attack Israel in the last great battle, the battle of Armageddon (Zech. 13:8-9).

There are two other kinds of furnaces mentioned in the Word of God. The first is a "smoking furnace", which is emblematic of God's past judgment (no more fire). We see this emblem in the Abrahamic covenant, i.e., the Old Testament covenant of grace (Rom. 4:1-5). In connection with this, we see in Gen. 15:9-17 that a smoking furnace and a burning lamp passed through the midst of three sacrifices (types of the shed blood of Christ) to establish the unconditional covenant of grace with Abram. The smoking furnace typifies the past judgment of God that fell on Jesus Christ on the cross, while the burning lamp is a type of the Word of God (Psa. 119:105). Hence, these two types point to the Christian who has, by grace through faith (Eph. 2:8-9), received the smoking furnace (the complete work of Christ on the cross) and is continuing to receive the burning lamp (the witness of Christ living through him).

The second kind of furnace mentioned in God's Word is the "iron furnace," which is used as a type of Israel's suffering while they were under bondage to Egypt (Deut. 4:20; 1 Kings 8:51; Jer. 11:4).

Matt. 13:42 speaks of the heavenly furnace; a furnace that will be located in heaven at the judgment seat of Christ. All Christians must appear at the judgment seat in their raptured, redeemed bodies to be judged for the things done in their bodies after they were saved, whether good or bad (2 Cor. 5:10); for all things must be tested in the heavenly furnace. If the Christian's works (wood, hay, stubble) are burned up in this baptism of fire (Matt. 3:11c), he will suffer loss (be disinherited from the kingdom); yet, he will still be saved. If his works (gold, silver, precious stones) survive this fire, he will receive a reward (1 Cor. 3:11-15). So we see that God has two different judgments for His people; an earthly one, which will be in Jerusalem for His earthly people and a heavenly one for His heavenly people.

In the final portion of our text (Matt. 13:42b), we read that there will be **"wailing and gnashing of teeth."** Most Christians believe that this expression speaks of the suffering in hell of the lost. But this cannot be, since this expression in God's Word is always found in the context of the judgment seat of Christ or the outer darkness (Matt. 22:13; 24:51; 25:30; Luke 13:28). Confusion arises from this because of the popular pulpit, which does not believe that rewards must be attained. They teach that every Christian will automatically receive crowns and they will throw them back at the feet of Jesus. However, the scripture used (Rev. 4:10) has been grossly misinterpreted. The four and twenty elders do not represent the church, but angelic rulers of the universe, under God, who will joyfully relinquish their rulership when Jesus Christ becomes heir of all things (Heb. 2:5).

It is true that the eternal council of the Godhead has predetermined the position of every child of God in the eternities (kingdom of the Father), and that all sorrow, pain, sickness, and death will be wiped away. But the judgment seat of Christ is not heaven; it is the place of induction into and assignment of position in the kingdom of heaven. It is here that one may "suffer loss" when his works are burned up and he fails to win a reward in the coming kingdom of heaven. This startling realization of being assigned the position of subject rather than sovereign, or of being cast into the outer darkness or the blackness of darkness rather then automatically inheriting the kingdom will bring wailing and gnashing of teeth to the disinherited Christian. The apostle Paul, in his use of the phrase *suffer loss* in 1 Cor. 3, backs this up with the use of the Greek word *zemioo,* which means to injure, to experience detriment, to be cast away, to receive damage. It is plain that a lost man cannot suffer loss in the same way, since he has nothing to lose.

"Then shall the righteous shine forth as the sun in the kingdom of their Father. Who hath ears to hear, let him hear" (Matt. 13:43). This last verse views past the kingdom of heaven to the kingdom of the Father. This kingdom will not begin until the millennial reign of Christ is over; and it will continue throughout the eternal ages. Since the "kingdom of heaven" is totally ignored in this verse, we understand that the Holy Spirit is speaking mainly to the Christians who will fail the fiery tests of the judgment seat of Christ (the furnace of fire) and will as a result, spend one thousand years in outer darkness or in Gehenna, where they will weep and gnash their teeth. Only after that will they be resurrected out of their place of punishment into a glorified body to live in the kingdom of the Father forever (1 Cor. 15:51-54; Psa. 47:5). In the kingdom of the Father, all Christians will shine as the sun. It is the writer's belief that those who gain the reward in the kingdom of heaven will retain the reward forever in the kingdom of the Father. But those who lose their reward in the kingdom of heaven will lose it forever; they will shine as a heavenly body, but without reward.

The apostle Paul spoke of the kingdom of the Father in 1 Cor. 15:24-25, when he wrote, **"Then {cometh} the end, when he shall have delivered up the kingdom to God, even the Father; when he shall have put down all rule and all authority and power. (25) For he must reign, till he hath put all enemies under his feet."**

The content of these verses, which gives great glory to the Lord Jesus Christ, is a grand finale to the parable.

CONCLUDING THOUGHTS

The parable of the wheat and the tares teaches separation. First, there is a separation of the tares from the wheat when they are bundled together while standing in the field. Second, there is a separation of the wheat from the tares at the rapture of the church. Third, there is a separation, within the wheat, of those who gain a reward from those who suffer loss. Fourth, there is a separation of all the righteous into the kingdom of the Father from all the unrighteous, who will be in the lake of fire forever.

This fourth and final separation will take place after the one thousand year reign of Jesus Christ here on earth with His bride. It is here on the earth that He will rule and reign until all enemies are placed under His feet. He will defeat the last two enemies, "death" and "hell," at the "great white throne" of judgment after His earthly reign is over (Rev. 20:14). The kingdom of the Father will then commence and will continue through the eternal ages. All who are saved will be there, regardless of their rank and station, and will shine forth as the sun. Only then will all sorrow, pain, tears and death be wiped away (Rev. 21:4).

Summarily, this parable reveals the entire history of the church and its glorious future throughout the eternal ages.

CHAPTER NINE

THE MYSTERIES OF THE KINGDOM: PART TWO

In chapter eight, we studied the parable of the "wheat and the tares," which revealed the history and future of the church. In this chapter, we will be considering the parables of the "mustard seed" and the "leaven," which reveal the history and future of the tares (the false church). These two parables were given by our Lord between His teaching and His interpretation of the wheat and the tares. Hence, their location indicates that they added some information to the parable of the wheat and the tares; information that will reveal the details of the external and internal structures of the tares.

THE PARABLE OF THE MUSTARD SEED

"Another parable put he forth unto them, saying, The kingdom of heaven is like to a grain of mustard seed, which a man took, and sowed in his field: (32) Which indeed is the least of all seeds: but when it is grown, it is the greatest among herbs, and becometh a tree, so that the birds of the air come and lodge in the branches thereof. (33) Another parable spake he unto them; The kingdom of heaven is like unto leaven, which a woman took, and hid in three measures of meal, till the whole was leavened" (Matt. 13:31-33).

Fewer passages, if any, have suffered more at the hands of commentators then the third and fourth parables of Matthew 13, because they have misinterpreted the term *kingdom of heaven*. Those who have erred have done so by believing that the kingdom of heaven is Christianity (kingdom in the heart of the believer), when, in reality, it speaks of the literal and visible coming of our Lord to earth to establish and rule over the kingdom. Because they will not believe this essential truth, they make the parables mean the very opposite of what our Lord taught. The writer remembers well one of his seminary professors who taught the popular view of the third parable. He taught that the parable of the mustard seed represented the glorious success of the gospel in the world, because the great tree that grew from the mustard seed portrayed the rapid growth of Christianity until it covered the earth. As plausible as this sounds, it is false. The Bible teaches that Christianity will not generate until it covers the whole earth, but will degenerate until it is unnoticed on the earth. Keep in mind, as we begin the exposition of this parable that the gospel does not produce loftiness and prominence in the world as the great tree shows, but lowliness, meekness and suffering. Our Lord would not portray His bride as being rooted in the world with her branches stretched out over the earth. This is a worldly scene, not a spiritual one.

The true interpretation of the tree lies in understanding the nature of the mustard seed. Since the mustard seed grows into an herb, and herbs always grow into bushes, then it is clear that the Word of God is teaching that something happened to the early church (the mustard bush) that caused it to grow, against its nature, into a monstrosity that scripture calls a "great tree."

The church began from a mustard seed, the least of all seeds, which is an emblem of faith (Matt. 17:20); faith that was first placed in Jesus Christ as Saviour for the salvation of the spirit (objective salvation), then daily exercised in Jesus Christ as Lord of the life for the salvation of the soul (subjective salvation). This continuous faith caused the early church to grow into seeing and hoping for the kingdom, which matured them into the mustard bush; a bush that is not lofty, but lowly; a bush whose purpose, among others, was to provide spiritual seasoning and healing to the world. This is the structure of the church. It was made up of the fruit-bearers of the first parable; believers who had the three-fold doctrine of Christ, i.e., the word of salvation, the word of power (Lordship of Christ) and the word of the kingdom. But beginning in the third century, the mustard bush began changing into the monstrous great tree. What caused this to happen?

To find the answer, we must interpret by scripture the three central figures of this parable — the mustard seed, the birds of the air, and the great tree.

The Mustard Seed

According to horticulturists, the mustard seed will grow just about anywhere and under any condition. Therefore, scripture uses it as a figure of faith; overcoming faith. In Matt. 17:20, Jesus referred to the seed as an emblem of faith. In this verse, He did not say, "if ye have faith as *small* as a grain of mustard seed," as so many preach, but "if ye have faith *as* a grain of mustard seed." Hence, the teaching does not emphasize the mustard seed's size as much as its nature, a nature that will overcome all obstacles.

The Birds of the Air

The birds or fowls, of the air always represent the *evil agents of Satan.* In Gen. 15:11 (the first place of mention), Abraham had to drive away the fowls from the prescribed sacrifice of animals that was necessary for the giving of the Abrahamic covenant (a covenant of grace, see Rom. 4:1-5). These sacrifices typified the death and shed blood of Jesus Christ on the cross. In Rev. 18:2, the birds are identified with the "habitation of demons" and "every foul spirit." In the first parable of Matt. 13 they represent agents of the devil taking away the seed that was sown by the wayside.

The Great Tree

The "great tree" of scripture is first mentioned in the book of Daniel. By using the "law of first mention," we will be able to interpret it and establish its meaning, which will not change throughout the Word of God.

"Thus {were} the visions of mine head in my bed; I saw, and behold a tree in the midst of the earth, and the height thereof {was} great. (11) The tree grew, and was strong, and the height thereof reached unto heaven, and the sight thereof to the end of all the earth: (12) The leaves thereof {were} fair, and the fruit thereof much, and in it {was} meat for all: the beasts of the field had shadow under it, and the fowls of the heaven dwelt in the boughs thereof, and all flesh was fed of it....(22) It {is} thou, O king, that art grown and become strong: for thy greatness is grown, and reacheth unto heaven, and thy dominion to the end of the earth" (Dan. 4:10-12, 22).

Daniel clearly establishes the great tree as an emblem of a great world-wide kingdom; a kingdom that has a physical structure with its power centered in a king. Such was the kingdom of Babylon with its king Nebuchadnezzar in 580 B.C. This great tree also had fowls (agents of Satan) resting within its branches, which undoubtedly pointed to the "Babylonian caste," a religious-political system of that day called the "Magism." When the Persian empire conquered Babylon, Magism was driven out of Babylon and replaced by Zoroastrianism, the religion of the Persians. With their temples broken down, the greater number of Magians fled to Asia Minor, during the Persian reign of Emperor Darius Hystaspes and fixed their central college and headquarters in Pergamum (See G.H. Pember, *The Great Prophecies of the Centuries Concerning Israel and the Gentiles,* p. 271, Schoettle publishing Co., Miami Springs, Florida, 1984). Thus, the political-religious structure of the great tree was moved west.

The Beginning of Magism, or the Babylonian Mystic Cult

The political structure and idolatrous religious system of Magism originated with Nimrod's wife, Semiramis. Nimrod was the founder of Babel and the kingdom of Babylon. Semiramis became the first high priestess of this idolatrous system. She had apparently heard (by oral tradition) of the Seed that was promised to Eve by God and claimed this promise for herself. When she gave birth to a son, she proclaimed that he was miraculously conceived by a moonbeam, and she offered her son as the promised deliverer of the earth. His name was Tammuz. She claimed that when he was grown, a wild boar slew him; but after forty days of her weeping, he was raised from the dead.

This idolatrous system grew rapidly and soon covered the world. In Assyria, Semiramis was call Ishtar. It was probably here that the practice of giving Easter eggs began. They were known then as Ishtar eggs, the sign of new life, and they were given at the close of a forty day period (modern day lent) each year that celebrated Tammuz's resurrection from the dead. In the Phoenician pantheon, Semiramis was known as Ashteroth, or Astarte. In Egypt, she was known as Isis. The Greeks called her Aphrodite. Among the Latins and the Romans, she was known as Venus. Her son, Tammuz, was also known by different names in the ancient world; names such as Baal, Osiris and Horus. In Greece, he was called Eros, and in Rome, Cupid.

"The cult of the worship of mother and child spread throughout the whole earth. She was worshiped by the offering of a wafer (a little cake) to her as 'queen of heaven.' And there was always forty days of Lent, of weeping over the destruction of Tammuz before the feast of Ishtar, at which time his resurrection was celebrated" (Dr. W.A. Criswell, *Expository Sermons on Revelation,* p. 183, Zondervan Publishing House, Grand Rapids, Michigan, 1969). The temples of this idolatrous system were known as Taus, and its faithful worshipers always made the sign of the Tau with their hands (the letter T). Their worship consisted of altars, sacrifices, vestments, magic and mystic languages. Their priestesses practiced prostitution, which drew the masses. Later on, they also began an order of vestal virgins, the real slaves of their religion (nuns). "The secret of the Babylonian mystery (the Magism) was to be found in priestly ablutions and in sacramental rites and rituals, in the dedication of virgins to the gods, in purgatorial fires, and in a thousand other things that are familiar to us today." (Dr. W.A. Criswell, *Expository Sermons on Revelation,* pp. 183-184, Zondervan Publishing House, Grand Rapids, Michigan 1969). The real power of this secret religious system was in the practice of confession. Before a member could be initiated into the cult, he had to confess to the priest the secrets of his life. The priest then had him in his power. This practice (the confession of sins in a confession box) is also the secret power of the Roman Catholic church of today.

God has much to say against this abominable and idolatrous system. In Jeremiah 44 and Ezekiel 8, we read of the time when Israel turned away from God, worshiped the "queen of heaven" (Semiramis), and mourned for Tammuz; and God's judgments fell on Israel for this idolatry.

From Pergamos to Rome

When John wrote the book of Revelation in about A.D. 95, the "Babylonian mystic cult" was still considered by God to be headquartered in the city of Pergamos (same as Pergamum). Jesus revealed this in His letter to the church at Pergamos in Rev. 2:12-17, when He called the city of Pergamos "Satan's seat" (verse 13). Apparently, the seat of Satan would not change in God's view until A.D. 387, when it would officially be united with the Roman state.

The move to Rome began in 133 B.C., when Attalus, the pontiff and king of Pergamos, bequeathed the headship of the "Babylonian priesthood" to Rome. Sometime after his death, it was brought to Italy by the Etruscans, who came from Lydia, the region of Pergamos. They brought with them the Babylonian cult and all its rites. They set up a pontiff who was the head of the priesthood. Later, the Romans accepted this pontiff as their civil leader. Julius Caesar was made pontiff of the Etruscan Order in 74 B.C. and, in 63 B.C., he was made supreme pontiff of the Babylonian Order. Therefore, he became heir to the rights and titles of Attalus, pontiff of Pergamos, who had made Rome his heir by will. Thus, the first Roman emperor became the head of the Babylonian priesthood and Rome, the successor to Babylon. The Emperors of Rome, in succession, continued to exercise the office of "supreme pontiff" (Pontiff Maximus) for many years.

In A.D. 323, Constantine became sole ruler of Rome and adopted

Christianity. This was more for a political reason than a religious one. Constantine did not divorce himself from the religious support of the pagan devotees of the Babylonian mystic cult. He retained the title of Pontiff Maximus and became one of their deities after his death in A.D. 337. In the last fourteen years of his life, he showered favors upon Christians. He ceased their persecution; he destroyed pagan temples and filled their official positions with Christians; he exempted Christians from military service and their churches were allowed to hold property without taxation. They were given buildings called bascilicas for worship, and he made their day of worship a civil holiday. He also issued a general exhortation to his subjects to become Christians. To retain the support of Constantine, pagans by the hoards, answering this call, began joining the church, bringing with them their pagan customs.

It is highly doubtful that Constantine was a Christian, although his mother was. In his day, the empire was declining rapidly. It needed a strong internal unity, which could engender loyalty. History tells us that his embracing of Christianity was the cement that held the empire together. In spite of this, Constantine never gave any indication that he was Christian. As a matter of fact, he thought that baptism was for the washing away of sins. Thus, he delayed receiving this rite until he was at the point of death.

After the Emperor Constantine died, his office of Pontiff Maximus, over the priesthood of the Babylonian mystic cult, was offered to the Emperor Gratian. He refused it; for what reasons, history cannot be sure. As a result, Damasus, the bishop of the church at Rome, was elected to this position. Before the election, Damasus had been bishop of Rome for twelve years. He had received this office through the influence of the monks of Mt. Carmel, a college of Babylonian religion, originally founded by the priests of Jezebel. As a result, the head of the Babylonian priesthood and the Babylonian mystic cult became the ruler of the Roman church. Hence, the church was officially united with paganism.

Finally, under Emperor Theodosius (A.D. 378-395), Christianity was declared the official state religion of Rome. This made Rome the official seat of Satan. Consequently, the mustard bush (the church) was officially united with the tree (the Babylonian mystic cult) and, in turn, grew into the great tree; an empire that is both a church and a state.

Babylon and Rome in One Religious System

"Soon after Damasus was made 'supreme Pontiff' (Pontiff Maximus) the rites of Babylon began to come to the front. The worship of the Virgin Mary was set up in A.D. 381. All the outstanding festivals of the Roman Catholic Church are of Babylonian origin. Easter is not a Christian name. It means Istar, one of the titles of the Babylonian Queen of Heaven, whose worship by the children of Israel was such an abomination in the sight of God. The decree for the observance of Easter and Lent was given in A.D 519. The 'Rosary' is of pagan origin. There is no warrant in the Word of God for the use of the 'Sign of the Cross.' It had its origin in the mystic 'Tau' of the Chaldeans and the Egyptians. It came from the letter 'T' the initial name of 'Tammuz,' and was used in the 'Babylonian Mysteries' for the same magic purposes as the Roman church now employs it. Celibacy, the Tonsure, and the Order of Monks and Nuns, have no warrant or authority from scripture. The Nuns are nothing more than an imitation of the 'Vestal Virgins' of pagan Rome.

"As to the word 'Mystery,' the Papal Church has always shrouded herself in mystery. The mystery of 'Baptismal Regeneration'; the mystery of 'Miracle and Magic' whereby the simple memorials of the Lord's Supper are changed by the mysterious word 'Transubstantiation,' from simple bread and wine into the literal Body and Blood of Christ; the mystery of the 'Holy Water'; the mystery of the 'Lights on the Altar'; the 'Mystery Plays,' and other superstitious rites and ceremonies mumbled in a language that tends to mystery, and tends to confusion which is the meaning of the word Babylon" (Clarence Larkin, *The Book of Revelation,* p.

152, Philadelphia Pennsylvania, Clarence Larkin Est., 1919). God uses the same word *mystery* to identify the woman of Rev. 17:1-10. Upon the woman's forehead is written, "MYSTERY, BABYLON THE GREAT, THE MOTHER OF HARLOTS AND ABOMINATIONS OF THE EARTH" (verse 5). She is clothed in purple and scarlet, the colors of the papacy. She is decked with gold and precious stones and pearls, which represent the wealth she has received from her worldwide harlotry. She has a golden cup in her hand, full of abominations and filthiness of her fornication. This represents her pagan ceremonies and, in particular, the cup that is used in the Roman Catholic Mass. In verse 1, she is called the "great whore that sitteth upon many waters"; i.e., rules many nations (waters are always emblematic of nations and peoples). In verse 9, we see her seated on seven mountains, which identifies her headquarters as Rome. Rome is built on seven mountains, or hills. In verse 3, we see her sitting on a scarlet colored beast full of names of blasphemy, the coming antichrist.

Summarily, the woman represents a false religion shrouded in "MYSTERY," which had its beginning in "BABYLON," and has become the "MOTHER OF HARLOTS" by selling her religious and idolatrous "ABOMINATIONS" to the peoples of the earth from her headquarters, which sits on seven hills (Rome). She has spawned a multitude of false religions, whose members are tares. A few of these include "Mormanism," "Jehovah's Witnesses," "Christian Scientist," the "New Age Movement," "Astrology," "Spiritualism" and "Free Masonry." Also included are thousands of counterfeit churches bearing the names of main-stream churches, who preach "self-love," "positive thinking" and "prosperity." All of these have come out of the fountainhead, the MOTHER OF HARLOTS, identified by God as the Roman Catholic Church, who will be burned in the field (world) with all the tares under God's wrath during the great tribulation. However, during the first three and one-half years of the tribulation period, this woman (bride of the antichrist) will have finally reached her goal of total worldwide dominance. This is revealed by her sitting upon the back of the beast (the antichrist), which signifies control. In the last three and one-half years (the "great" tribulation), God will use the antichrist and ten kings of this world who will follow him to utterly destroy her world wide kingdom; then antichrist will assume control. (Rev. 17:16).

When the apostle John (the human author) wrote the book of Revelation, he did not know what to call this religious system, since it had not yet come into existence. All he could do was describe what he saw. But in these last days, we know that the false religious system is called the Roman Catholic Church, the great tree of Babylon with fowls in its branches.

THE CONCLUSION

The parable of the mustard seed shows the beginning of the church, which grew into a mustard bush and was united with the great Babylonian tree in the fourth century. This is a picture of the outward structure of the tares, which will be destroyed in the field (the world) after the rapture of the church.

The True Church

To understand what Christ had to say concerning the true church (those not influenced by the Babylonian mystic cult), we need to read and understand the parable of the mustard seed as it is recorded in Mark. **"And he said, Whereunto shall we liken the kingdom of God? or with what comparison shall we compare it? (31) {It is} like a grain of mustard seed, which, when it is sown in the earth, is less than all the seeds that be in the earth: (32) But when it is sown, it groweth up, and becometh greater than all herbs, and shooteth out great branches; so that the fowls of the air may lodge under the shadow of it"** (Mark 4:30-32). Mark tells us that the seed was sown in the earth, not in the world; and when it grew up, it became greater than all herbs, not a tree. Its branches were great (thick) so that the fowls of the air could lodge *under* the shadow of its branches, not *in* its branches. So has been the true church down through the centuries. It has not been a great tree ruling the world, but a spiritual herb (medicinal) bush for the sin sick world, growing in any place and over any obstacle to dispense the gospel of grace. The true church began from the mustard seed, an emblem of overcoming faith, and grew in the earth separate from the world. Though the agents of Satan (fowls) could not lodge in its branches, they have received a benefit by lodging under its spiritual shadow (representing the grace of God through the church in this dispensation).

We who are members of the mustard bush must ever be on guard to not fall into the same satanic trap that the fourth century Roman church did. The enemy is still trying to convince us that we cannot be successful unless we become a large church with big and beautiful buildings having stained glass windows, pipe organs and paid choirs. Only by making these religious trappings our goal can we gain huge memberships (establishing our own little kingdom) and great amounts of money. This will make us (particularly the pastor) successful in the eyes of God, and will impress our denomination and the world.

This is a satanic lie. The Bible warns us that we are not to become a great tree, utilizing the programs of the flesh, but we are to remain a bush. If a church is to become physically large, let it be of God, and not of our own self-efforts. God is not interested in successful Christians — only faithful ones. We are not to seek the plaudits of the world or the denomination that we are a part of, but we are to seek the approval of our Lord at the judgment seat of Christ, which will be, **"Well done thou good and faithful servant: thou hast been faithful [not successful] over a few things, I will make thee ruler over many things"**(Matt. 25:21b).

THE PARABLE OF THE LEAVEN

"Another parable spake he unto them; The kingdom of heaven is like unto leaven, which a woman took, and hid in three measures of meal, till the whole was leavened" (Matt. 13:33).

The fourth parable will also reveal added information concerning the tares. As the parable of the "mustard seed" spoke of the tare's *external* structure, the parable of the "leaven" will speak of their *internal* structure (doctrines).

The Popular False Teaching of the Fourth Parable

Before we can give a true exposition of the fourth parable, we need to categorically refute the popular interpretation being taught in these last days by many self-styled scripture authorities who are amillennial and liberal in their views.

The popular interpretation teaches that the leaven represents the gospel and its power, the meal is the human race, and the woman is the church. As the woman hid the leaven in the meal until it was all leavened, so will the gospel, hidden in the world by the church, spread until it reaches all of mankind.

First, if this popular view is correct, it follows that, ultimately, all of the human race will be evangelized. But this is not so! God has stated that He is taking out of the Gentiles a people for His name (Acts 15:14). Therefore, not all of the world will be saved.

Second, if this popular view is correct, Christ was in error in His choice of figures when He gave this parable. Consider these two points: (1) Jesus never committed the preaching of the gospel to women. (2) Leaven cannot represent the gospel moving on the burdened hearts of Christians for the lost, since leaven works alone — by itself.

Third, if the popular view is correct, the results of the leaven's work is error; because leaven puffs up the meal which is emblematic of sinful pride. How can a scriptural emblem for evil be a figure for the successful evangelizing of the world?

Fourth, if the popular view is correct, God has contradicted Himself in the second parable. There, He gives a picture of Christianity by using the figures of wheat and tares, with the tares being destroyed instead of being evangelized.

Fifth, if the popular view is correct, the word *leaven* is an emblem of good, not evil, throughout the Bible. This would make the leaven of the Pharisees and the Saduccees that Jesus warned against good, not bad. Sadly, those that teach this popular view seem to forget that once a figure is established by the law of first mention, it cannot change. Thus, leaven is always an emblem of evil in God's Word, with no exception. In Ex. 34:25, He warned against using it with blood offerings. In the Levitical law, He excluded it from all offerings (Lev. 2:11). In Lev. 23:17, He uses it as a type of the "old nature" of both Jewish and Gentile converts to Christ. In Amos 4:5, it is the language of irony, which means the opposite. We know this by the context established by Amos in 4:4. In 1 Cor. 5:6-7, He warns us to purge out the old leaven. In Gal. 5:7-9, it is a picture of hindering men from obedience to the truth.

The True Interpretation

By letting scripture interpret itself, we will clearly see that the *woman* represents the Roman Catholic Church, while the *three measures of meal* represent the three-fold doctrine of Christ; i.e., the word of salvation, the word of power and the word of the kingdom. As the woman hid the *leaven* in the meal until all was leavened, Romanism hid the *doctrine of works* (legalism) in the three-fold doctrine of Christ until all was leavened.

In elaborating on this parable's three principles, we see immediately that it teaches a continuation of the third parable through a different view. As the third parable (the great tree) symbolizes the *outward* appearance of the false church, the fourth parable symbolizes the *inward* view, or its false doctrine. As the third parable reveals what is visible to the eye, the fourth shows what is hidden from the eye. As the third reveals the *institution,* the fourth shows the *teaching of that institution.* When we connect the tares in the second parable to the great tree in the third and to the leaven in the meal of the fourth, we get an unmistakable picture of the apostatizing of the church period. When the tares were sown in the fourth century, the leaven was placed in the meal and the nature of the mustard bush was changed to that of a tree. When the Lord returns He will find tares, a great tree, and the true doctrines of Christ leavened and puffed up, filling the earth; but not much wheat.

The Self-Righteous Works of Leaven

The leaven of the Roman Church is "self-righteous works." To understand where this Biblical emblem, *leaven,* originated and how it works, we must first understand from where its type, the literal leaven of the early church period, came and how it worked. The literal leaven, used to bake bread, was made from a small portion (a lump) of fermenting bread dough that was taken out of a new batch of dough and left by itself (sometimes on the window sill over night) where it continued to ferment. The next day, the woman baking the bread would place the old lump from the day before into a new batch of bread dough, causing its fermenting action (leaven) to spread throughout the bread and make it rise (puff up) before she baked it. Hence, each day she would take a small lump out of the bread dough to ferment for the next day's bread. Today, we do this a little differently. We use a fungus called yeast in order to make our bread rise.

Our Lord's use of the figure, leaven, tells us that the leaven of the Pharisees and the Sadducees (the fungus of self-righteous works) was probably received by Israel from Satan before the church began and later introduced into the Roman church before it became the state church. Later, this leaven, fermenting together with the pagan works of the Babylonian mystic cult, to which the church had been united, permeated all of its three measures of meal, i.e., the three-fold doctrine of Christ, and caused it to be puffed u Consequently, the doctrine of the kingdom was first leavened in the fourth century. Then the doctrine of the Lordship of Christ was leavened and, finally, the doctrine of salvation.

All of the three-fold doctrine of Christ became leavened and remained so for 1300 years, up until the time of the reformation period, when Martin Luther, a Catholic priest, was saved and the doctrine of "salvation by grace through faith" was rediscovered. Later, in the nineteenth century, the true church began rediscovering the doctrine of the Lordship of Christ; and in these last days of the twentieth century, a few are beginning to rediscover the doctrine of the kingdom.

Notwithstanding, there are many non-Catholic churches of today that are leavened. They are preaching a doctrine of salvation by works, and a service to God by self-effort through the programs of man. They believe that the kingdom is only a spiritual kingdom, which comes into the heart of man when he is baptized and has joined the church. Of these churches, there are many variations of leavened doctrine. The writer once attended a Bible conference hosted by a church that featured the "kingdom truths." Feeling that this church must have already rediscovered the doctrines of salvation and the Lordship of Christ, we anxiously awaited the series of messages on the kingdom. To our surprise, we found that the doctrine of the *word of power* (the Lordship of Christ) had not yet been rediscovered by this church's pastor or congregation; though they did believe that they were saved by grace and could not lose their salvation. This came to light when their pastor stated that the Bible was only the source of the knowledge of God, not the power. They believed that one must pray aloud, and simultaneously with other people, particularly, to have the Holy Spirit come down and anoint him in power. By trying to reenact over and over the day of Pentecost to cause the Holy Spirit to come upon them to fill them with power, they demonstrated that they had not yet rediscovered the *word of power,* which was already in them. True doctrine teaches that we are sealed by the Holy Spirit when we are saved, and then continually filled with the Holy Spirit to the same degree that we are yielded to the teachings of God's Word. This can be seen by comparing Eph. 5:18-19 with Col.3:16, which teach that the action of the Word of God and the fullness of the Spirit are equated as the same. Pentecost could happen only one time. The Holy Spirit is presently sealed in the believer, waiting to fill him over and over again as the believer daily presents to Him a surrendered and yielded life through the conviction of His Word (Rom. 10:17; 12:2; 2 Cor. 3:18).

The Woman of the Fourth Parable

The leavening of the three-fold doctrine of Christ by the woman in the fourth parable is God's way of describing the action of the Roman Catholic Church. The woman is the same figure that we saw in Revelation 17; a woman on whose forehead a name was written, "MYSTERY, BABYLON THE GREAT, THE MOTHER OF HARLOTS AND ABOMINATIONS OF THE EARTH." She is the counterfeit church and counterfeit bride to a counterfeit Christ who will reign over a counterfeit kingdom for three and one-half years. She will be destroyed with the tares in the field (the world) and, later, will be judged and cast into the lake of fire. At the coming of Christ, the antichrist will be defeated by our Lord and cast alive into the lake of fire.

To summarize this parable, the devil has managed through false doctrine to corrupt all of the three-fold doctrine of Christ in this age by using the Roman Catholic Church, the great tree of Babylon, as his chief tool. This teaches that this age will not end in a great spiritual revival in which the world will turn to God, nor will the church be revived; but it will end in apostasy by false doctrine. In 2 Thess. 2:3 the apostle Paul called this apostasy the "great falling away." It is the opinion of the writer that we are presently living in the portion of the "great falling away," signifying that the Lord is at the door preparing to once again invade human history and to take out His church.

A CLOSING THOUGHT

Always love and pray for the people caught up in this idolatrous system that God, through His mercy, might save them.

CHAPTER TEN

THE MYSTERIES OF THE KINGDOM : PART THREE

THE PARABLE OF THE HID TREASURE

"Again the kingdom of heaven is likened unto treasure hid in a field..." (Matt. 13:44a)

In expounding upon this parable and the next one, we must caution the reader to beware of the modern day interpretations. The false, but popular, interpretations by modern day theologians are a product of the corruption of the three measures of meal (three-fold doctrine of salvation) by the leaven (false doctrine). It is amazing how much leaven has crept into the teaching of scripture, causing relentless violence to sound exegesis. Even those who call themselves "conservative" have, in many cases, fallen victim to this puffed-up doctrine of Satan. Before we expound upon the true interpretation, let us focus on God's Word to expose these erroneous teachings for what they really are.

The popular view interprets this parable (the hid treasure) and the next (the pearl of great price) to mean that salvation is found when the buyer of the field finds the treasure and the merchant finds the pearl. It fallaciously teaches that both parables are figures of a sinner finding salvation. The only difference is that the man in the field "accidentally" finds it, while the merchant "seeks" to find it. As plausible as this sounds, this false interpretation, if believed, will actually destroy the truth of the plan of salvation. Consider these six points: (1) Man never seeks salvation (Rom. 3:11), God seeks man (John 15:16). (2) Man does not find the Lord, since the Lord is not lost; the Lord finds the lost man (Luke 15:4). (3) Salvation is not hid in the world, but is separate from the world. (4) When one is saved he does not hide his salvation in the world, but lets it shine that the world may see it. (5) A man cannot purchase salvation for it is a free gift; and he cannot sell all that he has to purchase it, for he has nothing to sell. (6) He cannot purchase the field to obtain salvation, for the field is the world (Matt. 13:38).

Introduction to the Parable's True Meaning

The "mysteries of the kingdom of heaven" is an expression used by our Lord at the beginning of these seven parables to identify two different kinds of saints who will inherit the kingdom of heaven. They are: (1) certain Old Testament saints, who were called out of the saved of Israel, and (2) the bride of Christ, who will be called out of the body of Christ at the judgment. In the parable of the "treasure," Jesus unveils the mystery of the Old Testament saints.

The Interpretation

"Again, the kingdom of heaven is like unto treasure hid in a field; the which when a man hath found, he hideth, and for joy thereof goeth and selleth all that he hath, and buyeth that field" (Matt. 13:44).

There is no problem in discovering the principles of the fifth parable. The "field" is an emblem of the world (already interpreted in the parable of the wheat and the tares). The "man" is Christ and the "treasure" represents all the Old Testament saints of Israel (the national seed of Abraham), including the remnant who will be saved at Christ's second coming.

Jesus further identifies the "treasure" in Matt. 13:52, when He says: **"Therefore every scribe {which is} instructed unto the kingdom of heaven is like unto a man {that is} an householder, which bringeth forth out of his treasure {things} new and old."** Our Lord calls the *treasure* a repository from which the householder (Jesus) takes things "new" and "old". In light of this truth, the *treasure* represents all the saved members of Israel. The things "old" represent the *peculiar treasure* taken out of saved Israel; i.e., those of Israel who will gain a portion of the spiritual kingdom of heaven. The things "new" represent the church, the New Testament saints also taken out of the *treasure*, who will gain the highest privilege in the spiritual kingdom of heaven. We recognize this because both groups come out of the *treasure*, both are of the seed of Abraham (Rom. 4:11-12; Gal. 3:29), and the church has the apostles (Israelites) as its foundation.

Our Lord further reveals that unless a scribe (a teacher of the Word) understands the "new" and the "old" and whence they come, he is not properly instructed in the truths of the kingdom of heaven. Therefore, at the end of these seven parables, our Lord gives us the "key" to understanding who the "mysteries of the kingdom of heaven" are. The order of the things "old" and "new," as taught in the fifth and sixth parables, are reversed in the key. In the key (verse 52), it first says things "new" and then things "old". We understand why when we learn that the order in which rewards will be given in heaven will be reversed. Scripture teaches that the *peculiar treasure* of the Old Testament cannot be made perfect until after the "church of the first born" is made perfect (Heb. 11:40).

The Treasure versus the Peculiar Treasure

The identities of the *treasure* (Jacob) and the things "old" (Israel), coming out of the *treasure*, are clearly seen in Psalm 135:4. **"For the Lord hath chosen Jacob [the treasure] unto himself, {and} Israel for his *peculiar treasure*."** "Jacob" represents Jacob's life being lived through his "old sin nature," for its meaning is "supplanter." This is further established when we see that Jacob was called "Jacob" by God for twenty-one years after he was saved at Bethel (Gen. 28:12-22) and before he was renamed "Israel." This was apparently due to Jacob allowing his old nature to rule over his life for this period of time.

It was at Bethel that he dreamed of the ladder to heaven (a type of Christ) with the angels of God ascending and descending upon it (Gen. 28:12; John 1:51). Jacob awoke out of his sleep that night believing what God had told him in his dream. As a result of his faith, he was saved by grace and became the *treasure* of Israel (Gen. 28:16-17). God had told him in his dream that He would give to him and his seed (plural) the land where he slept that night. This spoke of the physical portion of the coming millennial kingdom (Gen. 28:13b-14a). He had told him that his Seed (singular) would be a blessing to all the families of the earth. This spoke of the Promised Seed of Abraham (Christ) who would come through the lineage of Abraham, Isaac and Jacob (Gal. 3:16). Therefore, "Jacob," as God uses it in the above verse, represents the national seed of Abraham, Isaac and Jacob who, by grace, were saved by believing in the coming Promised Seed (Christ) and God's promises of the millennial land. It speaks of salvation only and corresponds to the "carnal Christian" of 1 Cor. 3:1-3. "Jacob" denotes his spiritual posterity in only the physical portion of the kingdom — the millennial land.

It was about twenty-one years after Jacob was saved, became the *treasure* of Israel, and forgot his vows to God (Gen. 28:20-22) that his name was changed to "Israel," which represented his new nature. This name was given to him by God after he had wrestled with the Lord and was blessed by Him (Gen. 32:31). From that time on, Jacob walked with a limp as a sign from God that his walk (life) had been changed (Gen. 32:25). He returned to God and committed himself to obey Him and make Him first in his life. Therefore, "Israel," as used by God in the above verse, represents the *peculiar treasure* of the house of Jacob; those who were not only saved, but obeyed God's voice and kept His commandments. It speaks of the salvation of the soul and corresponds to the "spiritual Christian" of 1 Cor. 2:15-16. Its meaning is "he will rule as God," or the "prince of God," and it denotes his spiritual posterity in the spiritual portion of the kingdom.

God further revealed this division of Israel coming out of Jacob in

Ex. 19:5, **"Now therefore, if you will obey my voice indeed and keep my covenant, then ye shall be a *peculiar treasure* unto me above all people: for all the earth is mine."** At this time, after their exodus from Egypt, the children of Israel were already God's *treasure,* through the Abrahamic covenant; but according to this verse, at the beginning of the Mosaic covenant, they also had the right to become His *peculiar treasure.* The expression *peculiar treasure* was first used by our Lord to identify the new nature of Jacob (Israel) four hundred years before; now, it was used to identify those of the children of Israel who would inherit the spiritual portion of the kingdom under the Mosaic covenant. God used this expression to distinguish between the Jews who were merely children of Jacob (saved only, with rights to enter the earthly portion of the kingdom) and the Jews who were the children of Israel (saved with an inheritance into the spiritual portion of the kingdom) (compare Psalm 78:5,71). One was the *treasure*; the other, the *peculiar treasure.*

We learn from Ex. 19:5 and Psa. 135:4 that "Jacob" (all believing Israelites) was chosen by God to be saved, under the Abrahamic covenant of grace, into the physical portion of the kingdom (later known as the kingdom covenanted to David). On the other hand, "Israel" (believing Israelites who further heard God's voice, obeyed and kept His commandments) was chosen out of Jacob, under the Mosaic covenant, to be saved into the spiritual portion of the kingdom (later known as the kingdom of heaven). Hence, Jacob is the *treasure;* Israel is the *peculiar treasure.* This corresponds to the Christians of the church dispensation. Some have only been saved by grace (salvation of the spirit), while others are being saved into the kingdom by obeying and keeping the commandments of Christ (salvation of the soul). The first group is known Biblically as the body of Christ; the second is the bride of Christ.

Under the Abrahamic Covenant

As difficult as it is for the Christian's mind to understand the salvation of the Old Testament saints, we must let scripture speak for itself. Under the "Abrahamic covenant," God saved Abraham and his national seed by grace through faith; faith in the promise of God concerning the coming Seed of Abraham, Jesus Christ (Gal. 3:16), and His promise of the millennial land. The covenant of grace was not conditional on any works of Abraham or his seed — only on their faith in God's word (Rom. 4:1-5). Once they were saved, they could not lose their salvation, though they could become apostates (fall away from God). There were those who did not believe God concerning these promises, and they died in their sins as lost men. The report of the "rich man and Lazarus," in Luke 16, is one example.

Under the Mosaic Covenant

Under the "Mosaic covenant," God elected into the spiritual portion of the coming kingdom all the believers (those under the Abrahamic covenant) who obeyed His voice and kept His commandments. The Old Testament believers who did not continue to obey His voice and keep His commandments became apostates and lost the privilege of entering the spiritual portion of the kingdom. Since the Mosaic covenant (unlike Abraham's covenant of grace) was a covenant of works, it was a conditional covenant. In Ex. 19:5, God placed conditions upon the children of Israel that they must keep to enter the spiritual portion of the kingdom.

The reader might assume that God was speaking of salvation here (same as the Christian's salvation of the spirit); but that would be in error, since all of Israel was already saved when He gave them conditonal promises under the Mosaic covenant. Consider this: By faith Israel had applied the blood of the passover lamb (a type of Christ) in Egypt and was saved from the death angel (a type of salvation); by faith, they crossed the Red Sea on dry ground (Heb. 11:29); they were under the cloud and passed through the sea and were all baptized unto Moses in the cloud and in the sea (1 Cor. 10:1-4). How, then, can one mistake the Mosaic covenant for a covenant of salvation? No, it was a covenant of works to produce obedience to God's voice and to keep His commandments — not for salvation, but for the inheritance in the spiritual portion of the kingdom.

The Overcomers of Israel

The *peculiar treasure* represents the overcomers of Israel, who were invited to inherit their portion of the spiritual kingdom of Christ. In later chapters, we will learn that a part of this assigned portion was to be that of the "wedding guests" (Jewish wedding guests) at the heavenly marriage feast of the Lamb, when the overcomers of the church period become the bride of Christ. They had the opportunity to reign over Gentile cities of the earth from this spiritual portion of the kingdom. But, sadly, the unbelieving generation of Jesus' day lost that opportunity. It was given, instead, to a chosen group of believers out of the church period (Matt. 22:2-14). In Matt. 21:43, it is recorded that Jesus Himself took this portion of the kingdom away from Israel and gave it to the church. He said: **"Therefore say I unto you, The kingdom of God shall be taken from you, and given to a nation [the church] bringing forth the fruits thereof."**

Jesus' indictment of national Israel of that day did not preclude earlier individual saints of the Old Testament period from attaining to the spiritual kingdom. Scripture tells us that Abraham, Isaac and Jacob will sit down in the kingdom (Matt. 8:11; Luke 13:28). It is suggested by the scripture that the Old Testament prophets will be the "friends of the bridegroom" during the heavenly marriage of the Lamb. John the Baptist was the last of these prophets (John 3:29).

We see evidence in the book of Daniel that some Israelites of the Old Testament have attained the spiritual portion of the kingdom. **"And many of them that sleep in the dust of the earth shall awake, some to everlasting life, and some to shame {and} everlasting contempt. (3) And they that be wise shall shine as the brightness of the firmament; and they that turn many to righteousness as the stars for ever and** ever" (Dan. 12:2-3). In these verses, Daniel is not describing the resurrection of the church, as some have suggested. According to its context, he is describing the resurrection of three classes of Jews: (1) those who were saved by believing the promises of God through the Abrahamic covenant and will have everlasting life (the Jacobs); (2) those who failed to believe and will go to shame and everlasting contempt in hell; and (3) those who are the wise (the Israels), who are taken out of those who are only saved. The wise, in this verse, will have attained to this higher position by turning many to righteousness; i.e., to right living because of the hope of the spiritual kingdom of heaven. Like the church, they will shine as the brightness of the firmament and as the stars for ever and ever. The Jews who are only the saved (the Jacobs) will be raised into redeemed soulical bodies (like Adam's body before he sinned) and will be assigned the earthly portion of the kingdom.

Apparently, some of the wise of Israel are the heroes of faith listed in Heb. 11. They are identified in Heb. 12:23b as the "spirits of just men made perfect." However, according to Heb. 11:40, they are not yet perfect (have not yet received their spiritual bodies) and cannot be until the resurrection of the church. Their souls are presently in heaven, along with the general assembly of the church and the names of the "church of the firstborn" (Heb. 12:22-23).

The "church of the firstborn" identifies the wise of the church period, who, like the wise of Israel, will have turned many to righteousness. They, however, will be called out of the general assembly of the church as the bride of Christ and, like the *peculiar treasure* of Israel, will have bodies that will shine as the stars in glory (compare 1 Cor. 15:40-41; Matt. 13:43).

We are given another glimpse of the *peculiar treasure* in Mal. 3:16-17, when God calls them His "jewels." They are the ones chosen out of Jacob; those who feared God, obeyed Him, kept His commandments and exhorted others to do so (verse 16). These verses tell us that God recorded their names in a book of remembrance so that in "that day" (after the church of the firstborn has received their reward), they may make up His jewels (Heb. special or *peculiar treasure*).

Summarily, the *peculiar treasure* (the Israels) represents the saved individual Israelites of the Old Testament who will inherit a heavenly portion of the kingdom. Apparently, they are the "wise" of the Old Testament, mentioned by Daniel, who will shine as the brightness of the firmament; they are also the "jewels" of Malachi. The hidden *treasure* (Matt. 13:44) of Israel (the Jacobs) represents the individual Israelites of the Old Testament period who were saved, but will have no reward (corresponding to the general assembly of the church). They will be raised at the close of the tribulation period and will enter the earthly portion of the kingdom along with the remnant of Israel who will be saved at Christ's coming (Ezek. 37:1-13).

The earthly portion of the kingdom, the land that God promised to Abraham, is part of the Abrahamic covenant of grace and will be given as a possession to all believing Israelites forever. This portion of the kingdom could not be attained to by works, through the Mosaic covenant; but only by grace, through the Abrahamic covenant. It corresponds to heaven for the believers of the church period, since like heaven, it will last forever. It will exist, first, under the Davidic covenant for one thousand years on this present earth, and then forever on the new earth (Luke 1:33a; 1 Chron. 16:15-17).

The Purpose of the Mosaic Law

The Mosaic law, which included the moral law (Ex. 20:1-20;26), the civil law (Ex. 21:1-23:35) and the ceremonial law (Ex. 30:1-38), was given by God to the Israelites, not for their salvation, but because of their transgressions (sin). It was to serve as a schoolmaster to point them to Christ that they might be justified by faith (Gal. 3:19,24). Hence, the responsibility of the succeeding generations of Israelites, who lived from the time of the giving of the Mosaic law down to the time of Christ, was to repent of their sins, turn from the traditions of their fathers, and believe on the coming Promised Seed of Abraham, Christ (Gal. 3:16). Those who did this had their sins "covered," though they could not be "paid for in full" until Christ had come and died for them (Heb. 10:1-14). Therefore, the Israelites who believed and died in past centuries waited for this coming event with great excitement in the paradise section of sheol (John 8: 56); waited for Jesus to come and "pay" for their sins on the cross and to, then, move them into the paradise of the third heaven (Eph. 4:8-10).

The Israelites who had believed in God's promises to Abraham also had the opportunity to enter the coming spiritual kingdom for reward as members of His *peculiar treasure* (Ex. 19:5). All they needed to do was to obey the voice of God and keep His covenant; a conditional covenant of works based on the law of Moses, which pointed, through typology, to the coming Christ as their sin bearer.

The Traditions of Men

In light of this, one may ask, "How could these people have fallen away from God?" After all, they had been privileged to hear the voice of God proclaiming the law to them (Deut. 4:11-13; 5:2-4). They were privileged to read the written words of the law, which God had given to Moses, containing, among other things, the ten commandments and the ceremonial laws of sacrifices and feast days; all filled with meaning through types and symbols. Every Hebrew sacrifice that was burned on the brazen altar of their tabernacle was an object lesson (type), pointing to Christ's coming and dying on the cross for their sins. But as time went on, the Israelite believers began to fall away from the commandments of God's Word. They began to corrupt the Mosaic law and to set aside the Abrahamic covenant of grace through their own invention called the "traditions of the fathers"; a tradition of "oral law" that had evolved over the centuries and they had come to believe in for eternal life. As a result of this corruption of God's Word, an untold number of Jews died in their sins.

By the Jews following this unwritten law, known as the *Cabala*, the

Lord Himself tells us they **"transgressed and made void the commandment of God."** Nevertheless, in order to create a credence for these inventions, the Jews taught that Moses himself had received this traditional law from Sinai, and delivered it to Joshua, Joshua to the elders, the elders to the prophets, and the prophets to Ezra's great synagogue. Afterwards, it was transmitted orally through the centuries from the elders to the prophets, etc. The Roman Church, learning from the conduct of the Jews, later did the same thing by instituting its apostolic succession and tradition (inventions of doctrine that made void the Word of God) from pope to pope. The traditional law of the Jews, however, "was not in written form until several centuries after the New Testament times. It existed during this period in the form of 'oral tradition,' committed to memory verbatim in the rabbinical schools. The oral law, or the elaboration of the Torah, was organized into a systematic arrangement by Rabbi Juda about A.D. 200, but none of it was reduced to writing until later." (H.E. Dana, *The New Testament World*, p. 65, Broadman Press, Nashville, Tennessee, 1937).

This oral tradition began with Ezra's great stress on observing the law after the Jews had come out of captivity. He had the post-exile Jews to begin studying it diligently and in depth to get the greatest possible knowledge of it. From this arose a class of people in Judaism known as the scribes, or rabbis, from which, later came the Pharisees. They not only gave themselves over to the study of the law, but also to the defending of the "traditions of Israel." Thus, by combining their oral traditions with the law, they devised more detailed regulations for personal conduct. These traditions and regulations were transferred down through the years in oral form and regarded as authoritative. Later generations came to conceive this tradition as a "hedge about the law," and it filled volumes of Hebrew books. It extended to the most trivial matters and became preposterous, unbearable and rigid. Jesus referred to this when He rebuked the Pharisees as those who **"bind heavy burdens and grievous to be borne, and lay them on men's shoulders" (Matt. 23:4).** The apostle Paul also referred to this tradition when he described his own zealous attitude for it before he was saved: **"And [I] profited in the Jews' religion above many my equals in mine own nation, being more exceedingly zealous of the traditions of my fathers"** (Gal. 1:14). Additionally, the apostle Peter reminded the early Jewish church in his first epistle that they **"were not redeemed with corruptible things, {as} silver and gold, from your vain conversation {received} by traditions from your fathers"** (1 Pet. 1:18).

Before the Jews were led captive into Babylon in 606 B.C., they were all for idolatry; but after their return from captivity, having learned their lesson not to worship other gods, they abhorred idolatry; instead, they were all for traditions: "they changed naught for naught, or rather naught for worse. For, indeed, their traditions, one may justly say, were more destructive than their history." (G.H. Pember, *The Church, the Churches, and the Mysteries,* p. 475, Schoettle Publishing Co., Miami Springs, Florida, 1984). Consequently, those following the traditions of the Jews when Jesus appeared did not believe the promises of the Abrahamic covenant and, as a result, rejected Jesus, crucified Him and, afterwards, died in their sins. They thought by "searching the scriptures" (through their own invented oral law) and keeping the "Mosaic" law (according to the oral law) that they would have eternal life. Jesus Himself even said to them, **"Search the scriptures; for in them ye think ye have eternal life: and they are they which testify of me"** (John 5:39).

Heaven on the New Earth

As bizaare as this may sound to some, scripture reveals that God will ultimately have an earthly people who will live forever on the new earth, which He will create (Rev. 21:1-5). They will be composed of the nations, with Israel as their head, living in natural, or redeemed, bodies (like Adam's body before he sinned), without the possibility of dying. This is what the writer terms God's "Adam plan"; for if Adam had not sinned, he would still be alive today, along with all of humanity. Apparently, God will return to that "Adam plan" after all things are reconciled to Christ at the great white throne of judgment and He destroys all enemies, including death and hell, by casting them into the lake of fire (1 Cor. 15:24-28; Rev. 20:14). Hence, the "Adam plan" includes: (1) those of Israel who will be raised at the beginning of the millennium (Ezek. 37:7-12) and will live in the promised land in their resurrected and redeemed bodies; (2) those of the remnant of Israel who will be saved at His coming; (3) the Gentile nations saved during the tribulation period under the preaching of the "gospel of the kingdom" by the 144,000 Jewish evangelists (Rev. 7:4-8; Matt. 24:14); and (4) all those saved during the millennium, both Jew and Gentile.

According to scripture, the rule of Christ, after His millennial reign, will continue throughout the ages for ever and ever and will be known as the "kingdom of God," or the "kingdom of the Father" (I Cor. 15:24). The eternal kingdom will begin when the new heavens and new earth are brought into existence. However, before God destroys this present earth at the close of the millennial kingdom (2 Pet. 3:12-13), He apparently will remove all living saints from the earth; for we see, in Rev. 21:1-5, the holy city descending out of heaven onto the new earth where people with flesh and blood bodies will be living who can no longer die (Rev. 21:4). How is God going to remove all the saved people from the earth before He destroys it? He has not told us how, but We assume He will rapture them, change their bodies into redeemed bodies (bodies like Adam's before he sinned) at the close of the millennium and, after the new heaven and new earth are established, unrapture them (to coin a word) back to the earth. Is this process un-Biblical? I think not; for Elijah was raptured into heaven and will be placed back upon the earth (unraptured) during the great tribulation period to be killed as one of God's two witnesses.

The final heaven will be upon the new earth in the midst of new heavens (probably only that portion of the heavens that Satan had control over). God's earthly people will be living on the new earth in redeemed, flesh and blood bodies (like Adam's before he sinned). Apparently, they will procreate as Adam was told to do before he sinned. They will not die, since death and hell will have been destroyed; and the tempter, Satan, will have been cast into the lake of fire forever.

Also upon the new earth will be God's spiritual people, dwelling with Christ in the holy city. These will be all the saved from the church age, including those called out of the saved; i.e., the chosen and the bride of Christ, who will have rulership over the earth and the universe as co-heirs with Christ (Rom 8:17b). In addition, the *peculiar treasure*, or the *jewels of God*, will apparently be living in the holy city in their spiritual bodies. These may be the saints who were raised from the dead immediately after Christ's resurrection (Matt. 27:52-53). They, too, will probably have rights to live in the city, since the names of their tribes are written over its twelve gates (Rev. 21:12). Finally, all the saved, i.e., all whose names are written in the Lamb's book of life (Rev. 21:27), will have the right to enter the city, though they probably will not be permitted to live there.

In summary to this section, there will be two kinds of people in the final heaven. Those who have earthly bodies (the *treasure* and the saved nations) and those who have spiritual bodies (the saved saints from the church age and the *peculiar treasure*).

Finally, the calling out by God of the *peculiar treasure* from the treasure corresponds perfectly to the saved of the church period, when, at the judgment seat of Christ, He will call out the bride of Christ from the body of Christ to be co-heirs with Him (Rom. 8:17b).

Back to the Parable

"Again, the kingdom of heaven is like unto *treasure* hid in a field; the which when a man hath found, he hideth, and for joy thereof goeth and selleth all that he hath, and

buyeth that field" (Matt. 13:44). Let us expound on our parable point by point. First, the *treasure* was hid. This has reference to Israel's national history beginning in Egypt. It was there that they were slaves among the brick-kilns, hidden in the world literally and typically, for Egypt is a type of the world. Later, the ten northern tribes of Israel were so hidden in the world by God through their Assyrian captivity that they are still hidden today, and are referred to as the "ten lost tribes of Israel."

The second point is that Christ found this *treasure* (the national seed of Abraham) when He came to fulfill His earthly ministry. In the word *found,* the meaning is extended to all the tribes of Israel, including the ten lost tribes, through their representatives, the Jews (Judah). If all the Jews had repented at the preaching of John the Baptist or of Christ, and had turned to Him as their King (the Promised Seed of Abraham), the remaining ten tribes would have been made part of the earthly portion of the kingdom, and the kingdom would have been established at Christ's first coming. God, however, had other plans that required the setting aside of the kingdom to include the church, which is not seen in the Old Testament. Hence, the union of both houses of Israel will not occur until Christ comes again. This truth is established in the prophetic scriptures of Ezekiel 37:15-28, where the Lord promises, through the sign of the two sticks, that all twelve tribes will be brought back together to dwell in their land in the coming kingdom.

Third, our text tells us, **"...when a man hath found, he hideth..."** These words do not mean that when Christ came the first time, He found the *treasure* (the national seed of Abraham), and then hid it back in the world; for to do so, He would have had to hide it again before His crucifixion. Even if He did so, it cannot be said that the Jews were hidden. For the population of the earth has always known where they were, and have persecuted them from the day they were scattered. There exists in these last days a nation of Jews that everyone can see. They are certainly not hidden. No, Christ did not hide them again; He hid Himself! The writer believes that the word *hideth* in this verse refers to the man, not the *treasure;* after He found the *treasure,* He *hideth* Himself.

The prophet Isaiah made reference to this in Isa. 8:14-17, when he wrote: **"And he shall be for a sanctuary; but for a stone of stumbling and for a rock of offense to both the houses of Israel, for a gin and for a snare to the inhabitants of Jerusalem. (15) And many among them shall stumble, and fall, and be broken, and be snared, and be taken. (16) Bind up the testimony, seal the law among my disciples. (17) And I will wait upon the Lord, that *hideth His face* from the house of Jacob, and I will look for him."**

Notice, in verse 17 that the Lord prophesied that He would hide His face from all twelve tribes because of their rejection of Him. In verse 14, He spells out that rejection in terms of the crucifixion by using the expression *a stone of stumbling and a rock of offense.* The Lord clearly chose these terms to show that the crucifixion would be offensive to the Jews and a stone that they would stumble over, since, nationally (through their religion of Judaism), they cannot accept that their Messiah came and was crucified by them (Rom. 9:33; 11:7-12; 1 Pet. 2:8). Furthermore, the word *hideth* could have reference to Jesus purposely hiding Himself from Israel while in His earthly ministry so that only the Israelites who repented to God would have their eyes opened to His person.

Fourth, our text tells us, **"...he hideth, and for joy thereof goeth and selleth all that he hath..."** Here, our text teaches that our Lord, through His sovereignty, looked forward to that day when He would claim His *treasure;* therefore, with joy, He sold all that He had on the cross of Calvary to purchase the object of His joy. Notice that the "hiding" came before the crucifixion, for He first hides and then goes and sells all that He has. This, in the writer's opinion, proves that *hideth* does not refer to the scattering of the Jews throughout the world in A.D. 70, as this occurred after the crucifixion.

Fifth, our text tells us, "**...He selleth all that He hath and buyeth that field.**" The buying of the field does not refer to just the salvation of the Jews, but to all creation; because creation fell with man when he first sinned, and is now awaiting its redemption at the coming of the Lord when He will renew all things (Rom. 8: 22-33). It was at the cross that Jesus sold all that He had, even Himself, to purchase the world and the *treasure* in the world. Though the world and the *treasure* in it are His, he has not yet claimed legal title to it. However, one day in heaven, He will break the seven seals on the title deed to the world, which only He is worthy to open (Rev. 5). He will come forth for the second time, will cast out Satan, and will take possession of and redeem what is rightfully His. Notice that the *treasure* is in the world when he comes the second time. There is no mention of His saving the *treasure* out of the world as He will the church, but of leaving the *treasure* where it is and buying the world (the field). Though the *peculiar treasure* (those who will inherit a spiritual portion of the kingdom) comes out of the *treasure*, this portion of the parable teaches that the *treasure* (Jacob) is God's earthly people, who will inhabit the earthly portion of the kingdom at Christ's return.

Concluding Thoughts

This parable has enabled us to see three divisions of the Jews: first, the unsaved, who, through many generations, came to trust in the "traditions of their fathers" (their own invented oral law) instead of the promises of God through Abraham; second, those represented by the term *Jacob* (the *treasure*), who, by believing in the promises of God, i.e., the coming Seed of Abraham (Christ), under the Abrahamic covenant, were saved out of the unsaved Jews and into the coming earthly portion of the kingdom (later their heaven). The apostle Paul said, "**... they {are} not all Israel, which are of Israel**" (Rom. 9:6b). The third division is the Jews represented by the term *Israel* (the *peculiar treasure*), who are saved out of Jacob into the coming spiritual kingdom of heaven by obeying God and keeping His commandments under the Mosaic covenant.

THE PARABLE OF THE PEARL OF GREAT PRICE

"Again, the kingdom of heaven is like unto a merchant man, seeking goodly pearls: (46) Who, when he had found one pearl of great price, went and sold all that he had, and bought it" (Matt. 13:45-46).

There are two modern day interpretations concerning the "pearl." Both views are in error.

The first represents gross error. We call it the "popular view," as it is aligned with the modern day seminary and is taught in the majority of pulpits. Like the parable of the "treasure," the popular view is a product of the leavened three-fold doctrine of Christ, which has spread throughout the theological world. It is a doctrine of Satan and violates all the cardinal principles of salvation. Like the erroneous teachings of the parable of the treasure, it teaches that salvation can be bought by the sinner; that man seeks after God, rather than God seeking after man; and that man has something to sell, in opposition to the scriptural teaching that man is totally depraved.

The second interpretation is a more conservative view, and is only in minor error in comparison to the popular view. This view is the product of serious minded Bible students who have not discerned the deep teaching of the scriptures, and thereby are in error because of shallowness. They properly identify the man as Christ, but wrongly identify the pearl of great price as all the saved of the church period.

The True Interpretation of the Parable

To properly interpret the parable of the "pearl of great price," we must keep in mind two things. First, the parable is in a group of three parables told by Jesus only to His intimate few, teaching the identity of the "mysteries of the kingdom of heaven": the parables of the treasure, the pearl of great price and the drag net. Second, the pearl of great price cannot represent all the saved, as taught by the more conservative view, as that has already been dealt with by the figure of the wheat. Why would the Lord be repetitious? The pearl of great price, necessarily, begins where the parable of the wheat ends, at the judgment seat of Christ. Its figure can be nothing but the wheat after it has been tried and rewarded; an emblem of the few who will attain to the inheritance of the kingdom, and not the believers who will suffer loss of the kingdom for a thousand years. This is a beautiful picture of the Gentile portion of the mysteries of the kingdom, who will gain their position in the coming kingdom in the same manner as the peculiar treasure of Israel; first, by being saved by grace through faith (the salvation of the spirit); and, then, by continually hearing the voice of God through His Word, obeying Him and keeping His commandments (through a Christ-controlled life), which leads to the salvation of the soul. Since the "pearl of great price" will reign with Christ in His coming kingdom as His queen consort, He calls her the "bride of Christ."

Points of Interpretation

First, the parable shows Christ seeking goodly pearls. Since He is seeking more than one pearl, we must conclude that the pearls (plural) represent all who would be saved during the church period; for Jesus came "to seek and to save that which was lost."

Second, the parable shows Christ finding one pearl of great price among the other pearls. This discovery of the one among many speaks of the coming division of all the saved, at the judgment seat of Christ, into two major groups: the "body of Christ" and the "bride of Christ," or the "general assembly" and the "church of the firstborn" (Heb. 12:23). Notice that Christ found the pearl before He bought it, thus showing the sovereign election of the bride by the Lord. This is in harmony with scripture that teaches that the bride has been known and predestinated by God from before the foundation of the world (Eph. 1:4-6).

Third, after Christ found the pearl of great price (the bride), he went and sold all that He had and bought it. This can only be His finished work on the cross of Calvary to purchase His bride.

Notice that He sold all that He had. This has reference to God giving His Son, the Lord Jesus Christ, even to His death (1 Pet. 1:18-20).

There may be an objection to this interpretation on the grounds that the Lord Jesus Christ died for all who are saved. Although that is true, the salvation of the general assembly of the saved is not in view in this parable; nor are the "chosen," who are identified only as the wedding guests at the heavenly wedding. In view here are those selected out of the "chosen," who will be called "faithful" by the Lord Jesus Christ at His coming (Rev. 17:14). They will make up the pearl of great price — His bride.

Points of Typology of the Pearl

First, by using the pearl as an emblem (type), the Lord teaches the unity of the "body of Christ." The pearl is the only gem known to man that cannot be divided into two parts without destroying it. One may cut a diamond or a ruby in half and get two gems, but to cut a pearl would result in its destruction. Likewise, the body of Christ cannot be divided spiritually, though its members can gain various levels of reward in the kingdom while others suffer loss.

Second, the pearl is formed from a living creature and is a product of suffering. This happens when a piece of foreign matter (perhaps a grain of sand) enters the oyster's side and wounds it. The oyster transforms this into a pearl by attempting to cover it with the substance of its inner shell. By using the emblem of the oyster, the Lord teaches that the bride of Christ is formed by the living God and is a product of suffering. When a piece of corrupt foreign matter, i.e., the sin-sick man, enters by faith into Christ, he is saved and his sins are continuously covered by the blood of Jesus from His wounded side. This transforms him into a pearl. Notice that the process of forming the pearl is caused by two works. First, there is the entering in of the foreign matter, and then, the long, slow process of the oyster in forming the pearl. This is accomplished by a continuous buildup of countless layers of pearl placed around the foreign matter. Likewise, there are two works in forming the bride. First, there is the act of justification by entering into Christ through faith (salvation of the spirit). Second, there is the continuous process of being covered (cleansed) by the blood of Jesus Christ when we walk in the light as He is in the light (the truths of the Word of God) (1 John 1:7), which causes us to continually confess our sins (salvation of the soul) (1 John 1:9). Those who are saved, but fail to be continually cleansed, cannot be the pearl of great price (the bride of Christ), though they are a member of the body of Christ and are represented by the other pearls of our parable.

Third, the pearl begins its development with a corrupt center, which cannot be seen by its owner, since it has been covered by the substance, representing the suffering, of the oyster. All the owner can see is a thing of beauty; a live gem formed from a living creature. Likewise, the bride of Christ begins with a corrupt center of sin that cannot be seen by God, since it has been covered countless times with the substance (blood) of Christ's suffering.

Fourth, the oyster is a creature found in the depths of the sea where the eye does not normally penetrate; a place of slime and silt at the bottom of the ocean. Normally, it is the last place that man would look to find priceless beauty. Likewise, Christ was made flesh and dwelt among us. He lived as "a man of sorrows and acquainted with grief," yet without sin in the depths and slime of the sea of humanity. The world (the sea of nations) still has not recognized Him. Nevertheless, it was here that He suffered and died for us; it was here that His side was wounded for us. All who enter into Christ by faith will become a pearl (salvation of the spirit); but only those who avail themselves of the cleansing blood of Jesus Christ (a process for the saving of the soul) can be candidates for the pearl of great price.

Fifth, the pearl is formed in layers. This is accomplished by the oyster secreting a special substance called "nacre" around the foreign particle that enters into the oyster. Before this can occur, the foreign particle is first encompassed by a sac of the oyster called the "epithelium sac" (a one time work of the oyster). Only then can it become coated many times with thin layers of pearl; and after many years of this process, a lustrous pearl is formed. A pearl of great price not only has quality and color, but is made up of many layers. Likewise, the bride is formed by many layers of the work of Jesus Christ; not by being constantly saved over and over, but by being constantly cleansed over and over. This, then, gives proof that the "pearl of great price" is not an emblem of all the saved, but of layers of cleansing and recommissioning by the Lord through the trials, tribulations and persecutions of the world, the flesh, and Satan. **"If we confess our sins, he is faithful and just to forgive us {our} sins, and to cleanse us from all unrighteousness"** (1 John 1:9).

THE PARABLE OF THE DRAG NET

"Again, the kingdom of heaven is like unto a net, that was cast into the sea, and gathered of every kind: (48) Which, when it was full, they drew to shore, and sat down, and gathered the good into vessels, but cast the bad away. (49) So shall it be at the end of the world: the angels shall come forth, and sever the wicked from among the just, (50) And shall cast them into the furnace of fire: there shall be wailing and gnashing of teeth" (Matt. 13:47-50).

The careful reader of this seventh parable will note a difference in its construction and that of the fifth and sixth parables. As the fifth and sixth are given without further explanation, the seventh seems to interpret itself. We said "seems," for in reality, its added material is not an interpretation at all, but a second division, which speaks of a different subject hidden from the casual observer.

While the first division of our parable uses the figures of sea, seashore, net and fishes, the second division uses angels, the wicked and the just and the furnace of fire. Between these two divisions, there is a common denominator, which will aid in the interpretation of both divisions. It is the expression, *So shall it be at the end of the world...*

The First Division

"Again, the kingdom of heaven is like unto a net, that was cast into the sea, and gathered of every kind..." At the beginning of this first division, we find no difficulty in interpreting the figures of the "sea" and the "seashore." In prophetic language, the Bible clearly uses the "sea" as an emblem of all nations of the world (Isa. 17:12; Rev. 17:15), while the "seashore" is used to speak of the land of Israel (Israel is never numbered with the nations and cannot be a part of the sea) (Gen. 22:17; Heb. 11:12). Of these emblems, the most difficult for most expositors to interpret is the "net"; i.e., the drag net used to drag fishes to the shore. Some try to make it mean the rapture, while others turn to the fishermen's nets of the gospels and try to make it mean evangelism. While it is true that Jesus used the nets of His fishermen disciples to teach evangelism, the net in this seventh parable is different from those of the gospels. It is prophetic in its scope and, as such, must be interpreted in light of other prophetic scriptures.

The first prophetic mention of this net is found in Eccl. 9:12, **"For man also knoweth not his time: as the fishes that are taken in an *evil net* [drag net], and as the birds that are caught in the snare; so {are} the sons of men snared in an evil time, when it falleth suddenly upon them."** The net, here, is a type of device that arrests (brings under control to others) men of all nations in an "evil time." The "evil time" spoken of here is a prophetic utterance pointing to the great tribulation, which is to come upon the whole earth after the rapture of the church has occurred. Notice that this evil time will fall *suddenly upon them*. By letting scripture interpret scripture, we find that this is the same language the apostle Paul used when he described the coming great tribulation. **"For yourselves know perfectly that the day of the Lord so cometh as a thief in the night. (3) For when they shall say, Peace and safety; *then sudden destruction cometh upon them*, as travail upon a woman with child; and they shall not**

escape" (1 Thess. 5:2-3).

A prophetic utterance about the great tribulation was given by the prophet Habakkuk, when he wrote: **"They take up all of them with the angle, they catch them in their net, and gather them in their drag: therefore they rejoice and are glad. (16) Therefore they sacrifice unto their net, and burn incense unto their drag; because by them their portion {is} fat, and their meat plenteous. (17) Shall they therefore empty their net, and not spare continually to slay the nations?"** (Hab. 1:15-17)

In Habakkuk's prophecy, the past and the future merge; the type and the antitype meet; for as the ancient Babylonian Empire (the conqueror of the world at that time) is prophesied in Habakkuk, so is the coming kingdom of antichrist, which it foreshadows. Through other prophets of the Old Testament, we learn that the king of Babylon, mentioned in Habakkuk, is a type of the coming antichrist. We see this in the titles given to him by God; for during the great tribulation period, God calls him the "Assyrian" and the "Chaldean" (king of Babylon) (Isa. 10:24; 14:25; 23:13; 30:31; 31:8;).

According to Habakkuk, it will be the antichrist (the Assyrian, or the Chaldean) who will use both the angle (fish hook) and the drag net to arrest, capture, control and continually slay the nations during this time. The drag net, then, must speak of the times and circumstances of the coming antichrist. Habakkuk further tells us that they will worship the net, which represents the power, or god, of the antichrist. This they will do with sacrifices and the burning of incense. It is clear to the writer that the drag net and the angle (used to prevent a single fish escaping his control) are not only symbols of the power of antichrist (Satan himself), but also his times, which incorporate his laws, devises, schemes and circumstances to capture all men. The net will be cast into the sea of nations and will gather every kind. The expression *every kind* not only speaks of all nationalities, but every kind of person within those nationalities, including the "good" and the "bad."

"**Which when it was full, they drew to shore, and sat down and gathered the good into vessels, but cast the bad away.**" This verse switches our thoughts from the net to those who drew the net. Beautiful is God's Word; for even as it tells of terrible times that will come upon the whole world by the antichrist (slaying of the nations), it also tells of the net that will be cast into the sea and drawn to shore by the work of God's providence. This is the meaning of the word *they*, which speaks of the angels of God who work His providence. Here, in the parable, His eye is on the good fish that have been made righteous by hearing and believing the "gospel of the kingdom" preached by the 144,000 sealed evangelists of Israel during the tribulation (Rev. 7:4-8; Matt. 24:14). Even though millions of the good fish will be killed by antichrist (Rev. 7:14), God will not suffer all of them to perish in the evil times; for many will be alive when Christ comes to establish His kingdom. Thus, while the net represents the devices and circumstance used by antichrist to draw all the armies of all the nations to Israel for the final battle, Armageddon, it also represents the circumstances used by God to draw all Gentile nations to Israel to be judged by Christ at His coming (Matt. 25:31-46). Though antichrist will rule during this time, God always overrules to accomplish His purposes.

"**And sat down and gathered the good into vessels, but cast the bad away.**" It is evident that the good fish speak of the Gentiles who will be saved during the great tribulation. The Greek word for good is "kalos," which means intrinsically valuable, or with a right heart toward God. Only one who is saved can have this kind of goodness. Hence, in our parable, they are gathered into vessels. The bad fish speak of the opposite of the good, and represent the lost nations that will be cast away into everlasting fire prepared for the devil and his angels (Matt. 25:41,46).

Notice the words *sat down* in our text. This is ever the emblem of sovereignty, showing the presence of our Lord. For it is then that He will judge the nations. Jesus gives us further details of this coming event in Matthew 25, when He prophesies: "**When the**

Son of man shall come in his glory, and all the holy angels with him, then shall he sit upon the throne of his glory: (32) And before him shall be gathered all nations: and he shall separate them one from another, as a shepherd divideth {his} sheep from the goats" (Matt 25:31-32).

Here our Lord speaks of coming in His glory with His *angels, sitting* on His throne of glory, and *gathering* all nations and *separating* them one from the other (language similar to our parable). Those of the nations who are sheep will inherit the earthly portion of the "kingdom of heaven" (verse 34); those of the nations who are goats will be executed. The word *nations* is used in this passage to show that the whole world, or "all kinds," as our parable states, will be gathered there with the exception of Israel, since Israel is not numbered among the nations. Strictly speaking, this will not be a judgment, but a separation; for no books of judgment will be opened. The Lord will merely divide those who are lost from those who are saved. He will separate people according to what they are, as a shepherd divides his sheep from his goats. After He slays the goats, they will automatically go into hell because of their unsaved condition. One thousand years later, at the close of the millennium, they will be raised and judged individually at the great white throne of judgment, along with all the lost, and sentenced to the lake of fire, according to their evil works. For all practical purposes, this separation could be called an antirapture, since the goats are taken from the sheep. As our Lord, at the rapture, will separate by translating the sheep from the goats into heaven, so, at the judgment of the nations, He will separate by executing the goats from the sheep into hell (sheol).

The basis of this separation is taught in our parable. Notice that the good fish are separated from the bad and placed in vessels; whereas the bad are cast away. On what basis does He separate? The answer is found in Lev. 11:9, where the law establishes what the marks of a good fish are. According to this verse, the Israelites were only allowed to eat fish that had scales and fins, while all others were to be looked upon with abomination (verse 10). Typically speaking, the scales of the good fish speak of the believer's armor (Christ in him), while the fins speak of his power (Christ through him). The good fish of our parable, then, will be separated from the bad on the basis of having spiritual scales and fins. They will be put into vessels, and represent the believers who have been saved during the tribulation period. They are the same as the sheep in Matt. 25, who will be allowed to enter alive into the kingdom of heaven, which will be established at this time.

Second, the separation of the good fish from the bad is understood by examining how Christ will separate the goats from the sheep. This is seen in Matt. 25:34-46, when Christ is separating the nations on the basis of how they treated the brethren. Since the word *brethren* speaks of the brethren of Christ according to the flesh, the Jews, then those who treat them kindly must be those who will be saved (the sheep) during the tribulation. It will be difficult for a Gentile to be kind to the Jews during this time, since the Jews will be proclaimed the enemy and hunted down by the antichrist. Nevertheless, the sheep will be willing to suffer for showing their love for God's elect. The goats, on the other hand, will hate the Jews and will join the armies of antichrist to destroy them.

It will be the goats who are slain at the second coming of Christ, during the battle of Armageddon. This harmonizes with the prophecy of Joel 3:9-16, which refers to this battle; for in this section of scripture, there is the call to battle, the assembly, the valley of decision and their destruction by the Lord. Notice, at the same time, the protection of both God's people (the tribulation saints and the elect of Israel, the remnant) from this destruction (verse 16b). All these truths are in the first division of our parable.

In summary to this first division, the parable of the drag net must be viewed as a double type. As it clearly foreshadows the times, devices, and circumstances that will be created by the coming antichrist, it also foreshadows the providence of God in gathering all nations to separate the bad fish from the good, and the goats from the sheep (the lost from the saved).

The Common Denominator

"So shall it be at the end of the world." This expression marks the division of the two sections of our parable by speaking of the time in which they both occur (the common denominator). The time is at the end of the world (Gr. *age*), just before the kingdom age begins. Scripture also refers to this time as the fulfillment of the *times of the Gentiles* (Luke 21:24b). Hence, both divisions of this parable must take place near the close of the tribulation period. This is why the drag net cannot represent the preaching of the gospel of grace during the church period, for at this time (the end of the age), the church will have already been raptured for seven years. Neither can it represent the preaching of the 144,000 sealed Jewish evangelists during the tribulation, for they will preach at the beginning of the tribulation period, not at the end. If by the stretch of our imagination we were able to make the drag net mean these evangelists, all the fish caught in the net by their preaching would have to be good fish. There could be no bad fish.

The Second Division

"So shall it be at the end of the world [age]: the angels shall come forth, and sever the wicked from among the just."

We now enter into the second division of our parable, which deals exclusively with the children of Israel. They, like the Gentile nations, will be gathered to the seashore (the land of Israel) for the purpose of being judged and separated. However, in this second division, God does not use the figure of the drag net to accomplish this; instead He uses the angels. Where in the drag net the angels are used to work the providence of God, here, the angels gather and sever the wicked from the just.

"And he shall send his angels with a great sound of a

trumpet, and they shall gather together his elect from the four winds, from one end of heaven to the other" (Matt. 24:31). In this verse, Jesus describes the activity of the angels of our parable. Where in the parable, they just "come forth," here, they come forth "with a great sound of a trumpet" for the purpose of gathering His elect (the Jewish remnant) from all over the earth. In accordance with our parable, they will be gathered into the land of Israel that the wicked of Israel may be severed from the just.

Notice that the angels come forth with the sound of a trumpet. This is not the gathering of God's spiritual people (the church) into heaven (the rapture), as some have tried to teach, but the gathering of God's earthly people into the land. Contextually speaking, this gathering will occur in connection with the time of Jesus' coming in the clouds to the earth with power and great glory (Matt. 24:30). All of this will occur at least seven years after the rapture of the church, at the end of the world (Gr. age). Keep in mind that there are two trumpets that are sounded for the assembly of God's people — one at the rapture of the church (1 Thess. 4:16) and the one here, which will sound seven years later at the close of the age (Matt. 24:31).

"And shall cast them into the furnace of fire." We have encountered the "furnace of fire" before. It was first seen in the parable of the wheat and tares and is the fire used by God to describe the judgment of the believer before the judgment seat of Christ, somewhere in heaven. The apostle Paul tells us that the Christians whose works do not burn up in this fire will receive a reward (inheritance of the kingdom), but those whose works are burned up will suffer loss of the kingdom (1 Cor. 3:13-14). The furnace of fire was also seen as the possible place of punishment in Gehenna for the apostate Christians for one thousand years, where there will be "wailing and gnashing of teeth" (Matt. 13:42).

Likewise, in this parable, the "furnace of fire" is a place of judgment. However, it is not located in heaven, but upon the earth, and is used by God to judge Israel as a nation. It will be set up at the end of the world (Gr. age) after the Jews have been gathered into the land by the angels. Isaiah describes this furnace as a "furnace of affliction," which will be located in Jerusalem (Isa. 31:9; 48:10). It will be composed of all the judgments of God upon Israel, as well as the wrath of antichrist. The wrath of antichrist includes the great holocaust that will come from all the nations in a last attempt, under Satan, to annihilate all the Jews in the battle of Armageddon.

The prophet Zechariah also gave details of this furnace of fire when he wrote: **"And it shall come to pass, {that} in all the land, saith the Lord, two parts therein shall be cut off {and} die; but the third shall be left therein. (9) And I will bring the third part through the fire, and will refine them as silver is refined, and will try them as gold is tried: they shall call on my name, and I will hear them: I will say, It {is} my people: and they shall say, The Lord {is} my God" (Zech. 13:8-9).** During the close of the great tribulation, Israel will be cast into this furnace of fire (affliction) in Jerusalem when the armies of the nations attack them. As a result, two-thirds of their number will be cut off (be killed). Only one-third will come through the fires and survive the holocaust. God likens this coming time to a time of refining for His earthly people. As silver and gold is cast into a furnace for the purpose of burning off the dross (other materials that will burn), Israel will be cast into this furnace of affliction by God to separate (burn-off) the wicked from the just. Through this process of refinement, God will save His elected remnant of the Jews, and they will enter the millennial land of promise.

Finally, a type of the furnace of fire is seen in the fiery furnace of Nebuchadnezzar (a type of antichrist), when the three Hebrew children were cast into it for not worshiping his image. They were saved by the presence of a fourth figure who had the form of the Son of God (Dan. 3:19-25). Thus, the furnace of fire in Israel will be the determined efforts of antichrist to destroy Israel because of their refusal to bow down and worship the image of the beast

(Rev. 13:14-15). Instead, they will be refined and saved by a "fourth" One, the Lord Jesus Christ Himself at His revelation (His second coming).

Concluding Thoughts

The tenth chapter completes the revelation of the two "mysteries of the kingdom." They are known as things "old" (the peculiar treasure) and things "new" (the chosen and faithful of the church). The tribulation saints and the Jewish remnant, revealed in the seventh parable, are apparently not a part of the old and the new things taken out of the treasure, but are numbered with the treasure, since they will have no part in the spiritual portion of the kingdom of heaven.

Only the Bible teachers who understand these mysteries will have the opportunity to be fully instructed in the kingdom truths presented in this book. For "**...every scribe {which is} instructed unto the kingdom of heaven is like unto a man {that is} an householder, which bringeth forth out of his treasure {things} new and old**" (Matt. 13:52).

NOTES

CHAPTER ELEVEN

THE CHURCH OF THE KINGDOM

In this chapter, our attention will be drawn to the many references that speak of the coming church. Christ will first prophesy of it in Matt. 16, revealing a miniature picture of its construction and spiritual power. In Matt. 17, we will see a miniature picture of the church as they accompany Christ on His return to earth to rule and reign with Him over His kingdom. In Matt. 18, we will see a miniature picture of the instructions given to the church that teach entrance into the kingdom, cleansing, forgiveness and church discipline.

THE CONSTRUCTION OF THE CHURCH

In this section of scripture (Matt. 12:50 to 21:46), national Israel is out of favor with Christ. In chapter twelve, they had failed to repent of their sins and had further committed the sin of blasphemy against the Holy Ghost, which could not be forgiven for two ages. Therefore, from the last verse of Matt. 12, Jesus was estranged from national Israel. He would do nothing more with them. Instead, instructing His disciples about the coming church that He would build and ministering to the individual lost sheep of the house of Israel became His main work.

When instructing His disciples, He would often retire to areas outside the scope of Judaism; places where the scribes and Pharisees, who dogged His steps, would not follow. In one case, He, with His disciples, retired near Caesarea-Philippi, a city north of the sea of Galilee at the base of beautiful Mt. Hermon, where three rivers flowed together to make up the river Jordan; a place of mulberry trees, fig trees, vines, cascades and bubbling fountains; a place near the city of many pagan gods. It was against this backdrop of natural beauty and paganism that Jesus asked His disciples...

> "...But whom say ye that I am? (16) And Simon Peter answered and said, Thou art the Christ, the Son of the living God. (17) And Jesus answered and said unto him, Blessed art thou, Simon Barjona: for flesh and blood hath not revealed {it} unto thee, but my Father which is in heaven. (18) And I say also unto thee, That thou art Peter, and upon this rock I will build my church; and the gates of hell shall not prevail against it" (Matt. 16:15-18).

This is another of the most misunderstood scriptures in the Bible, since it deals with the kingdom and not initial salvation. Because the majority of Christians do not understand the meaning of the kingdom, they grossly misinterpret the key words to this revelation of the church. What was Christ really saying? We will understand this after we understand the following three words.

The First Key Word Is "Christ"

"Thou art the *Christ*, the Son of the living God." Christ is the name and title given to Jesus that speaks of His second coming, not His first. When He came the first time, His name was announced as "Jesus" — the One who would save His people from their sins (Matt. 1:21). "Jesus" speaks of the cross. However, the name and title of "Christ" speaks of His coming as the Messiah of Israel, the anointed One of God and the King of kings. Peter did not say, "Thou art Jesus, the son of the living God," and Jesus did not answer that upon the statement that He was the Saviour (the rock), He would build an assembly of saved people.

The Second Key Word Is "Rock"

"Thou art Peter, and upon this *rock* I will build my church." Contrary to what Roman Catholic theology teaches, the rock does not represent Peter. The church was not built upon Peter. The Greek word for "Peter" is *petros*, meaning a piece of rock, or a pebble; the Greek word for "rock" is *petra,* meaning a mass of rock, or a boulder. It is clear, then, that the church would be built upon the "rock," or stone, which is an emblem of Jesus Christ at His second coming as King.

Others may disagree with this interpretation, citing that the rock is an emblem of the "smitten rock" of Ex. 17:5-6, which teaches of Jesus' death on the cross. Though this is true, the reader will come to see that scripture emphasizes, here, the "smiting stone," which is a type of Christ at His appearing, when He will come the second time to break down the Gentile kingdoms of the world (Dan. 2:34-35,45). While no apparent violence is done to the scripture by including the "smitten rock" with the "smiting stone" as the foundation to the church, it is the "smiting stone" that is emphasized here. Keep in mind that the church is not built upon the "smitten rock" alone. After one has had his spirit saved by faith in Jesus as Saviour, he needs to have his soul saved by a continuing faith in Jesus as Lord of his life. The first salvation gives him eternal life; the second gives him millennial life. The rock in our text, then, represents all the truths that are connected to the coming kingdom. It emphasizes a special people whose lives are grounded in the higher wisdom (wisdom of the kingdom) and, as a result, will inherit the kingdom of heaven.

The Third Key Word Is "Church"

"Upon this rock I will build my *church...*" Our Lord introduces the word *church,* a word misunderstood by Bible teachers and preachers, because most Christians have never heard the kingdom truths. They interpret everything in light of first tense salvation, making "church," in all cases, mean all the saved. But this is not true in every instance. In one place in the Bible, the Greek word for "church" is translated "assembly" (KJV) and used to designate a group of citizens called-out from other citizens to discuss the affairs of state (Acts 19:39). It is used in the Greek translation of the Old Testament to designate the gathering of Israel or representatives of the nation. It is also used to designate a local body of believers. But in the text before us, it is used to designate those who will be the bride of Christ, a higher selection of the "chosen" (the wedding guests), who will be called-out of the body of Christ at the judgment seat. They will enter the kingdom as the "faithful." The Greek word for church is *ekklesia,* which means "a calling out." We would naturally ask, "A calling-out of what?" The average Christian would answer, "Called-out of the lost." But that cannot be, for when God saves a lost man, the scripture tells us that he is "called," not "called-out." As a matter of fact, the Greek word for "called-out" (*eklektos*) is translated "chosen" in Matt. 22:14 and is used in conjunction with the word "called" (*kletos*): "many are called [saved] but few are chosen [called-out of the saved]." The church in its highest expression, as used in our text, must be an assembly of people who will be "called-out" (chosen) of all the saved at the judgment seat of Christ and made (built) into the bride of Christ.

The Typology of Adam and His Bride

This is seen in the typology of Adam and his bride, Eve, of whom Christ (the last Adam) and His bride are the antitype. Let us note carefully the scripture that forms the type in Genesis 2:21-22, **"And the Lord God caused a deep sleep to fall upon Adam, and he slept: and he took one of his ribs, and closed up the flesh instead thereof; (22) And the rib, which the Lord God had taken from man, made he a woman, and brought her unto the man."** God put Adam to sleep in the garden and took a rib out of his body; after which, He closed up the wound to his side. Notice that God did not take Eve, in a literal sense, out of Adam; He took a rib; a rib that represented a portion of Adam's body that was *chosen*-out by God, i.e., called-out of his body. Plainly, the rib represents another body of Adam. The scripture impresses this upon us when it says that after God took out the rib, He closed up the side of Adam, thus signifying it to be separate from Adam's main body. This action of God not only speaks of the impossibility of the second body ever becoming a part of the first, but it also speaks of the impossibility of any of the first becoming a part of the second. There is a finality about it.

Now, let us look at the antitype of Adam, Jesus Christ, the "last Adam" (1 Cor. 15:45). God put Him to sleep (death on the cross) in a garden (Calvary was located in a garden), where He opened His side with a Roman spear. Out of His side flowed a portion of His body, blood and water, signifying sanctification, i.e., being set apart (Heb. 9:19-22; 1 John 1: 7-9). Keep in mind that the antitype speaks of spiritual things and not earthly. The body of Christ (His first body), then, represents people; *all who would ever be saved by grace through faith,* for they were judicially placed in Christ on the cross and crucified with Him (Gal. 2:20a). On the other hand, the portion of his body that flowed out of His side represents those Christians *who are being set apart and, as a result, will be "chosen" out of His first body* (i.e., "called-out" of the "called") by God at the judgment seat of Christ. It will be at the judgment seat that the side of Christ (figuratively speaking) will be closed forever, separating His body into two separate bodies; one that will be the "called," the body of Christ, and the other that will be known as the "chosen" (Gr. the out-called).

We have not addressed the bride of Christ in our type, because the bride must yet be built by God out of the chosen (the out-called). To see this, let us return to the type. After God had chosen out of Adam's first body a second body (a rib) and had closed His side, He took the chosen (the second body) and "made [Heb. *built*]" a woman. Eve was not built from Adam's first body, for his side had already been closed up; but from his second body, which was chosen-out of his first. In the antitype, God will, likewise, take the chosen (Christ's second body) after His side is closed up (the finality of the judgment seat of Christ) and, from it, He will build (is now building according to His sovereignty) the bride of Christ. According to the parable that Christ taught concerning the bride, she will be called the "faithful."

The Appearing of the Bride

"These shall make war with the Lamb, and the Lamb shall overcome them: for he is Lord of lords, and King of kings: and they that are with him {are} **called,** and **chosen,** and **faithful**" (Rev. 17:14).

In this verse from Revelation, God further reveals the bride of Christ, who will appear with Him at His second coming. When we first read this verse, it may appear that there are three groups of people with Him — the *called,* the *chosen,* and the *faithful.* However, the Greek text, by using adjectives instead of nouns, indicates that God is showing us only one group, the faithful, and the stages through which they progressed This one group, then, will be those who have attained to the "faithful" (the bride of Christ) from out of the "chosen," who will be called-out of the "called."

"Upon this rock I will build my church." In Matt. 16, it seems spiritually correct to interpret the word *church* as those who represent a *higher selection* out from the *chosen* (who will be called-out of the saved at the judgment seat of Christ), who will rule and reign with Christ over His kingdom. The church (Gr. *ekklesia*), then, must be composed of all the saints whose foundation is built upon the rock of kingdom doctrines, and who are presently being called-out of the body as the *chosen* to be built into the bride of Christ. They will be known as the *faithful.*

Jesus' parables of the kingdom of heaven in Matthew seem to confirm what we have written here. Each of these parables teaches a different truth concerning the church, which, when taken as a whole, gives us a clear picture of the *called,* the *chosen* and the *faithful.*

The first parable confirms the heavenly "wedding guests," who are the *chosen.*

CONFIRMATION OF THE CHOSEN

"And Jesus answered and spake unto them again by parables, and said, (2) The kingdom of heaven is like unto a certain king, which made a marriage for his son, (3) And sent forth his servants to call them that were bidden to the wedding: and they would not come. (4) Again, he sent forth other servants, saying, Tell them which are bidden, Behold, I have prepared my dinner: my oxen and {my} fatlings {are} killed, and all things {are} ready: come unto the marriage. (5) But they made light of {it}, and went their ways, one to his farm, another to his merchandise: (6) And the remnant took his servants, and entreated {them} spitefully, and slew {them}. (7) But when the king heard {thereof}, he was wroth: and he sent forth his armies, and destroyed those murderers, and burned up their city. (8) Then saith he to his servants, The wedding is ready, but they which were bidden were not worthy. (9) Go ye therefore into the highways, and as many as ye shall find, bid to the marriage. (10) So those servants went out into the highways, and gathered together all as many as they found, both bad and good: and the wedding was furnished with guests. (11) And when the king came in to see the guests, he saw there a man which had not on a wedding garment: (12) And he saith unto him, Friend, how camest thou in hither not having a wedding garment? And he was speechless. (13) Then said the king to the servants, Bind him hand and foot, and take him away, and cast {him} into outer darkness; there shall be weeping and gnashing of teeth. (14) For many are called, but few {are} chosen" (Matt. 22:1-14).

The above parable of the "wedding feast" reveals how the *chosen* will be called-out of the *called* at the judgment seat of Christ, and will become the antitype of the blood and water that flowed from the wounded side of our Lord.

In verses 1-7, we see the kingdom being proffered to Israel and them refusing it. They were invited, as wedding guests, to come to the marriage of the Son of God (Jesus). The invitation went out from **"a certain king** [God the Father]**"** by His servants, the prophets (before the cross),**"to call them that were bidden [Israel] to the wedding: and they would not come"** (verse 3). God sent a second invitation to Israel by His apostles (after the cross) to invite them to the marriage (wedding feast); and they refused it the second time, treating His servants despitefully and slaying them (verses 4-6). As a result, God became angry and sent His armies to destroy the murderers and burn their city (Jerusalem) (verse 7). This occurred historically in A.D. 70, when the Roman armies destroyed Jerusalem and the nation of Israel was scattered throughout the world.

How marvelously and historically correct is this portion of our parable. In Matt. 21:43, before this parable was given, our Lord prophesied that the kingdom would be taken from Israel and given to a nation bringing forth spiritual fruit. **"Therefore say I unto you, The kingdom of God shall be taken from you, and given to a nation bringing forth the fruits thereof."** The apostle Peter, in 1 Pet. 2:9, identified this nation as the church. He called them **"a chosen generation, a royal priesthood, a holy nation, a peculiar people."** Notice that the kingdom was not to be given to those of the church period who were only saved, but to those who were saved and brought forth spiritual "fruit." Hence, those who will be in the kingdom will be those who are the "chosen" (saved, with fruit) out of those who are the "called" (saved, without fruit).

In the first part of our parable (Matt. 22:1-7), our Lord describes the time when the kingdom would be taken from Israel. This would be about forty years after the cross; forty years that God would give them (under the dispensation of grace) to repent of their sins and for crucifying Jesus Christ; a time during which the "gospel of the kingdom" would still be preached to the Jews, while the "gospel of grace" would be preached to the Gentiles.

However, the time of God's patience came to an end. After He destroyed Jerusalem and scattered the Jews, He said to His servants (apostles, evangelists, pastors and teachers), **"The wedding is ready, but they which were bidden [Israel] were not worthy. Go ye into the highways [places of the Gentiles], and as many as ye shall find, bid to the wedding."** This is God's invitation to the Gentiles to be saved and to come to the wedding feast; for the same dinner that was prepared, in verse 4, for Israel is offered, in verse 9, to the saved Gentiles of the world (compare Acts 28:28). However, for them to enter into this heavenly wedding feast as "wedding guests" (verse 10b), the saved Gentiles must qualify by bringing forth spiritual fruit.

Contrary to what is taught by most teachers today, entering into the wedding feast is not salvation, but reward. Those of our parable were saved on earth when they accepted the invitation to come. In heaven, after the rapture, they can enter the wedding feast only if they qualify by having brought forth spiritual fruit in this life. This qualification is incorporated in verse 10; for there, **"as many as they found,"** i.e., were saved, were **"gathered together,"** i.e., were raptured (2 Thess. 2:1), **"both bad and good,"** i.e., those who have bad works and good works (compare 2 Cor. 5:10).

Our parable further teaches that after the saved body of Christ arrived in heaven (those good and bad), **"the king came in to see the guests."** Notice the difference in the word *king,* here, and the words *certain king* in verse 2. The certain king, in verse 2, is God the Father, who is giving the feast for His Son's marriage. The king, here, is His Son, Jesus Christ, after He has received the kingdom. The king came in and **"...saw there a man which had not on a wedding garment"** (verse 11), to whom He inquired, **"Friend, how camest thou in hither not having a wedding garment?"**(verse 12b) And the man was speechless. **"Then said the king to the servants, Bind him hand and foot, and take him away, and cast {him} into outer darkness; there shall be weeping and gnashing of teeth. (14) For many are** *called* **[saved], but few {are}** *chosen* **[called-out of the called]"** (verses 13-14). Mark carefully that these scriptures are not teaching that a lost man came into the wedding feast, but a saved one who did not have on a wedding garment; a garment that, in the scriptures, is clearly an emblem of the righteous works (spiritual fruit) of the believer. This should become obvious when this wedding garment is compared with the bride's in Rev. 19:7-8, which is called the "righteousness [plural] of the saints," or "the righteous acts of the saints." Righteous acts cannot be produced by anyone other than Christ Himself as He lives through the yielded life of the Christian.

The wedding garment is not the garment of the righteousness of Jesus Christ, which is put on every believer by God at the moment he believes, but a garment that is produced by the continuing faith of the believer after he is saved; a garment that represents all the spiritual fruit produced by Christ through the believer who is yielded to the leadership of the Holy Spirit in obedience to the Word of God. How could this man represent the lost, when our parable shows him to be raptured and present at the wedding feast in heaven? The minute teaching of the parable itself reveals that the man accepted (through faith) the invitation to come (salvation) to the wedding. However, after he was raptured, he discovered from the King who came into the wedding feast (the judgment seat of Christ) that he had to bring his own wedding garment (righteous works after salvation). He apparently never prepared a garment for himself and, as a result, was cast out of the heavenly wedding feast into the darkness outside, where there is weeping and gnashing of teeth.

Summarily, the man of our parable represents all the "called," i.e., the saved, of the church period who will fail to surrender the control of their lives to the Lordship of Jesus Christ in obedience to the Word of God and, as a result, will be cast into outer darkness for one thousand years. The other invited guests, who each had a wedding garment, represent all the "chosen," i.e., those called-out of the saved, who, in this life, yielded their lives to the Lordship of Jesus Christ in obedience to the Word of God, produced fruit through their surrendered lives and, as a result, will be counted as the *wedding guests* at the marriage of the Lamb and will enter the kingdom in some capacity of rulership. For **"...many are *called*, but few are *chosen*"** (verse 14).

The Wedding Guests Historically:

To further help us understand the wedding guests, we must look at them historically through the customs of the Jews. The Jewish wedding feast on earth had two invitations for its guests. The first was a general, or preliminary, invitation given as much as a month in advance; a month during which they were to make themselves ready (*Midrash On Lament IV. 2*). The second invitation was given, sometimes, as little as one hour before the feast. Thus, they were to begin preparing themselves at the first invitation, which included making their own wedding garment, and then were to wait expectantly for the second invitation to come.

When they arrived at the feast, properly attired, they were ushered to their place at the feast table according to their rank. Those who were closer in friendship to the bridegroom sat closer to him, with his bride, at the head of the table. Those who were not as close were given places at the table according to how well he knew them. Jesus teaches this order of rank for the wedding guests in His parable in Luke 14.

> "When thou art bidden of any {man} to a wedding, sit not down in the highest room [place]; lest a more honorable man than thou be bidden of him; (9) And he that bade thee and him come and say to thee, Give this man place; and thou begin with shame to take the lowest room [place]. (10) But when thou art bidden, go and sit down in the lowest room [place]; that when he that bade thee cometh, he may say unto thee, Friend, go up higher: then shalt thou have worship in the presence of them that sit at meat with thee" (Luke 14:8-10).

Two things are revealed in this parable. First, there are ranks of honor in the heavenly wedding feast that correspond to the ranks of rulership in the kingdom to which the wedding guests may attain. Second, the sin of pride, of one thinking more highly of himself than he ought, will help determine the rank each member of the wedding guests will hold in the kingdom (Prov. 11:2; 29:23). Since pride comes from works of the flesh, the believer who is interested in ruling and reigning with Christ in His kingdom must be very careful in the making of his wedding garment to not allow pride to destroy it; for only those who take the humble position here will be given the highest position there.

The Making of the Wedding Garment

To understand specifically how righteous acts, which will form the wedding guests' garments, are accomplished, we need to read the "parable of the pounds."

> "He said therefore, A certain nobleman went into a far country to receive for himself a kingdom, and to return. (13) And he called his ten servants, and delivered them ten pounds, and said unto them, Occupy till I come. (14) But his citizens hated him, and sent a message after him, saying, We

will not have this {man} to reign over us. (15) And it came to pass, that when he was returned, having received the kingdom, then he commanded these servants to be called unto him, to whom he had given the money, that he might know how much every man had gained by trading. (16) Then came the first, saying, Lord, thy pound hath gained ten pounds. (17) And he said unto him, Well, thou good servant: because thou hast been faithful in a very little, have thou authority over ten cities. (18) And the second came, saying, Lord, thy pound hath gained five pounds. (19) And he said likewise to him, Be thou also over five cities. (20) And another came, saying, Lord, behold, {here is} thy pound, which I have kept laid up in a napkin: (21) For I feared thee, because thou art an austere man: thou takest up that thou layedst not down, and reapest that thou didst not sow. (22) And he saith unto him, Out of thine own mouth will I judge thee, {thou} wicked servant. Thou knewest that I was an austere man, taking up that I laid not down, and reaping that I did not sow: (23) Wherefore then gavest not thou my money into the bank, that at my coming I might have required mine own with usury? (24) And he said unto them that stood by, Take from him the pound, and give {it} to him that hath ten pounds. (25) (And they said unto him, Lord, he hath ten pounds.) (26) For I say unto you, That unto every one which hath shall be given; and from him that hath not, even that he hath shall be taken away from him. (27) But those mine enemies, which would not that I should reign over them, bring hither, and slay {them} before me" (Luke 19:12- 27).

The elements of this parable are as follows: (1) The nobleman is Jesus Christ. (2) The far country where he would travel to receive his kingdom (the kingdom of heaven), and then return, represents His ascension into heaven and His return at His second coming. (3) The ten servants represent all the saved of the church period. (4) The ten pounds represent that which each of the saved received equally when they first believed — the sealing of the Holy Spirit (Eph. 1:13). (5) The nobleman's return to receive an accounting of his servants' pounds is the rapture of the church and the judgment seat of Christ (2 Cor. 5:10). (6) The two servants who gained other pounds by trading represent those of the "wedding guests" who, by yielding their lives to the Lordship of Christ (the power of their pound), produced other Christians through their witness. These servants will become rulers over cities on the millennial earth. (7) The third servant, however, who hid his pound, represents those invited to be "wedding guests," who failed to yield their lives to the pound (Holy Spirit), i.e., failed to produce a wedding garment and, as a result, lost their position as wedding guest and lost the inheritance of the kingdom. (7) The remaining seven servants represent apostate Christians, who will lose not only the kingdom, but their lives for one thousand years at the judgment seat of Christ.

How the Wedding Garment Is Made

The parable of the pounds shows how righteous acts, which form the wedding garment, are accomplished. This is seen in the first two servants who gained interest on their pounds by placing them in the bank (same as trading), as opposed to the third servant who hid his pound and attempted to gain others by his own efforts. As the first two servants ceased from their self-efforts and put their pounds in the bank (power) of the Holy Spirit sealed within them, the third servant put his pound in a napkin (Gr. sweatcloth), which represents his own works. Hence, the first two servants allowed Christ to control their lives and their witness and to make interest (other believers) by the power of the Holy Spirit through them. All this was done in obedience to the Word, while they themselves (their inner-selves) sat down and rested by faith in Christ. The third servant, however, hid the power of his pound (the power of the Holy Spirit) in the works of his flesh (represented by the sweatcloth) and produced nothing, spiritually (John 15:5). As a result, he produced no wedding garment and lost a position in the kingdom as a wedding guest.

Disposition of the Ten Servants

The first servant received authority (as a king) over ten cities of the earth during the millennial kingdom, while the second received authority over five cities. Here, their ranks of rulership are established in accordance with what each had accomplished with the one pound that each was given. Therefore, the servant who gained ten pounds from his one pound became ruler over ten cities; the servant who gained only five pounds became ruler over five cities. The third servant worked in the efforts of the flesh (with his pound hidden in his sweatcloth), so he failed to gain any other pounds. Everything was taken from him, and he lost all hope of entering the kingdom and ruling over any cities. Finally, at the judgment seat of Christ, the last seven of the ten servants not only lost the kingdom, but also their redeemed bodies for a thousand years. For in this parable, Christ commanded that they be brought "hither" (Gr. *hode,* meaning to this same spot, i.e., the judgment seat of Christ, where He awarded crowns of rulership to the first two servants) and slain before Him. A careful study will show that these seven servants represent a great company of believers (citizens, verse 14) who will become enemies (verse 27) of their Lord by refusing to have Him rule over their lives, which He bought with His own blood. They will be apostates, fallen from grace (not out of grace) (Gal. 5:4), by totally dishonoring the pound (the Holy Spirit) that was given to them and sealed in them the moment they were saved (Eph. 1:13; 4:30).

All ten servants of our parable can be identified as living in these last days of the church period. The first two servants represent a very small minority of the church who allow Christ to control their lives and witness, while the third servant represents the majority of church members who are busily involved in church programs while trusting in their own abilities. A Christ-controlled life produces works of faith (1 Thess. 1:3), while self-effort produces works of self. A Christ-controlled life produces spiritual works, which glorify Christ; self-effort produces works of the flesh, which glorify self, the church, and the denomination. The third group (citizens who become enemies of the Lord), however, represents the believers who altogether leave Christ, the church, and the fellowship of other Christians and become totally involved in the world.

A Comparing of the Two Parables

It is the belief of the writer that the parables of the "wedding feast" and the "pounds" represent the same group of people, the wedding guests, who will gain a position of rulership in the kingdom. These, called the "chosen" by our Lord, are those who will be called-out of the called (the saved).

As the parable of the wedding feast speaks of the future *position* of the "chosen" in the kingdom, the parable of the pounds speaks of that which is necessary for them to *attain* to the kingdom. Where the parable of the wedding feast speaks of the honor and glory associated with the marriage of the Lamb, the parable of the pounds speaks of the honor, glory, and authority in the kingdom. As the parable of the wedding feast reveals various ranks of honor at the table of the wedding feast, the parable of the pounds reveals various ranks of rulership over the earth during the kingdom.

A Defective Viewpoint

A defective viewpoint can be taught by kingdom teachers and preachers by misinterpreting the parable of the "wedding feast." One such teacher whom the writer is acquainted with believes that the wedding guests of this parable represent the bride of Christ. But this cannot be for the three following reasons: First, Israel was originally invited to come to the wedding feast as the wedding guests, but they refused (Matt. 22:2-8). If they had accepted this invitation, they would have become, according to this view, the bride of Christ. This would, in turn, invalidate all the types in the Old Testament that speak of the bride, since they all show the bride of Christ as a Gentile bride. Second, the wedding guests, historically speaking, had no part in the actual marriage ceremony, only in the feast which took place after the ceremony. As an example, Jesus and his disciples were called to the wedding feast at Cana as guests (John 2:1-2), but were not part of the bride or the bridal party. Third, at all Jewish weddings, the guests wore a garment different from the bride's. How, then, can one say that both garments represent, spiritually, the bride's garment in heaven? It must be that each garment (the guests' and the bride's) has its own heavenly counterpart.

CONFIRMATION OF THE FAITHFUL

This section will introduce the "church which is built upon a rock"; a higher calling of saints who will be selected out of the "chosen" (the wedding guests) and the "called" (the body of Christ) and designated as the "faithful." In Rev. 17:14b, these "faithful," who are pictured with Christ at His coming, represent the "bride of Christ," and are described as **"called, and chosen, and faithful"**; or the "faithful" ones who have been selected out of the "called" (as the "chosen") and, then, out of the "chosen."

We get a further look at the "faithful" in Rev. 19:7-8, when she is called the "wife" of the "Lamb." **"Let us be glad and rejoice, and give honor to him: for the marriage of the Lamb is come, and his wife hath made herself ready. (8) And to her was granted that she should be arrayed in fine linen, clean and white: for the fine linen is the righteousness [plural] of saints."** It is important to see that at the time the apostle John first heard these words in heaven (before he wrote them down), the actual marriage ceremony of the Lamb had already taken place. The Greek language bears this out by placing verse 7 in the aorist indicative mood, active voice. Thus, it could have been better translated, **"...for the marriage of the Lamb came and His wife prepared herself."** It follows that because the ceremony is over and His wife had prepared herself for it, she is now given the right to be clothed in her bridal garment to take her rightful place at the next event — the wedding supper. Her garment is fine linen, clean and white (Gr. *bright and pure*), and stands for the righteousness (Gr. *righteous acts*) of the saints, which was continuously produced through her as she rested in Christ and obeyed His Word (verse 8). Apparently, the wedding garment of the bride will be a grander, loftier, more magnificent one than the garments of the wedding guests, who will be called to the marriage supper.

The Bride Historically

As we have revealed the historical elements of the Jewish wedding feast and the wedding guests, we will do the same with the Jewish wedding and the bride.

Tradition tells us that in New Testament times, the wedding ceremony was always preceded by a special formality of betrothal (we call this the engagement). The man, at the betrothal, would give the woman money and/or a letter that expressed that he was espoused to her. This espousal was binding under the law in all matters, such as inheritance and adultery. If the woman broke the espousal agreement by not being faithful to her espoused, there would be need of a formal divorce. This betrothal period lasted until the wedding ceremony was performed and generally preceded the wedding for no more than a year. A legal document at the time of the betrothal also fixed the dowry, which was brought by the woman to her husband at marriage.

On the evening (by custom, Wednesday) of the marriage (Heb. *Nissuin, Chathnuth*), the bride was led from her paternal home to either her husband's home or to a place where they would meet for the wedding. In this procession, she was led by the friends of the bridegroom with music, torch light, and light from lamp poles. Along the way, nuts were given to the children and other gifts to the adults. The bride could not be recognized because of her veil. When she arrived at the designated place for the weddding, she was led to her husband and the marriage formula was recited. In this formula, the husband made his vows much as the wedding vows are made today, promising to work and to keep her. The bride and groom were then crowned with garlands and the formal legal marriage instrument, called, in Hebrew, the *kethubah,* was signed. This was followed by the washing of the hands and the benediction, and they were escorted into the wedding feast. The marriage supper traditionally began with a filled cup of wine. Then the bridal prayer and benediction were given. Although most wedding feasts lasted for several days (some as much as a week), the bride and groom only attended the first night. After this, they left the feast and were led by the "friends of the bridegroom" to the bridal chamber and bed (Heb. *Cheder and the chuppah*).

With this historical division between the bride and the wedding guests, how can anyone interpret the *wedding guests* and the *bride* in our Lord's parables as the same?

The Spiritual Significance

Returning to Rev. 19:7-8, we will again consider the bride of Christ. But this time, we will examine her high position in relation to the wedding guests, who are revealed in the next verse (Rev. 19:9).

At this place in the scripture, God reveals that the people who are called to the heavenly wedding feast, in verse 9, represent a different group of people from those who will be the wife of the Lamb, in verses 7 and 8. For as the bride, at this point, has already been married to the Lamb and is called the "wife" of the Lamb (Gr. aorist indicative active), those in verse 9 are only now being called to the wedding feast as a result of a finished action of God in their lives (Gr. perfect participle passive). Therefore, our Lord is obviously showing us the heavenly counterpart of the earthly wedding, which has both a bride and wedding guests.

In the heavenly wedding, there is, first, the spiritual betrothal, i.e., our Lord, in His sovereign election, calling out certain saints of the church period to be His bride. At the time of this betrothal (our present time on earth), our Lord gives His first call to the other church saints to prepare to come to the wedding feast. Second, on the day of the wedding, the bride is escorted from her paternal home (rapture of all believers), with her veil on (she cannot be recognized as a member of the bride), to the Bridegroom's home, where she will be selected out from all believers. This will occur in the evening time, i.e., in the evening time of this present dispensation. Third, at the judgment seat of Christ, the faithful bride and the chosen will be revealed by being called-out of the called and given their spiritual bodies through the heavenly resurrection (Gr. meaning out-resurrection) of Phil. 3:11. It could be that this translation, or out-resurrection, of the redeemed body (Rom. 8:23) into the spiritual body is, in itself, connected to the wedding garment.

Whether or not there will be an actual wedding ceremony in heaven after the out-resurrection occurs is not known, though it seems to be implied in Rev. 19:7-8, when the bride is called the "wife" of the Lamb before the wedding feast begins. If there is such a ceremony, possibly the bride, the Lamb, God the Father and the friends of the bridegroom (certain Old Testament saints) will be the only ones in attendance, according to its earthly counterpart. Although we do not know what will take place at this ceremony (perhaps it will be the official establishing of the bride of Christ, as well as the various ranks of authority for its members), we do know, from scripture, that at its completion, the members of the bride will be granted the privilege of putting on the wedding garment, as seen in Rev. 19:8, and of entering the wedding feast; a feast that will be filled with wedding guests who have received their second invitation at the judgment seat of Christ; a feast where all the wedding guests will be seated around the table according to their individual rank of honor.

In Luke 12:35-40, Jesus gives us another parable concerning the heavenly wedding. This parable speaks of Him returning from the wedding, which has already been prepared in heaven, at the time of the rapture to catch out His bride.

The Wedding Garment of the Bride

The bride, like the wedding guests, will have on a wedding garment that will be emblematic of her righteous works accomplished in this lifetime; works that have been produced by the Lordship of Jesus Christ through her yielded life in obedience to the Word of God. However, the righteous acts of the bride will be of a much higher order than those of the wedding guests. They will not only have been produced by a continuing faith in the Lordship of Christ over their lives (salvation of the soul), but by a "lively hope" (1 Pet. 1:1-3), which the wedding guests will not have experienced in this life.

When this "hope" is seen by believers who are candidates for the bride, it becomes the most powerful motivating force in their lives. Hope is produced from understanding the "above knowledge" (Gr. *epignosis*), which speaks of the coming kingdom and the fear of the Lord (Prov. 9:10; 2 Cor. 5:10-11; Eph. 1:17). Hope is the understanding of the riches of His inheritance to the saints (Eph. 1:18); it brings forth fruit (Col. 1:5-6); it is a mystery that reveals the riches and glory of the kingdom (Col. 1:27); it is a crown of rejoicing given for soul- winning (not spirit-winning) (1 Thess. 2:19); it is the hope of a higher salvation — entrance into the kingdom (1 Thess. 5:8). Hope anticipates the appearing of Christ (Tit. 2:13); it makes us heirs in the kingdom (Tit. 3:7); it is an anchor to our souls (Heb. 6:19); it is the power of our witness (1 Pet. 3:15); it purifies our souls (1 John 3:3). If we hold fast to hope, it makes us members of Christ's house (the bride) (Heb. 3:6). Hope differs from faith. Faith claims what God says is already ours; hope anticipates that which can be ours if we hold fast the confidence and the rejoicing of hope firm unto the end (Heb. 3:6). Hope, which is a mystery to most Christians, produces a higher order of righteous works. Yet, this mystery is Christ Himself in us, "the hope of glory" (Col. 1:27). In summary, the righteous works of faith and hope make up the wedding garment of the bride.

The Making of the Bride's Wedding Garment:

To understand specifically how the bride's wedding garment is made, the reader must study two parables that speak of it; the parable of the "ten virgins" (Matt. 25:1-13) and the parable of the "talents" (Matt. 25:14-30).

The Parable of the Ten Virgins

"Then shall the kingdom of heaven be likened unto ten virgins, which took their lamps, and went forth to meet the bridegroom. (2) And five of them were wise, and five {were} foolish. (3) They that {were} foolish took their lamps, and took no oil with them: (4) But the wise took oil in their vessels with their lamps. (5) While the bridegroom tarried, they all slumbered and slept. (6) And at midnight there was a cry made, Behold, the bridegroom cometh; go ye out to meet him. (7) Then all those virgins arose, and trimmed their lamps. (8) And the foolish said unto the wise, Give us of your oil; for our lamps are gone out. (9) But the wise answered, {Not so}; lest there be not enough for us and you: but go ye rather to them that sell, and buy for yourselves. (10) And while they went to buy, the bridegroom came; and they that were ready went in with him to the marriage: and the door was shut. (11) Afterward came also the other virgins, saying, Lord, Lord, open to us. (12) But he answered and said, Verily I say unto you, I know you not. (13) Watch therefore, for ye know neither the day nor the hour wherein the Son of man cometh" (Matt. 25:1- 13).

This parable represents all the believers who will be saved during the church period, since the number *ten* is the Biblical number for "ordinal perfection," meaning *all*, i.e., all the saved. God further divides these ten into two groups of five, showing that both groups are saved (five is the Biblical number for "grace"). These two groups, then, represent two kinds of Christian believers who will appear at the judgment seat of Christ — one group is foolish and the other is wise (verse 2).

The foolish in this parable have only one portion of oil in their lamps, while the wise have a double portion — one in their lamps and one in a vessel with their lamps. The single portion of oil in the lamps speaks of the Holy Spirit, which was given to all ten virgins when they were saved (same as the pounds in the parable of the pounds); whereas the double portion speaks of the "higher wisdom" of the kingdom, which gives "hope" to the five who are wise. Thus, the wedding garment of the bride is not only made from the righteous acts produced by the single portion of Holy Spirit through their lives (same as the wedding guests), but also from the righteous acts produced by the second portion of the Spirit, i.e., "the hope of glory" (Col. 1:27). Notice that while all ten virgins were raptured, only five entered the wedding chamber (compare with Luke 13:24-25).

Summarily, the scope of teaching in this parable is to show the difference between those who will enter the marriage and those who will not. The five "wise" are the only ones of the ten who will enter the marriage, or bridal chamber, in heaven. The double portion of the Spirit, which the five wise possessed and which was necessary for them to have to enter the marriage, had to be purchased from those who sell, i.e., the Holy Spirit (verse 9); purchased daily with the price of a continuously surrendered life; surrendered to Christ as Lord of the life in obedience to His Word, and in the light of the hope of glory.

The Parable of the Talents

For {the kingdom of heaven is} as a man traveling into a far country, {who} called his own servants, and delivered unto them his goods. (15) And unto one he gave five talents, to another two, and to another one; to every man according to his several ability; and straightway took his journey. (16) Then he that had received the five talents went and traded with the same, and made {them} other five talents. (17) And likewise he that {had received} two, he also gained other two. (18) But he that had received one went and digged in the earth, and hid his lord's money. (19) After a long time the lord of those servants cometh, and reckoneth with them. (20) And so he that had received five talents came and brought other five talents, saying, Lord, thou deliveredst unto me five talents: behold, I have gained beside them five talents more. (21) His lord said unto him, Well done, {thou} good and faithful servant: thou hast been faithful over a few things, I will make thee ruler over many things: enter thou into the joy of thy lord. (22) He also that had received two talents came and said, Lord, thou deliveredst unto me two talents: behold, I have gained two other talents beside them. (23) His lord said unto him, Well done, good and faithful servant; thou hast been faithful over a few things, I will make thee ruler over many things: enter thou into the joy of thy lord. (24) Then he which had received the one talent came and said, Lord, I knew thee that thou art an hard man, reaping where thou hast not sown, and gathering where thou hast not strawed: (25) And I was afraid, and went and hid thy talent in the earth: lo, {there} thou hast {that is} thine. (26) His lord answered and said unto him, {Thou} wicked and slothful servant, thou knewest that I reap where I sowed not, and gather where I have not strawed: (27) Thou oughtest therefore to have put my money to the exchangers, and {then} at my coming I should have received mine own with usury. (28) Take therefore the talent from him, and give {it} unto him which hath ten talents. (29) For unto every one that hath shall be given, and he shall have abundance: but from him that hath not shall be taken away even that which he hath. (30) And cast ye the unprofitable servant into outer darkness: there shall be weeping and gnashing of teeth" (Matt. 25:14-30).

Unlike the parable of the pounds (Luke 19:12-27), this parable speaks of only three servants out of the ten. This draws our attention to the fact that Christ, here, is not dealing with all the saved, but only the few; those who, under the sovereignty of God, are called to be betrothed to Christ as His bride.

The man traveling into a far country is Christ (verse 14). Before He left, He called three of His servants and gave to them His goods (Gr. *huparchonta,* meaning His personal possessions) according to each servant's personal abilities, and then took His journey, i.e., went back to heaven (verse 15). The first servant received five talents, the second servant two, and the third, one. The first two servants went and traded their talents and, as a result, doubled their amount of talents (verse 16-17). The third, however, did nothing with his talent; instead, he hid it in the earth (verse 18). After a long time (two thousand years), the Lord of those servants came back to reckon with them regarding what they had done with His goods (verse 19). This reckoning refers to the judgment seat of Christ, which will occur immediately after the rapture of the church (1 Thess. 4:16-17; 2 Cor. 5:10). The results of that judgment in our parable shows us that the first two servants, who doubled their talents, were called "good and faithful" and were allowed to enter the "joy" of the Lord (the kingdom). The third servant, however, was cast into outer darkness, outside of the kingdom, for one thousand years.

All three servants in this parable were saved, since the Lord called them His "own servants" (no lost man is ever called a personal servant of the Lord). Also, they appeared before the judgment seat of Christ, where no lost man will ever appear. Some teach that the third servant was saved, but lost his salvation and went to hell. However, the Bible teaches that losing one's salvation is impossible. Others teach that the three servants of the parable represent the lost in their attempt to produce good works to get into heaven. Two of them made it and one did not. This false teaching is obviously in error in light of scripture, which explicity says "not of works lest any man should boast" (Eph. 2:9).

The true teaching of our parable is that while all three servants were saved and will have eternal life in heaven, only two attained to the millennial kingdom of heaven (the joy of the Lord), where they will be privileged to rule and reign "over many things" as the bride of Christ (verses 21, 23,). The third servant, on the other hand, was cast into the darkness (Gr. *skotos*, meaning obscurity) outside the kingdom for one thousand years. This was the result of his failure to produce any righteous works (representing the higher wisdom, or double portion of the Spirit) from his talent; thus, he failed to produce a bridal wedding garment for himself.

How the Bridal Wedding Garment Is Made

Unlike the wedding guest's garment, the bride's wedding garment will apparently be made from the righteous works of a higher wisdom; a wisdom that produces the "hope" of the kingdom in the lives of the betrothed. To be a candidate for the bride, a believer must, first, be surrendered to the Lordship of Jesus Christ over his life through the leadership of the Holy Spirit in accordance to the Word (same qualifications for the wedding guests). Second, he must go on into perfection (maturing of his faith) by receiving and being faithful to the personal property of Jesus Christ, i.e., His "goods," or talents, which represent this higher wisdom (Gr. *epignosis*). However, God does not permit all believers to go on into this perfection (Heb. 6:3); only those whom He has elected. If the reader has been privileged to see these truths during the course of this book, then he is obligated, as the betrothed bride of Christ, to go on into perfection (maturity) by being faithful to the Lord in these higher truths.

Our parable tells us that the first two servants (types of the bride) produced righteous works through a partnership that was made up of the power of the talents (His goods) and their personal abilities. Thus, by exercising their different abilities while resting in the power of "Christ, the hope of glory" (Col, 1:27b), they automatically produced the material for their wedding garments. The third servant, however, having seen the higher wisdom of the kingdom, failed to rest in its power and, as a result, produced no spiritual fruit. Instead, he hid his power in the earth (representing a worldly life) and lost his position as the bride, being called a "wicked and slothful" servant (Gr. hurtful and lazy servant) by his Lord.

Finally, by joining the truths from the parables of the ten virgins and the talents, we can clearly see two things that must be done by the believer in order to become a member of the bride of Christ. First, a believer must "see" the kingdom (become spiritually wise) and, then, "hope" for it to the end. Second, he must trust in Christ for the results that can be obtained from the talents as they flow through his personal abilities. This trust includes the losing of one's life here to gain it there; surrendering, or selling it, here to buy the double portion of oil for there; and depositing the talents in the bank (power) of the Holy Spirit here to earn interest through the believer's exercised abilities for there.

The Name of the Bride

By returning to Rev. 17:14, we see that the bride of Christ is called "faithful." Armed with this truth, we are able to identify her in the parables that deal with the kingdom of heaven; for wherever in scripture our Lord speaks of the bride, He calls her "faithful." We see this in comparing the parable of the pounds with the parable of the talents. For Christ, in the parable of the pounds, called his faithful servants *good* servants (Luke 19:17a); whereas in the parable of the talents, He called them *good and faithful* servants. This is further proof that the servants in the parable of the pounds cannot be a part of the bride; they do not have the title of the bride. They must, then, be the "chosen" and the same as the "wedding guests" (Matt. 22:14).

To further confirm this conclusion, there were ten servants in the parable of the pounds, representing all the saved. Each was given one pound (Gr. *mina*, worth one hundred days wages, or about twenty dollars). It is believed by the writer that the two servants in the parable of the pounds who gained authority over cities represent those from whom God is presently calling-out the candidates for the bride (the betrothed). This belief is on the basis that there are no others from whom they could come. According to our parable, they are the ones who were permitted to go on into maturity (Heb. 6:3) and, in accordance with their personal abilities, were given different amounts of talents (Gr. *denarii*, worth about six thousand dollars each, or three hundred times more than the pound). These gifts of great price should, by themselves, alert us to the fact that these two groups cannot represent the same group.

To each of the servants in the parable of the pounds, our Lord gave a pound, representing the doctrines that teach of the first coming of Christ, the cross, salvation of the spirit, cleansing of sins, the rapture, judgment and even the Lordship of Christ. These doctrines are better known as the "first principles of Christ" (Heb. 6:1-2), or the "milk" doctrines of the Word (Heb. 5:12; I Cor. 3:1-3). The talents of great price that were given to the candidates for the bride represent the doctrines that teach of the second coming of Christ, the salvation of the soul, the coming kingdom and the bride, who will rule and reign with Christ as co-heirs with Him over the kingdom (Rom. 8:17). These are better known as "meat" doctrines of the Word, which bring the believer to a "full age" (Heb. 5:14; 1 Cor. 3:2). Hence, the talent speaks of the great price of the hidden mystery that God ordained before the world unto our glory (1 Cor. 2:7).

The Two Levels of the Bride

The parables further reveal that two groups of believers will make up the bride of Christ. Both groups will be selected out of the "chosen" at the judgment seat of Christ and called the "faithful." The first group will be made up of selected Christian lay people with their scores of different personal abilities; the second will be made up of Bible pastors and teachers with the ability to teach the kingdom truths, i.e., to give meat in due season. The first is revealed in the parable of the "talents" (Matt. 25:14-30); the second in the parable of the "faithful and wise servant" (Matt. 24: 45-51). The first will be made rulers over "many things" (verse 21,23); the second will be made rulers over **"all his goods"** (verse 47), or according to Luke 12:44, over **"all that he hath."**

Closing Thoughts to this Section

It is the writer's belief that the "church" of Matt. 16:18b that Jesus said He would build upon a rock is none other than the bride of Christ, which would be established on the "hope" of the coming kingdom. The church, then, is synonymous with the bride of Christ; apparently, it will be built from the "chosen," who, in turn, will be called-out of the "called."

The coming kingdom of heaven may be structured to have hundreds of levels of rulers. In this section, we have seen the difference between the wedding guests, who will have various ranks of rule, and the bride, who will be ruling "over much" or ruling over "all that He hath." Finally, above this structure of kings and lords, there will be the "King of kings and Lord of lords," the Lord Jesus Christ Himself.

"...and the gates of hell [sheol] shall not prevail against it" (Matt. 16:18c). These last words of Christ concerning the church tell us that the graves ("gates of the dead") shall not prevail against the church, since the dead bodies will be resurrected at the coming of the Lord (the rapture) into redeemed bodies for the purpose of being judged at the judgment seat of Christ. **"For we must all appear before the judgment seat of Christ; that every one may receive the things {done} in {his} body, according to that he hath done, whether {it be} good or bad"** (2 Cor. 5:10).

THE POWER OF THE CHURCH

"And I will give unto thee the keys of the kingdom of heaven:..." (Matt. 16:19a).

Contrary to popular belief, the keys to the kingdom of heaven are not automatically given to every minister when he is called into the gospel ministry. Only Peter was given these keys by our Lord, and they were used to unlock the three doors to all the saved of humanity for the receiving of the power of the Holy Spirit that all believers might produce works necessary to enter the kingdom.

To the Jews

Because Peter was present, the first key of the kingdom of heaven opened the door to the believing Jews on the day of Pentecost. As a result, they received the filling of the Holy Ghost (Acts 2:4). Without delay, he preached to the multitude in Jerusalem, explaining the phenomenon of speaking in foreign languages by the disciples. He told them that this signaled the arrival of the Holy Spirit to fill and empower the church.

At no prior time had the Holy Spirit ever been on earth in this capacity, though God fills all His universe, all of the time, with His Holy Spirit. At Pentecost, however, the Holy Spirit came specifically to fill and empower believers to produce spiritual fruit necessary to enter the kingdom. So far, He has fulfilled this office for almost two thousand years, and He will continue to do so until the rapture of the church occurs. Then He will leave the earth and return to heaven along with all the saved of the church period. In this capacity, the Holy Ghost is the Spirit of truth (the resurrected Christ), who has been sent from heaven by Christ, the Head of the church (John 14:16-18). Furthermore, the coming of the Holy Spirit on the day of Pentecost could not have happened unless the Lord Jesus Christ Himself had been exalted and glorified at the right hand of God the Father (Acts 2:32,33; John 7:39). The Head of the church had to be established before the body of the church could be called into existence.

To the Half-Jew and Half-Gentile

By Peter laying his hands on the Samaritan believers, he used the second key to open the door to all half-Jew and half-Gentile believers that they might receive the filling and power of the Holy Spirit (no speaking in tongues was evidenced here — Acts 8:14-17). Notice that while the Samaritans were already saved under the preaching of Philip, they had not yet received the Holy Spirit in *power;* nor could they until Peter had laid his hands upon them.

To the Gentiles

By Peter preaching to Cornelius, a full-blooded Gentile, and revealing Jesus Christ as the only way to salvation, he used the third and final key to the kingdom of heaven. As a result of Cornelius' salvation under Peter's preaching, as evidenced by his speaking in tongues, all Gentiles everywhere can be assured that the door of salvation and power has also been opened to them (Acts 10:34-48).

Once Peter opened the three doors to all saved humanity (Jew, half-Jew and Gentile) with the keys of the kingdom, they would never be closed again during the dispensation of grace. Hence, all men who would live during the dispensation of grace (from Pentecost to the rapture) would have the privilege of being sealed and empowered by the Holy Spirit at the moment they believed on the Lord Jesus Christ for salvation. Thus, in this work of grace, they not only would receive the Holy Spirit as the *Spirit of life* for salvation, but also the *Spirit of power* to attain to the kingdom.

Spirit of Life versus Spirit of Power

Scripture tells us that all believers, whether Jew, partly-Jew, or Gentile, who live during the dispensation of grace (from Pentecost to the rapture), receive both the *Spirit of life* and the *Spirit of power* the very moment they believe on Jesus as Saviour.

In contrast to this, all believers who were saved after the time of the cross, but before the time of Pentecost (a fifty-day period), received only the the *Spirit of life* until Pentecost was come. At Pentecost, they received, in addition, the *Spirit of power.*

In further contrast to this, all the Old Testament saints, who lived and died before the time of the cross, could not receive the "Spirit of life" until Jesus Christ had come and paid for their sins on the cross and then descended to the paradise section of the lower earth, where they were waiting for Him. At this time, they received the "Spirit of life" (perhaps by Christ breathing on them), but not the "Spirit of power," since that could only be given at Pentecost to living believers.

Scripture tells us that after Christ had died on the cross and spent three days in the *paradise* section of sheol with the Old Testament saints, He emptied it by moving them all to the *paradise* section of the third heaven (2 Cor. 12:2-4). All this was done in an open show of victory over death and sin ("He led captivity captive") (Eph. 4:8) while He "gave gifts unto men." After His resurrection and before His ascension, Christ appeared back on earth and gave the *Spirit of life* to all believers who were alive. This is seen specifically in John 20:22, when "**...he breathed on {them} [His disciples], and saith unto them, Receive ye the Holy Ghost.**"

It is important, at this point, to understand that those who had received the Holy Ghost before Pentecost, received only *the Spirit of life,* i.e., eternal life, since the *Spirit of power* (the Holy Spirit in power) had not yet been given. The *Spirit of power* could not be given until after Jesus had been exalted and glorified at the right hand of the Father and had became the "Head" of the body of Christ. There could be no body without the Head; and there could be no power to the body until the Head had been established (John 7:39; Acts 2:32-33). This occured at Pentecost, fifty days after His resurrection.

Also, it is important to keep in mind that before the death and resurrection of Jesus Christ, the Holy Spirit was never "sealed" in believers; He only came upon them. After Pentecost, however, He was sealed in all believers the moment they believed in (Gr. *into*) Jesus as Saviour (Eph. 1:13). This sealing gave the believer not only the *Spirit of life,* but also the *Spirit of power;* life to enter heaven by grace through faith, and power (keys) to enter the kingdom of heaven by works of faith.

A believer, then, must believe that he has the authority (power) of the Holy Spirit to produce the works of God through a yielded life; a life daily surrendered to Christ that progressively dies to self, to the flesh, and to the world. Only then can he produce that preordained in heaven for him to produce, i.e., "**... whatsoever thou shalt bind on earth shall be bound in heaven: and whatsoever thou shalt loose on earth shall be loosed in heaven**" (Matt. 16: 19b). It is sad to say, but most Christians will never use the Spirit of power given to them when they were saved; because they are not willing to deny themselves, or take up their cross and follow Him, or lose their life (life in this world) for His sake. They want to profit from this world. They are eagerly willing to exchange their soul, giving up the riches of the glory of His inheritance in the coming kingdom, for the trinkets of this world. Therefore, when the Son of man shall come in the glory of His Father, they will not receive the reward of the kingdom, even though they are saved (Matt. 16:24-27). They will be cast into the outer darkness, or in the case of apostates, be consigned to Gehenna for a thousand years.

THE APPEARANCE OF THE CHURCH

> "And after six days Jesus taketh Peter, James, and John his brother, and bringeth them up into an high mountain apart, (2) And was transfigured before them: and his face did shine as the sun, and his raiment was white as the light. (3) And, behold, there appeared unto them Moses and Elias talking with him" (Matt. 17:1-3).

In the opening verses of Matthew 17, a miniature picture is given of the second coming of Christ, accompanied by His church. Its beginning words **("And after six days...")** speak of God's prophetic time calendar that means **"after six thousand years"**; because "one day is with the Lord as a thousand years...(2 Pet. 3:8b). Thus, the expression *after six days* must speak of the millennial reign of Christ, which is in the seventh day, or the seventh one thousand years. Bible chronologists presently place the human race near the end of the sixth day, or six thousandth year, of God's prophetic calendar, which began at the creation of Adam and Eve in the garden of Eden. Some have even estimated that our present time is in the 5990's.

In our text, Jesus takes Peter, James and John up into a high mountain (Mt. Herman). These three apostles typify the favored of Israel (the *peculiar treasure*), who will be privileged to be in the kingdom of heaven. The high mountain typifies the government of the kingdom. Jesus, in His transfiguration, typifies His second coming, in glory, to set up His kingdom. Moses and Elijah typify the church (His bride), who will accompany Him. Some of the church will be raised from the dead at the rapture, typified by Moses, who was raised from the dead (Jude 1:9). Others of the church will be translated at the rapture, typified by Elijah, who was translated into heaven. The nine apostles, who were not permitted to go up into the mountain to receive this special wisdom, typify saved Israel in the millennial land without any kingdom authority (note: these nine had no power to perform miracles during this time; verses 14-17).

To shed further light upon these types, our text is given immediately after Matt. 16:28, which reads: **"Verily I say unto you, There be some standing here, which shall not taste of death, till they see the Son of man coming in his kingdom."** Jesus was referring to Peter, James and John, who would not taste death until they had seen Jesus coming in His kingdom in type form. This occurance is recorded in the next three verses. Peter confirms this in his epistle (2 Pet. 1:16-19) when he states that he was an eyewitness to the majesty of Jesus Christ coming in His power, and that this occurred on the holy mount (the mountain of our text). Because of this experience, Peter further states, **"We [all three apostles who were present] have also a more sure word of prophecy...."** This sure word speaks of the importance of prophecy concerning Christ's return to establish His kingdom. It is as a light that shines into a dark place until the day dawns; it gives our lives spiritual illumination, hope and expectation until Christ comes. Many in these last days ridicule those who study prophecy. Yet, our Lord tells us that the personal **"testimony of Jesus is the spirit of prophecy"** (Rev. 19:10b). Prov. 4:18 reveals that the path of the just is as a shining light; a light that is a sure word of prophecy; a light that is the testimony of Jesus Christ; a light that is the path itself, i.e., the believer's walk of righteousness; a light that shines more and more unto the perfect day (the day of Christ's coming in power).

Returning to Matt. 17, we understand by the question they asked Jesus in verse 10 that the three apostles knew the meaning of the vision they had seen. For they asked, **"Why then say the scribes that Elias [Elijah] must first come?"** The scribes had taught, from Mal. 4:5-6, that before their Messiah would come to establish the promised kingdom, Elijah must come as a witness. The apostles, recognizing that the vision of the transfiguration spoke of Jesus as the Messiah, asked why John the Baptist came as a witness instead of Elijah. Jesus replied that John the Baptist was a type of Elijah (verse 12-13) and would have been Elijah if they (the Jews) would have received it, i.e., the kingdom (compare with Matt. 11:14). Hence, our Lord, knowing that the Jews would reject His kingdom, sent John the Baptist in the spirit of Elijah before His first coming. John the Baptist was that other messenger who had been prophesied as **"the voice of one crying in the wilderness"** (Matt. 3:3; Mark 1:3; Luke 3:4; Isa. 40:3; Mal. 3:1).

Elijah will truly come as one of two witnesses before that great day of the Lord. He will testify to the whole world of the coming of Christ, will be killed, along with the other witness (probably Moses), will lie in the streets of Jerusalem for three and a half days and will then be raised up again (Rev. 11:3-12). The clue to the identity of these two witnesses is found in Rev. 11:6, when they will have the power to keep it from raining (identifying Elijah) and to turn water into blood (identifying Moses). John the Baptist, on the other hand, never performed any miracles, and when questioned by the leaders of Israel, flatly denied that he was Elijah (John 1:21).

THE TEACHING OF THE CHURCH

Our last miniature picture of the church, in Matt. 18, reveals three major lessons that teach entrance into the kingdom: cleansing, forgiveness and church discipline.

Entrance into the Kingdom

> "And said, Verily I say unto you, Except ye be converted, and become as little children, ye shall not enter into the kingdom of heaven. Whosoever therefore shall humble himself as this little child, the same is greatest in the kingdom of heaven" (Matt. 18:3-4).

These words were spoken by Jesus in response to His disciples' question (verse 1), **"Who is [becoming] the greatest in the kingdom of heaven?"** (Note: the verb *is*, in the Greek, is in the present indicative active tense.) This chapter, then, begins with the disciples simply wanting to know who would be the greatest in the coming kingdom. Jesus' answer was given in two parts. First, He took a child and set him in their midst and said to his disciples that a believer could not enter the kingdom of heaven unless he changed and became as a little child. Second, He told them that those who enter the kingdom humble as a little child will be the greatest.

In this section of Matthew, we are immediately introduced to what the church of these last days should be teaching. However, they are failing to do so because of their lack of knowledge and disregard for the Word of God. For over a thousand years, all truths were lost under the papal church system. Beginning in the days of Martin Luther, they began to be slowly recovered. The first truth recovered was salvation by grace through faith — plus nothing. Later (between 1750 and 1900), the truths concerning the rapture, the tribulation and the primary knowledge surrounding the second coming of our Lord were recovered. Now, in these last days, the truths concerning the kingdom are slowly being recovered; truths that speak of inheritance for faithful believers; truths of the rewards that will be given to those who diligently seek Him (Heb. 11:6). The importance of these truths is mentioned throughout Matthew. But in the eighteenth chapter, they are clearly set forth as being the most important and significant to our Lord; truths that should be taught by the church to every believer.

According to our text, the believer must become as a little child who lives by totally depending upon his parents. As a little child never worries about the next meal, or where he will sleep, or of thousands of other details of his life, so must the believer live by faith in his heavenly Father. Therefore, only the believer who is converted from trusting in the flesh and the success of this world to totally trusting in God for all things will be qualified to enter the kingdom. Furthermore, the greatness of those who enter the kingdom will be measured according to their humbleness, i.e., their state of submissiveness, in remorse for their sinfulness.

In contrast to this teaching, our Lord reveals what will happen to the believers who fail to enter the kingdom; those who fall away and commit great offenses against the Lord. Emphasized, in this chapter of Matthew, is the great sin of the apostate believer who offends little ones who believe in Christ (verse 6). The Greek word for "offend" is *skandalizo*, which means "to commit an act that will lead someone unaware to ruin." The context, then, not only speaks of literal children who believe in Him, but of all believers who have become as little children and are totally trusting in Christ.

Not only is it possible for a believer to commit this great sin of offense against others, but, according to verses 8 and 9, he can also commit it against himself.

> "Wherefore if thy hand or thy foot offend [Gr. *skandalizo*] thee, cut them off, and cast {them} from thee: it is better for thee to enter into life [the kingdom] halt or maimed, rather than having two hands or two feet to be cast into everlasting [Gr. *aionian*, meaning age] fire. (9) And if thine eye offend thee, pluck it out, and cast {it} from thee: it is better for thee to enter into life [the kingdom] with one eye, rather than having two eyes to be cast into hell [Gehenna] fire" (Matt. 18:8-9).

Again, our Lord reveals to us the possibility of a believer suffering loss of the kingdom and losing his body to the fires of Gehenna for an age, i.e., one thousand years, while his soul goes to the "blackness of darkness" (Jude 1:13b) for an age. Here, our Lord tells us how extremely important it is for all believers to let the Spirit instead of their souls rule their lives. He stresses this importance by saying that it is better to cut off a hand or foot and pluck out an eye, if they lead you to ruin, i.e., keep you out of the kingdom, than to have them all and be cast into Gehenna fire.

To understand the greatest of all punishments for Christians, which will befall apostate believers at the judgment seat of Christ, keep in mind that Jesus was not addressing these words to the lost, but was instructing His disciples, who were saved (verse 1). He was not telling them that the lost may receive eternal life (salvation of the spirit) by cutting off their hands and feet and by plucking out their eyes. This would totally destroy the doctrine of grace which says: **"For by grace are ye saved through faith; and that not of yourselves: {it is} the gift of God: (9) Not of works, lest any man should boast" (Eph. 2:8-9).** No! It is clearly written in the scriptures that there will be a certain company of believers at the judgment seat of Christ who will be slain for their apostasy, i.e., for becoming enemies of Christ while in this life (Luke 19:14,27). Their bodies will be consigned to the fires of Gehenna while their souls spend the millennial age in the blackness of darkness (Psa. 88). Only after the kingdom age is over and the eternal ages are about to begin, will they be resurrected into their spiritual bodies.

The Word of God, in Luke 12:45-46, speaks of apostate teachers who will lose their bodies (be cut in sunder, i.e., bisected) for falling away from their commission to teach the kingdom truths (meat doctrines) and, in so doing, will "offend" others who are also teachers of the Word. They, too, will spend a thousand years in Gehenna before being resurrected. 1 Cor. 15:51-54 speaks of this resurrection, which will occur at the end of the millennial kingdom. Contrary to what traditional theology teaches, this passage is not about the rapture. Only 1 Thess. 4:16-17 teaches the rapture. This can be seen by comparing the two passages. Consider this: (1) 1 Thess. 4:16-17 teaches that the rapture is in two divisions; first the dead will be raised, then the living will be translated; 1 Cor. 15:15-54 speaks of the resurrection in one division; all will be changed at the same moment. (2) In First Thess., the Bible tells of a resurrection that will occur before the millennial kingdom; in First Cor., it speaks of one that will occur after the millennial kingdom when the last trump will sound (Psa. 47:5); when all tears will be wiped away (Rev. 21:4) (compare Isa. 25:8); when death and hell will be destroyed (1 Cor. 15:25-26, 55-56; Rev 20:14).

Most Christians do not want to hear this doctrine taught, for it disturbs their belief; a belief that says that after salvation, a believer can live his life any way he chooses, since all rewards will be automatically and equally given in heaven to all the saved. Therefore, because they are saved and cannot lose their salvation, they believe (because it is implied in the teaching of most churches) that they are free to get the most out of this life by satisfying their own desires and lusts; not knowing, or perhaps not caring, that they are willfully grieving the Holy Spirit, who is sealed in them (Eph. 4:30). Relaxed on their silken cushions of worldly goals and pleasures, they continue to recite to themselves over and over, "...not of works, lest any man should boast." Yet, God tells us in Heb. 10:26-27 that their lives of willful sin will be judged at the judgment seat of Christ, where they have nothing to look forward to except a "fearful looking for of judgment and fiery indignation" from the Lord. Saved? Yes! Have eternal life? Yes! Because Jesus paid it all on the cross. But rich? No! Will they inherit the kingdom? No! They will lose it all by trodding under foot the Son of God, counting the blood of the covenant by which they were sanctified (set apart unto God) an unholy thing, and insulting (doing despite to) the Spirit of grace (Heb. 10:29). Not only will they be spiritual paupers outside the kingdom of heaven — some in outer darkness, some in Gehenna; but after their resurrection at the end of the millennium, they will be spiritual paupers throughout the eternal ages.

Closing Thoughts to This Section

In light of the clarity and exactness of scripture, it is amazing that the church (except for a few individual ones) in these last days has missed these great truths concerning the kingdom; truths that are part of the "all things" of the great commission that the church is commanded to teach to all baptized believers (Matt. 28:19-20); truths that are the substance of the strong meat doctrines of the Word (Heb. 5:13-14). Perhaps for this reason alone, most Christians will suffer loss at the judgment seat of Christ. **"For we know him that hath said, Vengeance {belongeth} unto me, I will recompense, saith the Lord. And again, The Lord shall judge his people"** (Heb. 10:30).

THE FORGIVENESS AND CLEANSING OF THE CHURCH

> Then came Peter to him, and said, Lord, how oft shall my brother sin against me, and I forgive him? till seven times? (22) Jesus saith unto him, I say not unto thee, Until seven times: but, Until seventy times seven" (Matt. 18:21-22).

Another doctrine that should be of paramount interest to Christians who aspire to enter the kingdom is learning to forgive others who trespass against them; for they themselves will not be forgiven by God for their sins against Him (see the Lord's prayer) (Matt. 6:12,14-15) if they do not forgive others. Peter wanted to know how many times he should forgive someone who had sinned against him. He probably thought that seven times was a gracious number of times and, perhaps, too many times. But Jesus answered, "Until seventy times seven."

If taken literally, Jesus' answer would be four hundred ninety times. However, by using the perfect number, seven, and multiplying it by seventy (the perfect number times ten, the number for ordinal perfection), Jesus is saying that as long as the transgressor comes to us and asks for forgiveness, no matter how many times he comes, we are to forgive him. If we do not forgive, then neither will God forgive us our sins. This is seen in the parable of the "certain king and the account of his servant" (verses 23-35).

In light of inheriting the kingdom, a Christian must first be judged as clean. His sins must be forgiven. This is accomplished simply by confessing them to God and repenting of them while in this life (1 John 1:9). When this is done on a moment by moment basis, he is not only cleansed from the sins that he knows about, but, also, he is automatically cleansed from those sins he does not know about ("all unrighteousness"). However, before he can ask God for forgiveness, no matter how many times he has sinned the same sin, he must be willing to forgive others that come to him for forgiveness. In addition, to those who refuse to come to him, and instead, become his adversary, he is not to render evil for evil, but good for evil, while giving them over to the Lord in prayer. For God has said that He will be an adversary to our adversaries and an enemy to our enemies (Ex. 23:22).

THE DISCIPLINE OF THE CHURCH

The spiritual principle given by our Lord to the church in the matter of disciplining another church member is found in Matt. 18:15-17.

> "Moreover if thy brother shall trespass against thee, go and tell him his fault between thee and him alone: if he shall hear thee, thou hast gained thy brother. (16) But if he will not hear {thee, then} take with thee one or two more, that in the mouth of two or three witnesses every word may be established. (17) And if he shall neglect to hear them, tell {it} unto the church: but if he neglect to hear the church, let him be unto thee as an heathen man and a publican."

The smallest congregation of a local church can be two believers (verse 20). But no matter what its size, it must be in the unity of the Spirit, else the Holy Spirit in that church will be grieved and quenched. This is why the church is given the authority (according to our above passage), by our Lord, to dismiss a member from their congregation who refuses to repent. With this action, the church's unity and power from the Holy Spirit can be restored.

When the membership of a local church has removed the leaven from their members and committed themselves to live according to the will of the Lord Jesus Christ, everything done by their membership will already have been ordained in heaven (verse 18). Even two members praying in unity, separately in the will of God and asking for the same thing, will have their prayers answered, since the Holy Spirit, praying through them, can only ask for those things which are already in God's will for Him to give (verse 19).

CONCLUDING THOUGHTS

It has been the burden of the writer to show that the church of Matt. 16:18 does not represent all believers of the church period, but the bride of Christ; a people saved by the blood of Jesus and established on the rock of the kingdom. It was here that Jesus first used the word *church*, which is the highest expression of all the saved. Apparently, they are the "faithful" people of the "chosen," who will be called-out of the "called." They will rule over "all things" and "much" during the kingdom age; whereas the chosen will only rule over cities. Contrary to this, we looked further into the doctrines of outer darkness, the blackness of darkness and Gehenna; places outside the kingdom for all the "called" (saved) who will lose the kingdom and receive their just recompense of reward.

Matt. 17 revealed the church appearing with Christ in His coming kingdom. In Matt. 18, we saw the doctrine of the church, the power of the church and the cleansing of the church.

The writer has further labored to show the bride as a group of people separate from the wedding guests by using the scriptures and pictures from the first century Jewish wedding. While the details of the coming great heavenly wedding cannot be known, we can faintly see the outline of the Biblical truths that govern them.

(For more information, see the author's book *Shock and Surprise Beyond the Rapture*.)

CHAPTER TWELVE

THE TREES OF THE KINGDOM

Many of the church in these last days do not recognize Israel as being a separate people of God. They insist that God is finished with Israel forever and has made the church "spiritual Israel" to take their place. God, however, says something different. He tells us that He has not cast off Israel (Rom. 11:2), and that the church ought not boast against them (Rom. 11:18). Consequently, we know that we have only come out of Israel; we have not become Israel. The Bible, the Saviour who saved us, and the faith we exercise all came to us through Israel. Hence, the church, doctrinally and historically, was founded in Israel and was then brought out as a separate people. This will be seen in the two trees and the vine of the kingdom.

TREES IN SCRIPTURE

A tree in scripture is used to symbolize a national power (Judges 9:8-15; Dan. 4: 10-16, 19-27; Matt. 13:31-32). In Judges, the nations symbolized by the trees seek to elect a king over them. In Daniel 4, Nebuchadnezzar and the Babylonian Empire are symbolized by the great tree that was cut down for seven years. In Matthew 13, the mustard bush, an herb, becomes a tree, or world power. We find two trees and a vine being used to symbolize Israel. In Isaiah 5:1-7, the Lord tells us that the grapevine symbolizes Israel. In Romans 11:17ff, the Lord tells us that the olive tree symbolizes Israel, and in Matthew 21:19; 24:32; Mark 11:12-14, 20 and 21; and Luke 13:6-9, the fig tree symbolizes Israel. In Judges 9:8, the trees of the forest sought the olive tree to reign over them; she refused. In the twelfth verse, they sought the grapevine to reign over them; she refused. In the tenth verse, they sought the fig tree to reign over them; she refused. The olive tree symbolizes Israel in her *covenant relationship* to the Lord. The grapevine symbolizes the *spiritual blessing* Israel is to be to the whole world. The fig tree symbolizes Israel as God's *national witness* to all the world.

As these three symbols of Israel are presented, the reader will note that the vineyard was allowed to go to waste, some branches of the olive tree had to be broken off and the fig tree was cut down. Concerning the doctrinal and historical beginnings of the church, out of one vine (the Lord Jesus Christ) came the Gentile portion of the spiritual seed of Abraham; for Jesus said in John 15:5, "I am the vine, ye [the church] are the branches: He that abideth in me, and I in him, the same bringeth forth much fruit: for without me ye can do nothing." We, again, see this doctrinal and historical beginning in the olive tree, when some of the branches were broken off the natural olive tree (the rejection of Israel by our Lord) and a wild olive tree was grafted in. This wild olive tree symbolizes the Gentile nation (saved Gentiles out of all nations) that God calls the church (see Matt. 21:43; 1 Pet. 2:9).

THE GRAPEVINE

"Now will I sing to my wellbeloved a song of my beloved touching his vineyard. My wellbeloved hath a vineyard in a very fruitful hill: (2) And he fenced it, and gathered out the stones thereof, and planted it with the choicest vine, and built a tower in the midst of it, and also made a winepress therein: and he looked that it should bring forth grapes, and it brought forth wild grapes. (3) And now, O inhabitants of Jerusalem, and men of Judah, judge, I pray you, betwixt me and my vineyard. (4) What could have been done more to my vineyard, that I have not done in it? wherefore, when I looked that it should bring forth grapes, brought it forth wild grapes?" (Isa. 5:1-4)

Israel was chosen by God to be a blessing to the whole world through the symbol of the grapevine. In this parable, God describes how He planted a vineyard in a fruitful hill, protected it, cultivated it, planted the choicest vine and made preparation for the harvest; but it brought forth only wild grapes. This is a picture of God's call to Abram, in Gen. 12:2-3, when He made these seven promises: (1) I will make thee a great nation; (2) I will bless thee; (3) I will make thy name great; (4) thou shalt be a blessing; (5) I will bless them that bless thee; (6) I will curse him that curseth thee; (7) in thee shall all the families of the earth be blessed.

God's protection was upon Abraham, Isaac and Jacob. In our above text, He brought them out of Egypt to plant them in the land (the vineyard). He personally supervised them and gave them laws to govern every human relationship. He gave them the tabernacle and temple services with every detail described for their worship of Him. These details, through types, or foreshadows, even described the first coming of Christ, who would be sacrificed on the altar of the cross. God gave to them His Shekinah glory (His personal presence) and promises of earthly glory and blessings. He gave to them the Word of God and chose Israel to be the people from whom Christ would come. Then, when He looked for grapes, He found "sour grapes." In verse 4, God says, "WHAT MORE COULD I HAVE DONE?"

In Isa. 5:8-30, God pronounced six woes (judgments) upon Israel for their six sins that produced the sour grapes. These sins and judgments are as follows: (1) because of her selfish covetousness, desolation throughout the land would prevail (verses 8-10); (2) because of her joyous revelry and disregard for the services of the Lord, she would go into captivity in deepest humiliation (verse 11-17); (3) because she served iniquity (verse 18-19), (4) because she called evil good and good evil (verse 20), (5) because of self-complacent conceit (verse 21) and (6) because of drunkenness and merriment (verse 22-23), the Lord's anger would be kindled; His hand would be stretched out against her; the nations from afar would dispossess her, keep her captive and cause her unparalleled suffering. All six woes were fulfilled during the captivity of Israel and Judah in the sixth and seventh centuries before Christ.

But about 570 years later, after they were released from their Babylonian captivity, a far greater suffering awaited Judah for their rejection and crucifixion of Jesus, their Messiah. This suffering began by their losing the "kingdom of heaven" to the Gentile church and by being scattered into all the nations. Their rejection of Christ is seen in another parable of the vineyard (the reason for their rejection of Him is revealed in verse 38).

> "Hear another parable: There was a certain householder, which planted a vineyard, and hedged it round about, and digged a winepress in it, and built a tower, and let it out to husbandmen, and went into a far country: (34) And when the time of the fruit drew near, he sent his servants to the husbandmen, that they might receive the fruits of it. (35) And the husbandmen took his servants, and beat one, and killed another, and stoned another. (36) Again, he sent other servants more than the first: and they did unto them likewise. (37) But last of all he sent unto them his son, saying, They will reverence my son. (38) But when the husbandmen saw the son, they said among themselves, This is the heir; come, let us kill him, and let us seize on his inheritance. (39) And they caught him, and cast {him} out of the vineyard, and slew {him}. (40) When the lord therefore of the vineyard cometh, what will he do unto those husbandmen?" (Matt. 21:33-40)

In this parable, the scope of teaching is not on the fruit of Israel (sour grapes) as it was in Isa. 5, but on the husbandmen whom God had placed over His vineyard. After God had broken down the walls of the vineyard, in Isaiah 5, and caused Israel to be taken into captivity, He vacated His throne on earth. As a result, His Shekinah glory (the manifestation on earth of God's presence) went back to heaven (Ezek. 10:18; 11:23), or, according to our parable, "went into a far country" (Matt. 21:33b). At this point, God, in a dispensational way, assumed His eternal title, **"the Lord God of heaven."** When Israel had first entered the land, carrying the ark of the covenant where His presence was manifested, He had taken on His earthly title, **"the Lord of all the earth"** (Josh. 3:11,13). He relinquished that title to Cyrus, who became the ruler of the world at that time: **"Thus saith Cyrus, king of Persia, all the kingdom of the earth hath the Lord God of heaven given me..."** (2 Chron. 36:23). With the bestowment of this title, the Lord God also charged Cyrus to build Him a house at Jerusalem (Ezra 1:2). In the books of Ezra and Nehemiah, God gives us an account of the reestablishment of Israel in the land by Cyrus after the captivity was over. This included the rebuiding of the walls of Jerusalem and the restoration of the temple and of worship. Hence, the vineyard was replanted, the walls were restored, and it was let out to husbandmen.

As we have seen in other chapters, these husbandmen, over a period of time, assumed the titles of scribes and Pharisees and established the rabbinical system; a system that introduced the oral traditions of the fathers," which Jesus condemned. They were the husbandmen of our parable who beat and killed the prophets sent by God to receive the spiritual fruit of Israel (verse 35). They were also the husbandmen who killed the son of the vineyard's owner. The Son (the heir) was the Lord Jesus Christ, who was sent by His Father to receive the spiritual fruit of the vineyard (Verses 37-38). **"They caught him and cast him out of the vineyard [Jerusalem] and slew him [on the cross]"** (verse 39).

In this parable, Jesus prophesied His rejection and death on the cross by the leadership of Israel. As the builders of the temple had in the past stumbled over and rejected the chief cornerstone of the temple (Psa. 118:22; Isa. 28:16), so the leadership of Israel would stumble over and reject Jesus Christ, the spiritual cornerstone of the spiritual temple (Acts 4:11; Rom. 9:31-33; Eph.2:20; 1 Pet. 2:6-8). Because of this, the kingdom of God (same as the kingdom of heaven) would be taken from them and given to a nation (the church) bringing forth fruit (verse 43). Out of their own mouths (verse 41), Jesus would judge these husbandmen by destroying them (in A.D. 70) and letting out His vineyard to other husbandmen, i.e., the church.

The Vine and the Vineyard

Jesus continued to use the symbols of the vineyard and the vine after His rejection of Israel. In His teachings to the church, He used the parable of the "workers in the vineyard" (Matt. 20:1-16) to teach us of the work of the church, and the parable of the "grapevine" (John 15:1-8) to teach the work of the Holy Spirit through the church. Let us consider the vine first.

> "I am the true vine, and my Father is the husbandman. (2) Every branch in me that beareth not fruit he taketh away: and every {branch} that beareth fruit, he purgeth it, that it may bring forth more fruit. (3) Now ye are clean through the word which I have spoken unto you. (4) Abide in me, and I in you. As the branch cannot bear fruit of itself, except it abide in the vine; no more can ye, except ye abide in me. (5) I am the vine, ye {are} the branches: He that abideth in me, and I in him, the same bringeth forth much fruit: for without me ye can do nothing. (6) If a man abide not in me, he is cast forth as a branch, and is withered; and men gather them, and cast {them} into the fire, and they are burned. (7) If ye abide in me, and my words abide in you, ye shall ask what ye will, and it shall be done unto you. (8) Herein is my Father glorified, that ye bear much fruit; so shall ye be my disciples."

In this parable, our Lord uses the true grapevine as a symbol of Himself and the husbandman as a symbol of His Father. Through these emblems, we see the historical beginning of the church (in Christ) and its method of growth (Christ in us). The church grew out of the Jewish vine — specifically, Jesus Christ, the true vine (Isa. 5:7; John 15:1) — and became its Gentile branches. This is the fulfillment of God's promise to Abraham that out of his (singular) Seed — Jesus Christ (Gal. 3:16) — would come his spiritual seed who would be as numerous as the stars of heaven. God the Father, as the husbandman (cultivator of the soil, farmer, land worker), is everything to the vine. "The Son, as the true vine is the center of God's economy and the embodiment of all riches of the Father. The Father, by cultivating the Son, works Himself with all His riches into the vine, and eventually the vine expresses the Father in a corporate way through its [Gentile] branches." (Witness Lee, *The New Testament Recovery Version*, p. 437, Living Stream Ministries, Anaheim, California, 1991).

While the "branches" that come out of the vine are emblems of the "spiritual seed" and speak of all those who will be saved ("in Christ"), the "fruitful branches" coming out of the vine are emblems of the "ruling seed" and speak of all those who will inherit the kingdom ("Christ in you, the hope of glory") (Col. 1:27). These two kinds of branches are seen by comparing those that **"beareth not fruit"** (verse 2a) with those that **"beareth fruit"** (verse 2b). Our parable further reveals those branches that **"abide not"** in Christ, or those who **will not bear fruit** (verse 6). This third group foreshadows the apostates who will be cast away by Christ, withered, and gathered for the fire at the judgment seat of Christ (1 Cor. 3:13-15). They will lose the kingdom (not their salvation).

The Branch That Bears No Fruit:

The branch that bears no fruit does not represent a believer who loses his salvation. This is a mistake of many expositors in their attempt to interpret verse 2a of our parable. The branch, here, is not *taken away* from the vine (showing loss of salvation), but *lifted up* from the ground. This truth is revealed in our Lord's use of the Greek word *airo,* which is more accurately translated "lifteth up" instead of "taketh away." Since the branch is apparently on the ground where vine branches cannot bear grapes, God the Father is shown lifting it up and placing it on a trellis (a wooden device built above the vine to hold up its branches). This lifting up of the branch from the ground, which symbolizes a fruitless worldly life, unto the heavenly trellis, which symbolizes the fruitful spiritual life, is done chiefly by the power of the Word. Not all believers who are worldly are chastised, particularly if they have not yet learned of spiritual things; they are first gently lifted up to the trellis of sanctification. **"Sanctify them through thy truth: thy Word is truth"** (John 17:17).

The Branch That Bears Fruit:

While the above branch speaks of the majority of the saved in the church today, the branch that abides on the heavenly trellis and brings forth fruit speaks of those Christians who will rule and reign with Christ in His coming kingdom. Notice that there are three levels of fruit bearing for these branches; those who bring forth **"fruit"** (verse 2), those who bring forth **"more fruit"** (verse 2), and those who bring forth **"much fruit"** (verses 5,8).

These three levels of fruit bearing are comparable to the threefold levels of yield found in the parable of the "sower" in Matt. 13. They also speak of the three major levels of the kingdom as seen through parables that teach of the wedding guests and the two higher levels, the bride of Christ.

Salvations of the Spirit and the Soul of Man:

A careful study of verse 3 of our parable reveals the new birth of a Christian (the salvation of his spirit). Apparently, our Lord wants us to see this first before we try to understand how fruit is produced through us. **"Now ye are [already] clean through the word which I have spoken to you."** When the scriptures proclaim one already cleansed all over by water (an emblem of the Word), as it does in this verse, it always speaks of the salvation of his spirit.

This is seen in the typology of John 13:8-10, when Jesus tells Peter that he is already clean all over (a type of the salvation of his spirit) and needs only his feet (an emblem of his daily walk) washed (a type of continuous salvation of his soul). This type further teaches that if Peter had refused this cleansing of his feet (refused Christ's daily cleansing through the Word), he could not have produced any spiritual fruit, i.e., had any part "with" Him in the kingdom.

Another example of these two salvations is seen in Eph. 5:26. While the ASV of the Bible gives a clear understanding of this verse, we elect to quote the Emphatic Diaglott translation of Codex Vaticanus, a fifth century manuscript. **"So that, having purified her in the bath of water, He might sanctify her by the Word."** Here, again, our Lord tells us that a new believer has already been washed all over by the Word the moment he believes (salvation of the spirit) so that he might be sanctified (continuously cleaned) by the Word. Hence, one must first be born again before he can be sanctified (continually set apart by the Word) and bring forth fruit (the salvation of his soul). This is revealed in the fruitful branch of our parable, which has its unfruitful wood (works of the flesh) continuously cut away by the husbandman to enable it to bring forth more fruit.

Christ is presently working in the lives of all believers to make them fruit-bearers and qualify them for the kingdom of heaven. To do this, the husbandman (God the Father), through the Holy Spirit, is purging every branch that brings forth any spiritual fruit whatsoever. This purging is the pruning of the branch for the purpose of cutting off excess wood. Like a plant, when a Christian has his works of the flesh cut away, he will usually bear more fruit (verse 2b). The action of pruning, or cleansing, of the branch is accomplished by the application of the Word of God (verse 3), which, in turn, produces more fruit and causes the Christian to abide in Christ. It is important to note that the branch has no power of its own to bring forth fruit; for while its fruit comes from the sap that flows through it, it does not produce this sap. The sap comes only from the vine (the Lord Jesus Christ). This is why He tells us to abide in Him (by faith) and let His words (the Word of God) abide in us (verse 7). When this spiritual sap, i.e., the Holy Spirit through the power of the Word of God, flows unobstructed from the vine into our lives, we will abide in that Word and bear spiritual fruit.

Contrary to this, there are branches in this parable who obviously have been dealt with by Christ, but to no avail. They refuse to abide in Christ and, as a result, are cast forth and are withered, and men gather them for the fire (verse 6). This, again, does not speak of one losing his salvation, but his reward at the judgment seat of Christ. By not abiding in Christ, one has already separated himself and is in the process of withering. At the judgment seat, Christ will cast them out and they will be gathered to the baptism of fire, which will burn up all of their works. "**...but he himself shall be saved: yet so as by [through] fire**" (1 Cor. 3:13-15).

The Two Salvations and Justifications of the Branches

"Know ye therefore that they which are of faith, the same are the children of Abraham (Gal 3:7).

"So then they which be of faith are blessed with faithful Abraham" (Gal. 3:9).

According to our above text, it is clear that since we share the same faith that began with Abraham, we are called the children of Abraham. If we are children of the same faith, then we are children of his two salvations and justifications.

Contrary to what is taught by the popular pulpit, the Word of God informs us that there are two different kinds of salvations and justifications. These are first seen in the life of Abraham (the root of the vine) and are then reflected in the branches of the vine. He received the first of these *by faith* only, without works; and later, he received the second *by works* and not by faith only. Consider the following scriptures that teach this.

The first:

"For what saith the scripture? Abraham believed God, and it was counted unto him for righteousness. (4) Now to him that worketh is the reward not reckoned of grace, but of debt. (5) But to him that *worketh not, but believeth* on him that justifieth the ungodly, his faith is counted for righteousness" (Rom. 4:3-5).

"Therefore we conclude that a man is *justified by faith* without the deeds of the law" (Rom. 3:28).

The second:

"Was not Abraham our father *justified by works*, when he had offered Isaac his son upon the altar? (22) Seest thou how faith wrought with his works, and by works was faith made perfect? (23) And the scripture was fulfilled which saith, Abraham believed God, and it was imputed unto him for righteousness: and he was called the Friend of God. (24) Ye see then how that *by works a man is justified*, and not by faith only" (James 2:21-24).

Martin Luther, that great man of God from the reformation period, could not understand what James was saying here. To him, James was contradicting what the apostle Paul had written in Romans. As a result, he totally discounted James' epistle, calling it "an epistle of straw." However, as we study James' epistle under the leadership of the Holy Spirit, we will come to see that James was writing about a different kind of salvation and a different kind of justification. To be able to reconcile these two verses, the reader must come to a new understanding of the doctrine of salvation. In doing so, he will see that it covers more than just salvation from the *penalty* of sin (hell), it also covers salvation from the *power* of sin. These two salvations together will qualify one to enter the "great salvation" (the kingdom) spoken of in Hebrews 2:3. Hence, there are three salvations (not counting the redemption of the body, which is guaranteed if the spirit of man is saved), two justifications, two kinds of faith, and one hope.

Salvation of the Spirit:

In our text above (Rom. 4:3-5), we learn that this righteousness is imputed by God to everyone who believes on (into) Jesus Christ without works. This was how God imputed righteousness to Abraham, for Abraham believed that God would give to him a son (the Promised Seed) without any effort on his part or his wife's. God declares this truth in the 5th verse. **"But to him that worketh not, but believeth on him that justifieth the ungodly, his faith is counted for righteousness."** Hence, this act of faith without works causes God to impute righteousness that saves the sinner from the penalty of sin (hell) and gives to him eternal life. Nothing else is promised — just eternal life (John 3:16); eternal life that can never be lost, since, at the moment of belief, the believer is sealed with the Holy Spirit (Eph. 1:13). This sealing makes it impossible for the believer to ever lose his salvation when he falls into sin. However, he can lose his spiritual power and future reward (inheritance of the kingdom) if that sin remains unconfessed (Eph. 4:30; 1 John 1:9). Finally, it is worthy to note that this salvation occurs in the spirit of man (the place of the Holy Spirit's residence), and not in his soul. Therefore, this salvation can rightly be called the "salvation of the spirit."

Salvation of the Soul:

In James, we are presented with a different kind of salvation and a different kind of justification. The justifying of Abraham in our Romans passage is based on his faith in the Promised Seed without works; in our James passage, it is based on works which are produced by faith, i.e., obeying God's command. Notice that Abraham had to take Isaac (his lesser son) to the land of Moriah (probably Mt. Moriah) under God's command to sacrifice him. By this act of obedience, Abraham, through faith, produced righteous works and was justified by God. As a result, God guaranteed him — not eternal life — but life in the kingdom of heaven (He already had eternal life).

What gave Abraham the faith to produce this righteous work? It was the Word of God (Rom. 10:17), which promised Abraham that the land (a type of the kingdom) would be peopled by Abraham's seed through Isaac. Since it was impossible for God to lie, Abraham believed that God would raise up Isaac (his lesser son) from the dead to people the land and to be a blessing to the whole world (note: Isaac is a type of Christ [Abaham's greater Son] in His death and resurrection). Therefore, by believing God, he had no problem in obeying Him and producing righteous works.

In like manner, the Christian, who has already been justified by faith without works (salvation of the spirit), may also be justified by works and not by faith only (salvation of the soul). This justification will come at the judgment seat of Christ if his life has been lived in obedience to God's Word. In light of this, when the Christian arrives at the judgment seat of Christ (2 Cor. 5:10), he will present for testing either righteous works (works produced by the Holy Spirit through his faith) or unrighteous works (works of his own flesh, i.e., his old nature). If, at this judgment, he presents righteous works that cannot be burned up, he will be declared "justified" (justification of the soul) and will receive a reward. However, if he has failed to produce works of righteousness and, instead, can only present works of self, he will suffer loss (will not have attained to the privilege of being one of the kingdom people). Thus, while he may suffer loss, i.e., lose his position as a member of the ruling seed for one-thousand years, he will not lose his position as a member of the spiritual seed of Abraham through faith in Jesus Christ. He will still have the justification and righteousness that was accounted to him when he was saved; but he will not have a "fulfilled righteousness" (James 2:23) given to him on the basis of righteous works; nor will he have his soul justified (saved) or receive a reward in the coming kingdom.

THE OLIVE TREE

> "The Lord called thy name, A green olive tree, fair, {and} of goodly fruit: with the noise of a great tumult he hath kindled fire upon it, and the branches of it are broken" (Jer. 11:16).

In the above scripture, God calls Israel a green olive tree, which is symbolic of her covenant relationship with God through Abraham, Isaac and Jacob. "Green" speaks of it being an evergreen, pointing to an everlasting covenant.

The Parable of the Olive Tree

> "For if the firstfruit {be} holy, the lump {is} also {holy}: and if the root {be} holy, so {are} the branches. (17) And if some of the branches be broken off, and thou, being a wild olive tree, wert graffed in among them, and with them partakest of the root and fatness of the olive tree; (18) Boast not against the branches. But if thou boast, thou bearest not the root, but the root thee. (19) Thou wilt say then, The branches were broken off, that I might be graffed in. (20) Well; because of unbelief they were broken off, and thou standest by faith. Be not highminded, but fear: (21) For if God spared not the natural branches, {take heed} lest he also spare not thee. (22) Behold therefore the goodness and severity of God: on them which fell, severity; but toward thee, goodness, if thou continue in {his} goodness: otherwise thou also shalt be cut off. (23) And they also, if they abide not still in unbelief, shall be graffed in: for God is able to graff them in again. (24) For if thou wert cut out of the olive tree which is wild by nature, and wert graffed contrary to nature into a good olive tree: how much more shall these, which be the natural {branches}, be graffed into their own olive tree?" (Rom. 11:16-24)

In the parable of the "olive tree," the first fruit is holy, the lump is holy, the root is holy, and so are the branches. God chose and separated unto Himself a nation. Abraham, Isaac and Jacob are the roots; the twelve sons of Jacob, the trunk, and the branches are their descendents. The covenant that God made with Abraham was the covenant of salvation by grace (Rom. 4:1-4). Because of unbelief, some of the branches were broken off and the wild branches grafted in.

God did not break off all the branches; neither did He cut down the tree, as many Christians think. The Jewish root, trunk and branches still exist. Only some of the branches were broken off (Rom. 11:17) and the Gentiles, symbolized by the wild olive tree, were grafted in among them. God is not through with the Jew, and He will never be through with the Jew.

In Eph. 2:11-13, we see the relationship of Gentiles to God and that their salvation has come through the covenant that God made with Abraham — salvation through the shed blood of the Lamb of God. In Romans 11: 29, we read that the gifts and calling of God are without repentance; so God's purpose concerning Israel will yet be fulfilled. The Gentile Christians today — with the exception of a few — are doing exactly what God told them not to do in Rom. 11:18-20. They are boasting against Israel (verse 18-24). Some of Israel was cut off because of unbelief; some of the Gentiles will be cut off for the same reason (lose the kingdom) and the believers of Israel grafted back in. God tells us that the blindness of Israel is partial and temporary. The branches that were broken off symbolize those Jews who rejected Jesus Christ when He came the first time. However, they who believe (the descendants of the branches broken off) will be grafted back in at His second coming (Zech. 12:10-13:1). They are called the remnant.

Though the Jews are hated for the gospel's sake, they are still beloved for the fathers' sakes (Rom. 11:28). Israel is still God's firstborn son among the nations and will still be God's witness to the ends of the earth.

The Graft:

The actual grafting in of the wild olive tree (the Gentile portion of the church) is historically revealed in Matthew's parable of the "laborers in the vineyard."

The Matthew Mysteries *The Trees of the Kingdom*

"For the kingdom of heaven is like unto a man {that is} an householder, which went out early in the morning to hire labourers into his vineyard. (2) And when he had agreed with the labourers for a penny a day, he sent them into his vineyard. (3) And he went out about the third hour, and saw others standing idle in the market place, (4) And said unto them; Go ye also into the vineyard, and whatsoever is right I will give you. And they went their way. (5) Again he went out about the sixth and ninth hour, and did likewise. (6) And about the eleventh hour he went out, and found others standing idle, and saith unto them, Why stand ye here all the day idle? (7) They say unto him, Because no man hath hired us. He saith unto them, Go ye also into the vineyard; and whatsoever is right, {that} shall ye receive. (8) So when even was come, the lord of the vineyard saith unto his steward, Call the labourers, and give them {their} hire, beginning from the last unto the first. (9) And when they came that {were hired} about the eleventh hour, they received every man a penny. (10) But when the first came, they supposed that they should have received more; and they likewise received every man a penny. (11) And when they had received {it}, they murmured against the goodman of the house, (12) Saying, These last have wrought {but} one hour, and thou hast made them equal unto us, which have borne the burden and heat of the day. (13) But he answered one of them, and said, Friend, I do thee no wrong: didst not thou agree with me for a penny? (14) Take {that} thine {is}, and go thy way: I will give unto this last, even as unto thee. (15) Is it not lawful for me to do what I will with mine own? Is thine eye evil, because I am good? (16) So the last shall be first, and the first last: for many be called, but few chosen" (Matt. 20:1-16).

The Key Verse:

The key to understanding this parable is found in verse 16. Here, two expressions, always used separately in other scriptures, are brought together in one verse. The first expression, *the last shall be first, and the first last,* is used to show the results of the judgment seat of Christ for the early church that was made up of Jews (of the natural olive tree) and saved under the preaching of the gospel of the kingdom. The second expression, *many are called, but few are chosen,* is always used to show the results at the judgment seat of Christ for that portion of the church made up of Gentiles (of the grafted in wild olive branch) and saved under the preaching of the gospel of grace.

Doctrinally speaking, the grafting of the wild olive branch into the natural olive tree began before the cross and was prophesied by our Lord in the above parable. Its teaching began just prior to this parable after the rich man had rejected Jesus' offer of the kingdom in Matt. 19:22. Peter asked Jesus what the apostles would receive for following Him (verse 27). Jesus informed them that they would sit on twelve thrones and rule over the twelve tribes of Israel during the millennial kingdom. The other Jewish believers who had forsaken all would receive a hundredfold and inherit everlasting (Gr. age) life.

Then Jesus said to Peter in verse 30, **"But many that are first shall be last; and the last shall be first."** With this expression, Jesus set the stage for His parable of the "workers in the vineyard," which would show the grafting of the Gentiles (the wild olive tree) into the early Jewish church (the natural olive tree). The parable reveals all of the church age, beginning with the apostles. Those laborers of the parable who were first hired were hired by AGREEMENT (Matt. 20:2); whereas all the other laborers hired at various times, representing the church age, were hired under GRACE. When the time for payment came (the judgment seat of Christ), they all received the same wage — those who had been under agreement along with those who had been under grace (verse 9-10).

Verse 10 evidently points out the apostles as the ones who **"first came,"** for they had been hired under agreement. Peter's understanding of the kingdom had been on a commercial standard, i.e., a believer gets paid for the work he does by agreement. But Jesus was showing Peter that there would be a new standard of the kingdom; this would be introduced with the Gentile church period and called grace; a standard by which one would get far more then what he worked for if, indeed, he did work and was steadfast to the end. Thus, we see the grafting of grace into agreement and the Gentiles into the Jews. Both peoples and standards of the early and latter church period are expressed in verse 16. **"So the last shall be first, and the first last [the Jewish portion of the early church]: for many be called,**

but few chosen [the Gentile portion of the church]."

After this historical grafting had been completed and the early Jewish church had become the later Gentile church under grace, Jesus began to use the second expression of verse 16 to teach the Gentile church about the kingdom. In Matt. 22:2-14, He gave the parable of the "wedding feast," which revealed that all the Gentile church would be saved (called), but only a few would be called out of the saved (chosen). Under grace, the chosen would produce the fruit necessary to become the wedding guests at the marriage of the Lamb. **"For many are called, but few are chosen"** (Matt. 22:14).

In summary, Peter and the other apostles, in verse 2, represent the beginning of the Jewish portion of the church, those who would gain reward under "agreement." This is in keeping with the occasion of the parable in Matt. 19:27-30, Peter's question and Jesus' answer about what they would have in the kingdom. The other workers who were hired the third, sixth, ninth and eleventh hours represent all the Gentiles who would be saved and chosen to work in the vineyard. These appointments would occur during different centuries of the church dispensation, right up to the last (the eleventh hour). The chief teaching of this parable, then, is to show the wild olive tree, contrary to nature (Rom. 11:24), being grafted into the natural olive tree through faith, then producing fruit under grace.

THE FIG TREE

The fig tree is mentioned in Matt. 21:19; 24:32; Mark 11:12-14,20 and 21; and Luke 13:6-9 and symbolizes Israel as God's "national witness" to all the world. The vineyard was allowed to go to waste (except for one vine — Jesus); some branches of the olive tree were broken off; but the fig tree was cut down. Our Lord spoke three parables regarding the fig tree.

The First Parable

"Now in the morning as he returned into the city, he hungered. (19) And

> when he saw a fig tree in the way, he came to it, and found nothing thereon, but leaves only, and said unto it, Let no fruit grow on thee henceforward for ever. And presently the fig tree withered away. (20) And when the disciples saw {it}, they marvelled, saying, How soon is the fig tree withered away!" (Matt. 21:18-20)

Herein, the Lord turned aside to eat figs of the fig tree when He saw the tree in full leaf. This was emblematic of His hunger for a spiritual relationship with Israel and for their witness of Him to all the nations of the world. However, He found no fruit. As a result of this, He said, **"Let no fruit grow on thee henceforward forever."** Some expositors have interpreted this verse to mean that God is through with Israel forever and they will never again bear any fruit; but that is not what the Greek text is saying. The word *forever* is the Greek word *aion,* which means "an age" (the present age of the church). Hence, they would be unable to be a witness (bear fruit) to God during the church age. However, when this age is over and the millennial kingdom is established, Israel will again bear fruit. They will become Jehovah's witness to the whole world. The scriptures teach that God is not through with Israel. If He were, He would not have used the Greek word here that means "age," but the Greek words that mean the "age of ages" (forever and forever).

The Second Parable

> "He spake also this parable; a certain {man} had a fig tree planted in his vineyard; and he came and sought fruit thereon, and found none. (7) Then said he unto the dresser of his vineyard, Behold, these three years I come seeking fruit on this fig tree, and find none: cut it down; why cumbereth it the ground? (8) And he answering said unto him, Lord, let it alone this year also, till I shall dig about it, and dung {it}: (9) And if it bear fruit, {well}: and if not, {then} after that thou shalt cut it down" (Luke 13:6-9).

When the Lord turns aside to seek fruit from the fig tree in full leaf, He says, **"Behold these three years I come seeking fruit on this fig tree, and find none."** The experience recorded in this parable took place after three years of Jesus' earthly ministry. It tells us that He had sought fruit from Israel (their witness of

Jehovah to the world) during this time and found none. As a result, He told the vineyard keeper to cut it down (remove their nation out of the land and scatter them throughout the world). But the vineyard keeper, or husbandman (God the Father: see John 15:1), said to let it alone for another year. One more year, in the parable, symbolizes the probationary time that God gave to Israel beyond the cross. It was the answer to the prayer of Jesus on the cross when He prayed, **"Father, forgive them for they know not what they do."** It was another chance given to Israel through Peter's second sermon. It was still another chance given to Israel through Stephen's preaching. During this time, God waited for Israel as a nation to repent and turn back to Him. He sent preachers to them to preach the "gospel of the kingdom," but they would neither hear them nor repent for the sin of crucifying their Messiah. In about A.D. 63, His probationary period ended; His patience for Israel to repent ran out, and God set Israel aside and turned to the Gentiles (Acts 28:28). In Acts 1:8, we see that He chose another group to be His witnesses for the next two thousand years, until they would be raptured into heaven. In Romans 11:25, we find that the setting aside of Israel, as expressed by her blindness, is only in part and that it is temporary, not permanent. Romans 11:17 states conclusively that just some branches were broken off — not all the branches. The Gentiles, grafted in among the natural olive branches, bear fruit only as the sap from the Jewish roots flows out through the Jewish trunk and then through them.

The Third Parable

"Now learn a parable of the fig tree; When his branch is yet tender, and putteth forth leaves, ye know that summer {is} nigh: (33) So likewise ye, when ye shall see all these things, know that it is near, {even} at the doors" (Matt. 24: 32-33).

It is important to note that when the fig tree was cut down, symbolizing Israel being scattered throughout the world in A.D. 70, the stump of the fig tree did not die. Israel was not destroyed. Only their national structure was destroyed. In our above text, we find our Lord prophesying to the church that when they see the fig stump beginning to grow branches and leaves again, they will know that His second coming is near. History tells us that for almost two thousand years, the fig stump remained a stump. On May 14, 1948, Israel again became a nation. She was accepted as the fifty-ninth member of the United Nations and was recognized by over sixty-eight nations. The stump has produced branches and leaves; and the stage is set for the return of the Lord.

Luke reveals a secondary prophecy given with this parable that teaches of a great number of other nations being established for the first time just before the coming of the Lord. These nations are identified as "all the trees." **"And he spake to them a parable; Behold the fig tree, and all the trees; (30) When they now shoot forth, ye see and know of your own selves that summer is now nigh at hand. (31) So likewise ye, when ye see these things come to pass, know ye that the kingdom of God is nigh at hand"** (Luke 21:29-31). From the time that the fig tree stump put forth its tender branches and Israel became a nation in 1948, dozens of new nations have come into being. In 1962, over twenty-four black nations alone came into being, not counting those new ones of Asia and Europe. Still other nations have declared their independence from a union of states, such as the Soviet Union.

THE FIG TREE STUMP IN HISTORY

Jesus, in Matt. 24:4-31, prophesied what would happen to the scattered and rejected people of Israel during the church age. This passage, plus that of Luke 21:20-24, answers the three questions asked of Him by the apostles in Matt. 24:3b when Jesus prophesied the destruction of their temple. *The reader should pause and read this scripture from his Bible.*

The Three Questions Asked by the Apostles

"And as he sat upon the mount of Olives, the disciples came unto him privately, saying, Tell us, [1] when shall these things be? [2] and what {shall be} the sign of thy coming, [3] and of the end of the world?" (Matt. 24:3)

When Shall These Things Be?

The occasion for this first question is found in Matt. 23:38, when Jesus said to the Jews, **"Your house is left unto you desolate,"** and in Matt. 24:2, when He said, **"...There shall not be left here one stone upon another, that shall not be thrown down."** The apostles, knowing that Jesus was speaking of the destruction of the temple, asked Him, **"...when shall these things be?"** Jesus answered, **"And when ye shall see Jerusalem compassed with armies, then know that the desolation thereof is nigh"** (Luke 21:20). Notice that this answer is not recorded in Matthew, but in Luke. It speaks of the coming destruction of their temple, as well as their national structure. A rule of prophecy says that when a prophesied event first occurs, that first occurrence is the fulfillment of that prophecy. It necessitates, then, that Luke 21:20 was fulfilled in Oct., A.D. 66, when Cestius Gallus and his Roman legions moved against the city of Jerusalem for the first time, completely surrounding it. This was the sign of its approaching desolation, and the Christians living there knew it. Thus, by giving this sign, God was telling the Christians there to get out of Jerusalem. This is recorded in Luke 21:21, which says, **"Then let them which are in Judea flee to the mountains; and let them which are in the midst of it depart out; and let not them that are in the countries enter thereinto."** But how was this to be, since they were surrounded by an army? It presented a dilemma — commanded to flee and flight an impossibility. However, Jesus, being God, prophesied right. About a month later, in Nov., A.D. 66, after the city's food and water supply was exhausted and they were on the verge of defeat, Cestius Gallus and his Roman legions withdrew completely and left the territory.

Down through history, military tacticians have been baffled trying to explain why Cestius Gallus withdrew from Israel. However, by reading and believing the Bible, we can understand it. The encompassing of the city with armies was the sign of the imminent desolation of Jerusalem, a sign for the Christians to leave the city. Because they could not leave while the armies were there, our Lord removed the armies so the Christians could flee the city and not be a part of its desolation.

In A.D. 70 Titus returned with the Roman armies and threw up a siege that resulted in a sacking and desolation of the city. More than one million perished in the fall of Jerusalem. Josephus, in his *Antiquity of the Jews,* tells us that the wave of human blood flowing down through the gutters of the city reached such proportions that whole houses on fire in the southern part were extinguished by this wave of human blood. So far as could be ascertained, not a Christian perished in the fall of Jerusalem, because they believed the sign our Lord gave them and fled at the opportunity provided.

How did the temple fare? History records that when the siege was over there was not one stone of the temple left on top of another. Tradition has it that gold leaf was between the stones to enhance the beauty of the temple. The need of the Roman Empire for gold was such that each stone was removed, taken off by itself and the gold scraped from the stone and added to the coffers of the Roman Empire. Another tradition is that the dome of the temple was made of solid gold; the holocaust melted the gold causing it to run down between the stones; the stones had to be separated and the gold scraped off to rescue it for the Roman Empire. Thus was the prophecy of our Lord, concerning the desolation of Jerusalem and the temple, fulfilled. (See A.E. Wilson's book, *Selected Writings of A. Edwin Wilson,* pp. 10-11, Schoettle Publishing Co., Miami Springs, Florida, 1981).

What Shall Be the Sign of Thy Coming?

The second question asked of Jesus by the apostles was, **"What shall be the sign of thy coming?"** Contrary to the teaching of some fundamental scholars who say there are no signs given in the Bible concerning the second coming of Christ, Jesus took great pains in Matt. 24 to show there are. As we look closely at the following scriptures, keep in mind that Matt. 24:1-31 was written to the Jews and not to the church. It is prophecy that tells the Jews what will happen to them from the time of their rejection of Jesus Christ as their Messiah to His second coming. This is an example of scripture being addressed "to" Israel while, at the same time, being written "for" the church.

The sign of Christ's second coming comprises several events. The first will be false Christs (verse 5). This sign will continue across a two thousand year span of time and culminate in the coming antichrist in the latter days (the tribulation period). The second event constitutes wars and rumors of wars throughout the world until His return, beginning when **"nation shall rise against nation and kingdom against kingdom."** This was literally fulfilled in the First World-War when, for the first time, nations and kingdoms were part of a world wide conflict. The third event, following the great war, consists of continuous famines, pestilences (including diseases never heard of before) and earthquakes in different places of the world (note: there have been more devastating earthquakes during the 20th century than any other century). In verse 8, Jesus says, **"...these are the beginning of sorrows"** (Gr. birth pangs); sorrows that begin with the first World War and, like birth pangs, get closer together until the full birth pangs come. This full sorrow will culminate in the middle of the tribulation period for all Jews; a time known in the Old Testament as the **"time of Jacob's trouble"** and revealed by the apostle Paul in 1 Thess. 5:3. **"For when they shall say peace and safety [a false peace from antichrist]; then sudden destruction cometh upon them, as travail upon a woman with child [the great tribulation period]; and they shall not escape."**

The fourth event of this sign is given in verse 9. **"Then shall they deliver you up to be afflicted, and shall kill you; and ye shall be hated of all nations for my name's sake."** Notice the first word of this verse *then,* which relates this experience to the sign. Thus, sometime after the First World War there is going to be a world-wide persecution of the Jews, resulting from all nations hating them. This event is most notable when studying world history during the time between the First and Second World Wars. Before the Pearl Harbor tragedy, even our own country would not allow two shiploads of Jewish refugees from Germany to dock at any of its ports. Unable to find a place to dock, they were turned back to Nazi Germany. Eventually, many of these, along with an estimated one-third of all the Jewish population in the world, were destroyed by Adolf Hitler in the death camps of Germany. Despite this, the hatred and persecution of the Jew is still among all the nations of the world today. One-by-one, governments of the world are dropping assistance to the nation of Israel (the budding fig tree) and joining those who are against her. This will continue until the close of the "great tribulation" when all nations, under antichrist, will come against her in an attempt to utterly destroy her. Only then will the Lord appear and become the destroyer of Israel's enemies. All of this hatred was and is **"for my name's sake"** (verse 9b). How can these unsaved Jews be persecuted for Christ's sake? The Jews are hated for three particular reasons; for giving us the Bible (the human means); for giving us Jesus the Christ after the flesh; and for being chosen by God to be Jehovah's witnesses throughout the world. For these three reasons, Satan hates the Jew; and that is why the world hates the Jew.

The Budding of the Fig Tree:

In the same passage of Matthew, we have these verses. **"Now learn a parable of the fig tree; When his branch is yet tender, and putteth forth leaves, ye know that summer {is} nigh: (33) So likewise ye, when ye shall see all these things, know that it is near, {even} at the doors. (34) Verily I say unto you, This generation shall not pass, till all these things be fulfilled"** (Matt. 24:32-34). From this point in our text to Matt. 25: 31, our Lord leaves off speaking to Israel and speaks to the church — parables were never spoken to Israel. All that is written here is written "to" the church and "for" the church. Thus, in this beginning section, Jesus is telling us that when we see the fig tree stump once again grow into a fig tree with branches and leaves (a Jewish nation with people), then we will know that Christ is about to return (the rapture of the church).

Following the appearance of the fig tree, there will be times on earth likened unto the days of Noah (Matt. 24:37-39) and of Lot (Luke 17:28-29). Society will forget God and turn all their interest to sinful pleasure (**"eating and drinking"**), gross immorality (**"marrying and giving in marriage [wife swapping]"**), including homosexuality, the chief sin of Sodom, and the worship of money through commercial enterprise (**"they bought, they sold, they planted, they builded"**). The days in which we presently live have become a carbon copy of the days of Noah and Lot. The people of this world are flourishing in these sins and in their hatred of God, and will continue to do so into the great tribulation period. At the close of the great tribulation, our Lord will be revealed from heaven with His mighty angels. He will come "in flaming fire" to take "vengeance on them that know not God, and who obey not the gospel of our Lord Jesus Christ." He will punish them with "everlasting destruction from the presence of the Lord, and from the glory of His power." (2 Thess. 1:8-10) This final consummation of the age will occur seven years after the rapture of the church, and no more than a generation beyond the budding of the fig tree.

To summarize the answers to this second question, Jesus said that the generation that sees a world-wide war followed by famines, pestilences and earthquakes, world-wide persecution of the Jews in which untold numbers would be killed, and followed soon after by Israel becoming a nation — THAT GENERATION WOULD SEE HIS RETURN.

What Shall Be the Sign of the End of the World?

This is the third question asked of Jesus by His apostles and is recorded in Matt. 24:3c. The first question was, **"When shall** these things [the destruction of Israel] be?" The second question was, **"What shall be the sign of thy coming?"** Third and last, they asked, **"What shall be the sign of the end of the world?"**

The correct translation is not the end of the "world," but the end of the "age." The end of the world will not take place until one thousand years after the end of the age, and the end of the age will not take place until Jesus comes to establish His kingdom for one thousand years. In Matt. 24:15-21, we see the first sign of this present age drawing to a swift close. **"When ye therefore shall see the abomination of desolation, spoken of by Daniel the prophet, stand in the holy place, (whoso readeth, let him understand:) ...For then shall be great tribulation, such as was not since the beginning of the world to this time, no, nor ever shall be"** (Matt. 24:15,21). The abomination of desolation spoken of by Daniel (Dan. 9:27) refers to the placing of the image of antichrist in the holy of holies of the temple. This will be in the "midst of the week," i.e., the beginning of the last three and a half years of the tribulation period. Life will be given to this image by Satan, and worship of the image exacted from the people under the penalty of death for refusal (Rev. 13:15). The "great" tribulation (last three and a half years) will be consummated by the darkening of the sun, the failure of the moon to give light, the falling of stars from the heavens and the appearance of the sign of the Son of man in heaven (verse 29-30). **"And then shall appear the sign of the Son of man in heaven: and then shall all the tribes of the earth mourn, and they shall see the Son of man coming in the clouds of heaven with power and great glory"** (Matt. 24:30).

There are also a number of other events that will constitute signs of the end of this age. First, the rapture of the saints (1 Thess. 4: 13-17); the sudden catching away of the church, resulting in a vast number of individuals whose bodies will not be found on the earth, should be a sign to those remaining that the end of the age is fast approaching; but only those who will be saved during the tribulation will be able to discern this. Second, the appearance all over the world of 144,000 Jewish evangelists simultaneously beginning to preach the gospel of the kingdom will be a sign that the age is fast drawing to a close. Third, the rise of the antichrist, as seen in 2 Thess. 2, will be a sign to the earth dwellers that the end of the age is near. Fourth, the rebuilding and destruction of the city of Babylon, described in Rev. 18, will be another sign of the imminent end of the age. Fifth, the institution of a world-wide system of idol worship, headed by the worship of antichrist and his image, described in Rev. 13:15, will be evidence that the age is about to end.

CLOSING THOUGHTS

At the close of the seven year tribulation period, Christ will appear the second time with power and great glory (Matt. 24:30). In His wrath, He will invade human history and destroy the kingdoms of this world (Rev. 19:11-16; Dan. 2:44). At His coming, there will be such a great earthquake that every city of the world will fall (Rev. 6:12; 16:18-19). In total terror, the earth dwellers will frantically call for the mountains and rocks to fall upon them to hide them from His wrath (Rev. 6:15-16; Isa. 2:19-21; 34:4-6). Untold millions will perish. Many will literally be frightened to death (Luke 21:26-27). Others will perish by great hailstones weighing more than a hundred pounds falling on them from heaven (Rev. 16:21). Still others will have the flesh of their bodies instantly consumed away by the glory of His presence (Zech. 14:12). At His arrival, He will touch down on Mount Olivet and cause an earthquake of such proportions that it will make a valley in the mountains for approximately two hundred miles (Zech. 14: 4-5). Those of the elect of Israel, who are gathered from the four corners of the earth (Matt. 24:31), will escape down this valley of mountains as Israel escaped from Pharaoh through the valley of the sea (Zech. 14:5) Yet, this number will constitute only one-third of all the Jews. Two-thirds of them will have perished by the hands of the armies of the world sent against them. Only one-third will survive after being tried and refined in this furnace of affliction (Zech. 13:8-9; Isa. 48:10). In their escape through this valley, called Jehoshaphat (Joel 3:2,12-14), the armies of the world will attempt to follow (as Pharaoh and his armies did) and will be utterly trampled to death by Christ like grapes in a winepress. Blood will flow up to the horse's bridles for almost the entire length of the valley (Rev. 14:20; 19:15; Isa. 63:3-4). Antichrist and the false prophet will be cast alive into the lake of fire (Rev. 19:20), Satan will be locked up in the bottomless pit for one thousand years (Rev. 20:1-3) and the rest of the lost world will be condemned by Christ from His earthly throne of glory and slain (Matt. 25: 41-46). Not one lost person will be alive to enter the kingdom of heaven.

The third tree of scripture, the fig tree, is one of the signs that tells us we are near to the close of the age. In 1948, Israel again became a nation. At that time, the fig tree stump put out branches and leaves and became a tree. Jesus, in Matt. 24:34, tells us that the generation of people who were alive in 1948 when Israel became a nation will not all pass away until all these things be fulfilled. He also tells us that when the church sees the fig tree, they can know that the rapture is near; that He is at the doors, ready to secretly catch out His church. Will you be ready?

NOTES

SUBJECT INDEX

ABRAM/ABRAHAM......5-8-12-13-14
................16-23-43-91-120-161-167
.... 182-183
....186-189-190-254-255258-262-266
ABRAHAM'S BOSOM..................... 93
ADAM............... 5-9-10-11-13-43-49-12
ADAM PLAN........................... 192-193
AMILLENNIALISTS...................... 141
ANTCHRIST......10-23-88-154-158-173
.... 180-204-205-207-210-275-279-280
ANTIOCH.. 69
APHRODITE................................... 65
APOSTATES............226-243-247-248
AMMAGEDDON.............205-207-210
ARTAXERXES................................ 21
ATTALUS..................................... 170
BALAAM... 20
BAPTISM IN THE SPIRIT.........27-28
BAPTISM OF FIRE................ 162-261
BAPTISM OF THE HOLY SPIRIT ..
....71-72-73
BAPTISM OF REPENTANCE...... 27
BAPTISM THROUGH FIRE.......... 29
BATHSHEBA....................................5
BEAST......................................23-210
BELIEVE............................ 35-37-39-61
BETHSAIDA................................. 127
BLACKNESS OF DARKNESS...116-
.... 125-147
BODY OF CHRIST.............28-49-182
.... 185-194-199-200-201-216-228
BODY OF THE CHURCH.......... 240
BOOK OF REMEMBRANCE..... 188
BRANCHES................ 80-142-258-262-
.... .266-269-271
BRIDE OF ANTICHRIST............. 173

BRIDE OF CHRIST.........111-122-139
... 141-151-166-182-185-194-199-201
.... 216-217-218-227-228-230-231-236
.... 237-238-239-244-252-260
CAESAR, JULIUS.......................... 170
CAIN.. 11
CALLED......216-217-218-219-220-221
.... 222-228-239-252-269
CALVIN... 156
CAPERNAUM................................ 127
CARLYLE, THOMAS..................... 69
CARNAL......43-66-68-74-114-115-147
CHORAZIN................................... 127
CHOSEN..............141-194-200-216-217
.... 227-230-237-239-252-269
CHRISTIAN BAPTISM........28-61-62
CHRIST IN YOU........................... 150
CHRYSOSTOM, JOHN.................. 69
CHURCH..2-15-22-29-38-45-51-57-59
.....66-67-69-87-101-111-120-121-128
.... 137-139-147-174-183-188-213-220
.... 239-244-246-250-252-257-267-271
CHURCH OF THE FIRSTBORN.....
...................................99-183-188-199
CONIAH..6
CONSTANTINE...................... 154-170
CONSTANTINOPLE...................... 69
CORNELIUS.............................39-80
CRISWELL, W.A............................. 71
CROWN................................... 226-232
CYRUS.. 256
DAMASUS............................... 171-172
DANIEL................... 21-43-168-188-189
DAVID...................5-10-13-15-16-34-132
ELIJAH...............................26-244-245
EPAPHRODITUS........................... 85

283

ETHIOPIAN EUNUCH................ 39
ETRUSCANS 170
EVE 10-11-13-49-168-244
EVERLASTING GOSPEL.........34-41
EXTRA-BIBLICAL REVELATION
....64-82
FAITH................ 12-33-47-52-113-117
.... 120-148-166-175-186-188-201-215
.... 222-226-232-243-247-261-269
FAITHFUL.141-200-216-228-230-237
.... 238-252
FAITHFUL AND WISE......... 100-101
FALSE CHURCH....................... 139
FALSE PROPHET......................... 280
FIG TREE 253-269-276-280
FILLING OF THE HOLY SPIRIT....
....73-240
FIRST BODY 216-217
FIRSTBORN SON.....................46-120
FIRST TENSE SALVATION 1-215
FOUR & TWENTY ELDERS..... 162
FRIENDS OF THE BRIDEGROOM
.... 122-123-141-187-229-230-231
FRUIT...98-146
FURNACE OF AFFLICTION..... 161
.... 210-279
FURNACE OF FIRE.......161-202-209
GABRIEL.. 21
GALLUS, CESTIUS...................... 273
GATHERING OF iSRAEL............ 209
GEHENNA.106-123-147-243-248-252
GENERAL ASSEMBLY.188-199-200
GIFT............................ 1-42-49-182-248
GIFTS..81-82-83
GOOD AND FAITHFUL................ 235
GOSPEL OF GLORY 34-40-41
GOSPEL OF GRACE............33-36-38
. 40-44-50-60-61-79-123-208-220-267
GOSPEL OF THE KINGDOM...... 27
....33-36-40-53-55-60-64-70-75-79-80
93-119-123-193-205-220-267-271-279
GRAPEVINE..............253-354-257-258
GRATIAN... 171
GREAT SALVATION........43-149-263

GREAT TREE...166-167-171-174-177
GREAT TRIBULATION....22-29-139
.... 142-158-160-173-193-203-210-275
GREAT WHITE THRONE.. 157-193
.... 206
HABAKKUK............................... 204
HAGAR... 12
HARVEST............................... 157-159
HEALERS.................................56-75
HEROD... 19
HID TREASURE........................ 181
HIGH PRIEST 160
HOPE........ 46-50-112-145-148-166-231
...........................232-236-239-244-263
HUSBANDMAN 258-261
HUSBANDMEN 256-257
IRVIN, EDWARD 68
ISAAC............ 12-187-255-264-265-266
ISAIAH 27-43-196
ISHMAEL... 12
JACOB.13-16-20-183-185-187-255-265
JAMES 42-52-68-244-262
JEHOIAKIM...6
JEREMIAH...................................... 16
JEZEBEL.. 171
JOHN 29-84-127-136-174-228-244
JOHN THE BAPTIST...... 27-28-34-72
..................................91-187-195-245
JONAH.............................132-133-137
JOSEPH..5-6
JOSEPHUS....................................... 274
JUDAS.. 81
JUDE... 42
JUDGE... 160
JUDGMENT SEAT.2-14-29-42-49-52
.... 73-83-87-94-99-102-107-109-
113-116-
.... 121-125-128-139-141-146-153-160
.... 175-182-194-199-202-222-224-230
.... 235-238-248-249-261-264-267-268
KETURAH.. 12
KINGDOM OF THE FATHER..... 51
.... 163-169
KINGDOM OF HEAVEN...... 1-14-16

.... 100-103-105-111-116-119-125-130
.... 140-146-163-165-183-185-187-197
.... 200-205-311-213-218-223-232-223
................232-235-238-243-244
KNOX 156
LAKE OF FIRE 161-180-193-280
LAW OF CHRIST 103
LAW OF FIRST MENTION. 167-177
LAW OF GOD 103
LAZARUS 186
LEAVEN ....101-1'75-179-198-251
LORDSHIP .. 76-104-109-114--125-149
.... 166-179-215-222-224-231-234-236
LORD OF ALL THE EARTH..... 256
LORD GOD OF HEAVEN 256
LUTHER, MARTIN.154-178-246-262
MARK... 174
MARY 5-6-9-10-13-137
MARY MAGDELENE................... 136
MEAT 44
MILK.. 44
MOSES 190-244-245
MUSTARD BUSH....116-174-175-177
MUSTARD SEED 166-175
MY GOSPEL................. 34-41-46-50-62
MYSTERIES OF THE KINGDOM ..
.... 139-141-148-150-159-182-198-211
NATHAN...5
NATURAL BODY 192
NEBUCHADNEZZAR...168-210-253
NEW NATURE 113-185
NIMROD 168
NOAH... 43
OLD NATURE.... 98-113-177-183-264
OLIVE TREE........80-142-253-265-268
OUTER DARKNESS.............109-116-
.... 120-125
...................162-221-235-243-249-252
OUT-RESURRECTION................ 125
OVERCOMER 42-125-187
PARADISE.. 93
PAUL 66-74-80-85-108-146-163-180
PEARL OF GREAT PRICE. 181-198
..........................199-1200-201-202

....197-211-244
..................................191-206-238-240
SHEM 212
STRAIT GATE............................... 81
STRIVING...................................... 75
SPIRITUAL BODY 209-217-222
..................................225-233-234
TRUE VINE 26
WIDE GATE..................................67-72
WEDDING GARMENT................. 79
WILSON..1
PERGAMUS................................... 170
PETER.....39-42-50-68-80-146-214-240
..................................244-250-260-268
PHAROAH 57-279-280
PHILIP 39-80
PHILIPPIAN JAILER..................... 39
PILATE.. 20
PREMILLENNIALISTS................ 141
PRIZE................... 1-42-43-47-49-51-62
RAPTURE...... 2-22-36-39-41-46-52-58
.... 86-88-101-125-139-144-154-157
.... 160-174-203-206-208-209-221-222
.... 224-230-231-233-235-238-241-244
REDEEMED BODY........125-162-192
..................................226-230-231-239
REMNANT 142-266
REPENTANCE... 3-14-19-35-36-39-91
REST 149
RESURRECTION 188
REWARDS 2-14-42-95-130-144
.... 162-183-190-199-220-246-249-261
..................................263-264-265
ROCK 110-111-114
ROCK CHRISTIAN 110-115
ROCK OF OFFENSE..................... 196
ROOT OF THE VINE................... 262
RUTH...8
SABBATH 135
SALVATION OF THE SOUL 1-42
.....50-62-73-94-103-108-121-128-149
.... 153-166-185-199-201-231-238-260
.... 261-264
SALVATION OF THE SPIRIT...1-50

...... 58-62-73-97-103-108-128-149-166
.... 185-199-201-238-248-260-264
SAND CHRISTIAN................ 110-115
SARAI/SARAH................................ 12
SATAN....... 9-66-132-135-181-193-197-
.... 198-202-204-210-276-280
SATAN'S SEAT 170-171
SECOND BLESSING............. 71-72-73
SECOND BODY...................... 216-217
SECOND COMING ... 21-209-215-224
.... 238-243-244-246-271-274-275
SECOND TENSE SALVATION .. 1-2
.... 15
SEMIRAMIS.................168-169-170
SERMON ON THE MOUNT ... 91-92
.... 93-94-103-110-116
SIDON... 127
SIGNS AND WONDERS...... 19-23-55
.... 76-87-88-123
SMOKING FURNACE................... 161
SODOM... 127
SOLOMON...5
SPIRIT OF LIFE 214-242
SPIRIT OF POWER................ 241-242
SPIRITUAL BODY.......... 230-231-248
STONE OF STUMBLING............. 196
STUMP..........................271-272-277
SUFFER LOSS 3-42-95-114-162
.................................163-200-209
TARES.. 152-153-155-156-157-158-160
.... 174-175-176-177-180-182-209
THAMAR..8
THEODSIUS 171
THIRD HEAVEN........................93-94
THIRD TENSE SALVATION 2
THREE-FOLD DOCTINE OF
CHRIST........................178-180-181-198
TIME OF JACOB'S TROUBLE.... 22
TIMOTHY.. 85
TITUS 23
TONGUES ... 56-62-63-64-67-68-69-70
.... 71-73-74-75-82
TRADITIONS 190-191-197
TREASURE................182-183-185-197
TRIBULATION............................... 197
TRIBULATION PERIOD 157-158
.... 173-205-207-208-246-275-277-279
TRIBULATION SAINTS............... 139
TRUE GRAPEVINE...................... 258
TYPES; TYPOLOGY............11-23-48
.... 49-106-122-128-120-130-161
.... 167-177-186-190-195-200-204
.... 207-210-216-219-227-236-244
....245-355-260-264
TYRE.. 127
UNPARDONABLE SIN 131
VALLEY OF JEHOSHAPHAT... 124
VINEYARD........254-256-257-266-269
WAILING AND GNASHING OF
TEETH 161-162-163-202-209
WEDDING FEAST 123-187
.... 219-220-222-223-227-228-269
WEDDING GARMENT........ 122-221
.... 222-223-225-228-231-233
WEDDING GUESTS..... 14-15-42-107
.... 111-121-122-123-141-151-187-200
.... 216-218-220-222-224-225-227-228
............................230-231-237-260-269
WEEPING AND GNASHING OF
TEETH 109-221-222
WHEAT...... 153-155-156--159-176-178
....182-199-209
WILD OLIVE TREE........254-267-268
WISDOM 42-44-63-83-87-114-156
....212-323-244
WORD OF THE KINGDOM144-146
ZWINGLI... 156
ZECHARRIAH 210

SELECTIVE SCRIPTURE INDEX

GENESIS
1:5 135
1:26 9
2:21-22 49
3:15 8
3:20 11
3:21 11
4:1 11
5:2 11-49
12:1-3 12
12:2-3 254
15:9-17 161
15:18 13
22:17 203
28:12 184
28:13-14 184
28:16-17 184
28:20-22 184
32:25 184
32:31 184
49:10 20
EXODUS
4:22 120
7:1-6 110
7:10-12 57
7:20-22 57
8:5-7 57
13:21 135
17:5:6 215
19:5 185-186-190
20:1-20 189
21:1-23:35 189
2:3:22 251
30:1-38 189
34:35 177
LEVITICUS
2:11 177
11:9 206

23 135
23:17 177
NUMBERS
24:17 20
DEUTERONOMY
4:11-13 190
4:20 162
5:2-4 190
18:18 26
JOSHUA
3:11,13 256
JUDGES
9:5-15 253
1 KINGS
8:51 162
1 CHRONICLES
16:15-17 189
2 CHRONICLES
28:1-3 106
36:23 256
EZRA
1:2 256
NEHEMIAH
2:1-5 21
PSALMS
18:25 98
24:3-6 99
25:9 97
47:5 163-248
78:5 185
78:71 185
88 125-248
119:105 185
135:4 185
ECCLESIASTES
9:12 203
ISAIAH
2:19-21 279
5:1-4 254

5:7	258
5:8-30	255
6:9-10	80
6:11-12	142
8:14-17	196
10:20-24	23
10:24	204
14:25	204
17:12	203
23:13	204
25:8	249
30:27-33	23
30:31	204
31:7-9	161
31:8	204
31:9	210
34:4-6	279
40:3	245
48:10	142-161-210-279
53:1	131
53:4	58
53:5	58-59
63:3-4	280

JEREMIAH

7:30-33	106
7:32-34	124
11:4	162
11:16	265
19:5-6	106
19:6-15	124
23:5	16-140
25:11-12	21
29:10	21
31:33-44	25

EZEKIEL

10:18	256
11:23	256
22:19-22	161
37:1-13	189
37:7-12	193
37:15-18	195

DANIEL

2:23-35	140
2:34-35	110
2:35	215
2:44	279
2:45	215
3:19-25	210
4:10-16	253
4:19-27	253
7:13-14	140
9;2	21
9:24-27	21
9:27	278
12:2-3	188

JOEL

3:2	280
3:9-16	207
3:12-14	280
3:12-16	124

AMOS

4:4	177
4:5	177

MICAH

5:2	19

HABAKKUK

1:15-17	204

ZECHARIAH

6:12-13	25
12:10-13:1	266
13:1	25
13:8-9	142-161-210-279
14:4-5	279
14:9	140
14:12	279

MALACHI

3:1	245
3:16-17	188
4:5-6	245

MATTHEW

1:1	5-15
1:1-5	8
1:3	8
1:5	8
1:11-12	6
1:21	214
2:7	19

Reference	Page
2:16	19
2:21-22	216
3:2	26-23
3:3	245
3:11	162
3:12	29
4:17	19-33-34-38
5:1-2	92
5:13	101
5:14-16	102
5:28	105
5:29	105-124
5:30	105
6:12	250
6:14-15	250
6:24	147
6:31	115
6:33	112
6:34	115
7:13-14	115
7:21	106-112
7:22	107-112
7:23	107-112
7:24-27	110
8:11	187
8:12	14-119
8:16-17	58
9:15-17	121-122
10:5-6	40
10:5-8	55-60
10:6-7	34
10:9-10	40
10:32-33	126
10:37-39	126
11:14	245
11:20	127
11:21-24	127
11:28	129-130-149
11:29	129-130-149
11:30	129
12:24	130
12:32	130-131
12:39-40	132
12:43	131
12:45	131
12:50-21:46	213
13:1-9	144
13:1-35	142
13:3-23	149
13:4	145
13:5-6	145
13:7	147
13:10	123-143
13:10-17	142
13:11	123-139
13:18-23	144
13:19	144-145-150
13:20	145
13:21	145-145
13:22	147
13:23	148
13:24	152
13:24-30	159
13:25	153
13:26	155
13:27-29	156
13:31-32	253
13:36	159
13;36-50	142
13:38	158
13:40	160
13:41	160
13:42	161-162-209
13;43	51-163-188
13:44	181-182-189-194
13:45-46	198
13:47-50	202
13:52	182-211
15:24	33
15:26	33
16:15-18	214
16:18	237-252
16:19	239-243
16:27-27	243
17:1-3	243
17:10	245
17:12-13	245
17:14-17	244

19:22	268
19:27	268
19:27-30	269
20:1-16	257-258-267
20:2	268-269
20:9-10	268
20:16	268-269
21:18-20	270
21:19	253-269
21:33-40	256
21:35	257
21:37-38	37-38
21:39	257
21:41	257
21:43	14-187-219-254-257
22:1-7	220
22:1-14	14-121-219
22:2-7	121
22:2-14	187-269
22:3	14
22:10	107-151
22:11-13	122
22:13	109-162
22:14	46-216-222-237-269
23:38	273
24:1-3	272
24:1-31	274
24:2	273
24:3	272-277
24:4-31	272
24:9	275-276
24:14	36-193-205
24:14:30	234-238
24:15-21	278
24:30	209-278-279
24:31	209-279
24:32	253
24:32-33	271
24:32-34	276
24:34	280
24:37-39	277
24:45-47	15
24:45-51	239
24:47	15-151
24:48-51	125-147
24:51	109-162
25:1-13	111-232-233
25:10	107
25:14-30	121-132
25:21	236-239
25:30	109-162
25:31	276
25:31-32	206
25:31-46	205
25:34-46	207
25:41	107-205
25:41-46	280
25:46	107-205
27:52-53	194
28:19	28-92
28:20	92

MARK

1:3	245
4:3-20	149
4:4	150
4:11	150
4:15	150
11:12-14	253-269
11:20-21	253-269
15:42	135
16:16	61
16:17-18	59

LUKE

1:30-33	34
1:31-33	16
1:33	189
3:4	245
3:23	6
3:23-28	6
8:5-18	149
8:12	150
12:35-40	231
12:42	101
12:44	151-239
12:45-46	248
13:6-9	253-269-270
13:24	114
13:24-25	233

13:24-28	108
13:26-28	109
13:28	162-187
14:8-10	223
14:33-35	102
16:16	93
16:22	93
17:28-29	277
19:12-27	14-224-235
19:14-27	125-148
19:17-19	151
21:20	273
21:20-24	272
21:24	208
21:26-27	279
21:29-31	272
23:43	93

JOHN

1:11	131
1:19-23	26
1:21	245
1:51	184
2:1	137-227
3:5	62
3:16	30
3:29	122-187
5:22	160
5:39	192
6:37	130
7:39	228-242
8:56	190
11:9	135
13:8-10	260
15:1	271
15:1-8	257
15:2	259-261
15:3	260
15:5	225-254-259
15:6	259
157	261
15:8	259
16:13-15	75
17:17	259
18:28-31	20
19:31	136
20:1	136
20:22	242
20:31	1-37

ACTS

1:8	271
2:32-33	242
2:38	26-38
2:44	40
2:45	40
3:17	35
3:19	35-38
4:11	257
4:34	40
4:35	40
5:31	37
8:14-17	241
8:37	39
9:15	81
10:43	35
10:34-48	241
10:44-45	39
16:30-31	35
17:30	38
19:39	215
20:21	37
20:31	83
28:25-28	143
28:27	39
28:28	39-60-76-80-83-93-220-271

ROMANS

1:16	35-40
3:28	262
4:1-4	120
4:1-5	161-186
4:3-5	263-263
5:3	146
5:12	9
5:15	47
5:5-17	4
8:16	15
8:17	15-100-153
8:22-23	197
8:23	125

9:6 197
9:31-33 257
9:33 196
10:3-4 154
10:17 2-52-73-104-148-264
11:2 253
11:7-12 196
11:16-24 265
11:17 80-253-266-271
11:18 253
11:18-20 266
11:24 269
11:25 271
11:26 45
11:26-27 24
11:28 266
11:29 266
12:17 40
12:18 99
16:17-18 75-76
16:21 41
1 CORINTHIANS
1:22 ....
1:23 110
2:2 44
2:6-7 44
2:7 238
2:9-10 44
2:15-16 114
3:1-2 43-184-238
3:1-15 3
3:2 86-238
3:1-15 3
3:12 107
3:13-14 14-209
3:13-15 73-259-261
3:15 14-29-52
5:67 177
8:17 194
9:24-27 47
9:25 109
10:1-4 186
10:2 130
10:32 45

12:3 107
12:12-13 45
12:13 28-75
12:28 81-82
12:28-30 75
13:8 82
14:2 69-70-74
14:4 68
14:14 69-70
14:22 63-64
14:26 74
14:27 70-74
14:28 70
14:33 65-75
15:3-4 38
15:24 163-169
15:24-28 193
15:25 164
15:25-26 248
15:40-41 188
15:45 49-217
15:51-54 163-248
15:51-55 126
16:5-8 83
2 CORINTHIANS
3:18 86-87
4:4 40
5:10 2-14-29-42-43-95-114
.... -125162-221-235-239-264
5:10-11 232
10:1 97
11:13-15 154
12:2-4 242
12:4 93
GALATIANS
1:7-9 154
1:14 192
2:20 217
3:7 261
3:16 13-184-186-190-258-122-189
3:19 122-189
3:24 189
3:28 80
4:22-27 12

5:4 226
5:7-9 177
6:2 103
EPHESIANS
1:4-6 199
1:13 104-111-224-226-263
1:17 232
1:17-18 113
1:18 232
2:8-9 62-110-161-248
2:9 108-235
2:10 47
2:11-13 266
2:14 45
2:19-20 92
2:20 110-257
3:3-6 45
4:8 93
4:8-10 190
4:30 226-248-263
5:19 73
5:25-32 48
5:26 260
PHILIPPIANS
1:29 97
2:12-13 116
3:11 125
3:13 42
3:14 42-47
3:17-18 76
COLOSSIANS
1:5-6 232
1:22-23 113
1:26-27 46-150
1:27 232-233-258
3:16 73
1 THESSALONIANS
2:10 232
4:13-17 278
4:16 209
4:16-17 235-248-249
5:2-3 204
5:3 275
5:8 113-232

2 THESSALONIANS
1:8-10 277
2:2 279
2:3 180
2:8 158
2:11-12 159
1 TIMOTHY
5:8 40
6:9 148
6:17-19 40
2 TIMOTHY
2:5 49-109
2:12 100-141
3:12 100
3:16 76
4:7-8 108
TITUS
2:13 113-232
3:2 97
3:7 232
HEBREWS
1:3 14
1:14 2
2:1 43
2:2 43-95
2:3 43-263
2:4 79
2:5 162
3:6 232
3:6-19 130
4:9 149
4:11 149
5:12 238
5:13-14 250
5:14 238
6:1-2 238
6:1-6 146
6:3 150-236-238
6:19 115-232
9:19-22 217
10:1-14 190
10:19-22 99
10:26-27 248
10:29 248

10:30	250
10:30-31	57
11:6	246
11:12	203
11:29	186
11:40	188
12:22	188
12:23	99-188-199

JAMES

1:2-4	146
1:18-21	104
1:20	97
1:21	51-97
2:23	265

1 PETER

1:1-3	231
1:6-9	50
1:7	146
1:8-9	51
1:9-12	139
1:10-12	50
1:13	51
1:18	192
1:18-20	200
2:6-8	257
2:8	196
2:9	220-254
2:20	97
2:21	100
2:24	59
3:15	232

2 PETER

1:11	51
1:16-19	244
2:1-3	57-147
3:11-14	51
3:12-13	193
3:13	51
3:15	42
3:16	42

1 JOHN

1:7	201
1:7-9	217
1:9	37-50-58-96-131-202
2:28	49
3:3	113-132
5:14-15	58

JUDE

1:9	244
1:13	125-248

REVELATION

2:5	37
2:16	37
2:21	37
2:22	37
3:3	37
3:19	37
4:10	162
6:12	279
6:15-16	279
7: 4-9	193-205-158
7:9-14	158
11:3-12	245
13:14-15	211-278-279
14:6	41
14:20	280
16:18-19	279
16:21	279
17:1-10	172-180
17:14	200-205-218-228-237
17:15	203
19:7-8	15-122-221-228-230-231
19:10	245
19:11-16	279
19:11-21	24
19:15	280
19:20	280
20:1-3	24-280
20:13-15	57
21-1-5	164-193-249-192-193
21:12	194
21:27	194
22:18	64-82

Order Blank
(For you and your friends)

Check one:

☐ Please send me ___ copies of "Shock and Surprise Beyond the Rapture!" at $10.95 each plus $2.00 shipping

☐ Please send me ___ copies of "The Matthew Mysteries" at $10.95 each plus $2.00 shipping.

Name_____

Address_____

City_____Zip_____State___

Make your check out and send to: Gary T. Whipple Ministries, P.O. Box 196368, Winter Springs, Fla. 32719-6368 (Fla. residents add 6% sales tax).

------------------------------ CUT ALONG LINE ------------------------------

Order Blank
(For you and your friends)

Check one:

☐ Please send me ___ copies of "Shock and Surprise Beyond the Rapture!" at $10.95 each plus $2.00 shipping.

☐ Please send me ___ copies of "The Matthew Mysteries" at $10.95 each plus $2.00 shipping.

Name_____

Address_____

City_____Zip_____State___

Make your check out and send to: Gary T. Whipple Ministries, P.O. Box 196368, Winter Springs, Fla. 32719-6368. (Fla. residents add 6% sales tax).

MONUMENTAL WORKS
BY DILLOW, DODSON, GOVETT, LANG, MAURO, NEIGHBOUR, PANTON, PEMBER, STANTON, WHIPPLE, AND WILSON

JOSEPH C. DILLOW
- THE REIGN OF THE SERVANT KINGS

KENNETH F. DODSON
- THE PRIZE OF THE UP-CALLING

ROBERT GOVETT
- GOVETT ON ISAIAH
- GOVETT ON THE PARABLES
- GOVETT ON JOHN (2 vols in 1)
- GOVETT ON ROMANS
- GOVETT ON GALATIANS
- GOVETT ON EPHESIANS
- GOVETT ON PHILIPPIANS
- GOVETT ON COLOSSIANS
- GOVETT ON THESSALONIANS
- GOVETT ON II TIMOTHY
- GOVETT ON HEBREWS
- GOVETT ON I JOHN
- GOVETT ON REVELATION (4 vols. in 2)
- CALVINISM BY CALVIN
- CHRIST'S JUDGMENT OF HIS SAINTS
- CHRIST'S RESURRECTION AND OURS
- ENTRANCE INTO THE KINGDOM
- ESAU'S CHOICE
- ETERNAL SUFFERING OF THE WICKED AND HADES
- GOSPEL ANALOGIES
- HOW INTERPRET THE APOCALYPSE?
- IS SANCTIFICATION PERFECT HERE BELOW?
- KINGDOM OF GOD FUTURE
- KINGDOM STUDIES
- LEADING THOUGHTS ON THE APOCALYPSE
- REWARD ACCORDING TO WORKS
- SINS BEFORE FAITH AND SINS AFTER FAITH
- SOWING AND REAPING
- THE BEST MODE OF PRESENTING THE GOSPEL
- THE CHURCH OF OLD: I CORINTHIANS 12, 13, 14
- THE FUTURE APOSTASY
- THE JEWS, THE GENTILES, AND THE CHURCH OF GOD IN THE GOSPEL OF MATTHEW
- THE NEW JERUSALEM
- THE PROPHECY ON OLIVET
- THE SAINTS RAPTURE
- THE SERMON ON THE MOUNT
- THE THREE EATINGS: EDEN, PASSOVER & THE LORD'S SUPPER
- THE TWO WITNESSES
- TWO VIEWS OF THE SUPPER OF THE LORD

G.H. LANG
- AN ORDERED LIFE
- ANTHONY NORRIS GROVES
- ATONING BLOOD
- BALANCED CHRISTIANITY
- COMING EVENTS
- DEPARTURE
- DIVINE GUIDANCE
- FIRSTBORN SONS
- FIRSTFRUITS AND HARVEST
- GOD AT WORK ON HIS OWN LINES
- GOD'S PLAN, CHRIST'S SUFFERING, AND THE SPIRIT'S POWER
- IDEALS AND REALITIES
- ISRAEL'S NATIONAL FUTURE
- PICTURES AND PARABLES
- PRAYER: FOCUSED AND FIGHTING
- PRAYING IS WORKING
- THE CHURCHES OF GOD
- THE CLEAN HEART
- THE DISCIPLE
- THE EARLIER YEARS OF THE MODERN TONGUES MOVEMENT
- THE EPISTLE TO THE HEBREWS
- THE FIRST RESURRECTION
- THE GOSPEL OF THE KINGDOM
- THE HISTORY & DIARIES OF AN INDIAN CHRISTIAN
- THE HISTORIES AND PROPHECIES OF DANIEL
- THE LAST ASSIZE
- THE LOCAL ASSEMBLY
- THE MODERN GIFT OF TONGUES
- THE NEW BIRTH
- THE REVELATION OF JESUS CHRIST
- THE SINNER'S FUTURE
- THE UNEQUAL YOKE
- WORLD CHAOS

PHILIP MAURO
- GOD'S APOSTLE AND HIGH PRIEST

R.E. NEIGHBOUR
- IF BY ANY MEANS
- IF THEY SHALL FALL AWAY

D.M. PANTON
- RAPTURE
- THE JUDGMENT SEAT OF CHRIST
- THE PANTON PAPERS

G.H. PEMBER
- MYSTERY BABYLON THE GREAT
- THE ANTICHRIST BABYLON AND THE COMING OF THE KINGDOM
- THE GREAT PROPHECIES Vol. I
- THE GREAT PROPHECIES Vol. II
- THE GREAT PROPHECIES Vol. III
- THE GREAT PROPHECIES Vol. IV
- THE LORD'S COMMAND

GERALD B. STANTON
- KEPT FROM THE HOUR

A. EDWIN WILSON
- SELECTED WRITINGS

GARY T. WHIPPLE
- SHOCK & SURPRISE BEYOND THE RAPTURE

Available Through Your Local Christian Book Store or Consult Publisher